CAMBRIDGE
UNIVERSITY PRESS

CAMBRIDGE
Primary Mathematics

Learner's Book 4

Mary Wood & Emma Low

CAMBRIDGE
UNIVERSITY PRESS & ASSESSMENT

Shaftesbury Road, Cambridge CB2 8EA, United Kingdom

One Liberty Plaza, 20th Floor, New York, NY 10006, USA

477 Williamstown Road, Port Melbourne, VIC 3207, Australia

314–321, 3rd Floor, Plot 3, Splendor Forum, Jasola District Centre, New Delhi – 110025, India

103 Penang Road, #05–06/07, Visioncrest Commercial, Singapore 238467

Cambridge University Press & Assessment is a department of the University of Cambridge.

We share the University's mission to contribute to society through the pursuit of education, learning and research at the highest international levels of excellence.

www.cambridge.org
Information on this title: www.cambridge.org/9781108745291

First published 2014
Second edition 2021

40 39 38 37 36 35 34 33 32 31 30 29 28 27 26 25 24 23 22

Printed in Italy by L.E.G.O. S.p.A.

A catalogue record for this publication is available from the British Library

ISBN 978-1-108-74529-1 Paperback with Digital Access (1 Year)
ISBN 978-1-108-96416-6 Digital Learner's Book (1 Year)
ISBN 978-1-108-96417-3 Learner's Book eBook

Additional resources for this publication at www.cambridge.org/9781108745291

Projects and their accompanying teacher guidance have been written by the NRICH Team. NRICH is an innovative collaboration between the Faculties of Mathematics and Education at the University of Cambridge, which focuses on problem solving and on creating opportunities for students to learn mathematics through exploration and discussion: nrich.maths.org.

Introduction

Welcome to Stage 4 of Cambridge Primary Mathematics. We hope this book will show you how interesting Mathematics can be and make you want to explore and investigate mathematical ideas.

Mathematics is everywhere. Developing our skills in mathematics makes us better problem-solvers through understanding how to reason, analyse and reflect. We use mathematics to understand money and complete practical tasks like cooking and decorating. It helps us to make good decisions in everyday life.

In this book you will work like a mathematician to find the answers to questions like these:

- What are negative numbers and when are they used?
- How can you quickly find out if 1435 is in the 25 times table?
- Which is bigger: half a cake or 50 percent of a cake?
- What might you be doing at the time 23:30?
- What shape is a cone?
- What is a dot plot?
- What comes between the points north, east, south and west on a compass?

Talk about the mathematics as you explore and learn. This helps you to reflect on what you did and refine the mathematical ideas to develop a more effective approach or solution.

You will be able to practise new skills, check how you are doing and also challenge yourself to find out more. You will be able to make connections between what seem to be different areas of mathematics.

We hope you enjoy thinking and working like a mathematician.

Mary Wood and Emma Low

Contents

How to use this book

In this book you will find lots of different features to help your learning:

Questions to find out what you know already. →

Getting started

1 Write the term-to-term rule for finding the next term in these sequences.

a 185, 180, 175, . . . b 235, 245, 255, . . . c 901, 801, 701, . . .

2 Read these numbers to your partner, then write each number in words.

a 601 b 299 c 111

3 Write the number you make when you put the place-value cards together.

a

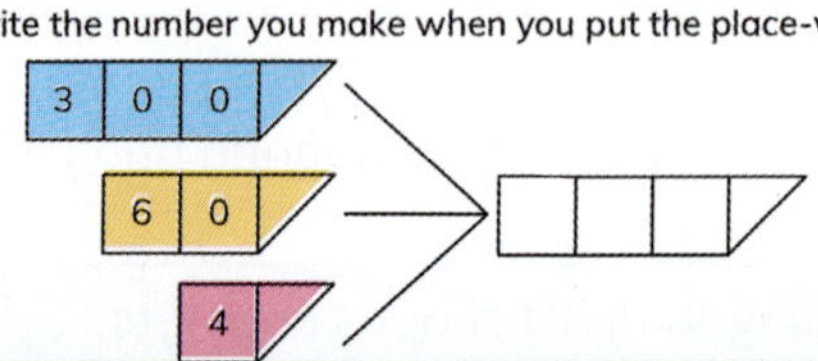

What you will learn in the unit. →

We are going to . . .

- count on and back in steps of tens, hundreds and thousands starting from any number
- count back through zero to include negative numbers such as −2
- recognise linear sequences and **non-linear sequences**

Important words that you will use. →

equivalent fraction
proper fraction

Step-by-step examples showing a way to solve a problem. →

Worked example 2

Written method of addition

Calculate 235 + 174.

Estimate 200 + 200 = 400	Start with an estimate.
235 = 200 + 30 + 5	
174 = 100 + 70 + 4	Decompose the numbers.
235 + 174 = 300 + 100 + 9	Add the hundreds, tens and ones together.
= 409	Then compose the parts.

Answer: 409

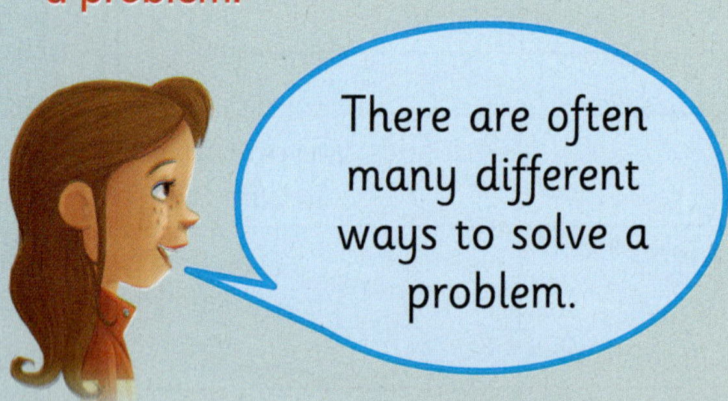

These questions will help you develop your skills of thinking and working mathematically. →

2 Choose any two of these three sequences.

How are they similar to each other and how are they different?

2, 4, 6, 8 . . . 2, 5, 8, 11 . . . 3, 5, 7, 9 . . .

An investigation to carry out with a partner or in groups. Where this icon appears, the activity will help develop your skills of thinking and working mathematically.

Think like a mathematician

Use each of the numbers 3, 4, 5, 6 and 7 to complete the cross pattern. The total going across must be the same as the total going down.

You will show you are **specialising** when you find solutions to the problem.

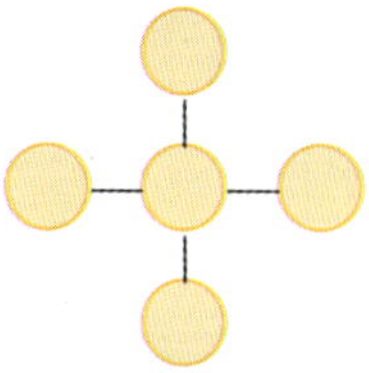

Questions to help you think about how you learn.

Number lines are useful for calculating and showing connections between values. Sometimes one is drawn for you, but sometimes you can draw your own to help.

Look at the questions in the exercise and write down how you have used number lines to help you.

This is what you have learned in the unit.

Look what I can do!

- [ ] I can find a missing number represented by a symbol.
- [ ] I can find a missing operation sign represented by a symbol.

Questions that cover what you have learned in the unit.

Check your progress

1 Write the missing number.

$100 - \square = 58$

2 Write the missing number.

$2 + 20 + \square = 100$

3 A total of 245 chairs are needed for a school performance.
169 chairs are already in place.
How many chairs need to be put in place?

At the end of several units, there is a project for you to carry out using what you have learned. You might make something or solve a problem.

Projects and their accompanying teacher guidance have been written by the NRICH Team. NRICH is an innovative collaboration between the Faculties of Mathematics and Education at the University of Cambridge, which focuses on problem solving and on creating opportunities for students to learn mathematics through exploration and discussion: nrich.maths.org.

Project 1

Deep water

Here is a picture of a bridge spanning part of the sea at an estuary. The scale marked on one of the bridge supports shows the level of the water.
The zero on the scale is at the base of the bridge. At the moment the water is 2 metres below the base of the bridge, shown by the −2 on the scale.

If the water level rose and reached the base of the bridge, how much would it have risen by?

If the water level then rose again and reached the number 2 on the scale, how much more would it have risen by? How much would it have gone up by in total?

Thinking and Working Mathematically

There are some important skills that you will develop as you learn mathematics.

Specialising
is when I choose an example and check to see if it satisfies or does not satisfy specific mathematical criteria.

Characterising
is when I identify and describe the mathematical properties of an object.

Generalising
is when I recognise an underlying pattern by identifying many examples that satisfy the same mathematical criteria.

Classifying
is when I organise objects into groups according to their mathematical properties.

Critiquing
is when I compare and evaluate mathematical ideas, representations or solutions to identify advantages and disadvantages.

Improving
is when I refine mathematical ideas or representations to develop a more effective approach or solution.

Conjecturing
is when I form mathematical questions or ideas.

Convincing
is when I present evidence to justify or challenge a mathematical idea or solution.

1 Numbers and the number system

Getting started

1 Write the term-to-term rule for finding the next term in these sequences.

a 185, 180, 175, . . . b 235, 245, 255, . . . c 901, 801, 701, . . .

2 Read these numbers to your partner, then write each number in words.

a 601 b 299 c 111

3 Write the number you make when you put the place-value cards together.

a

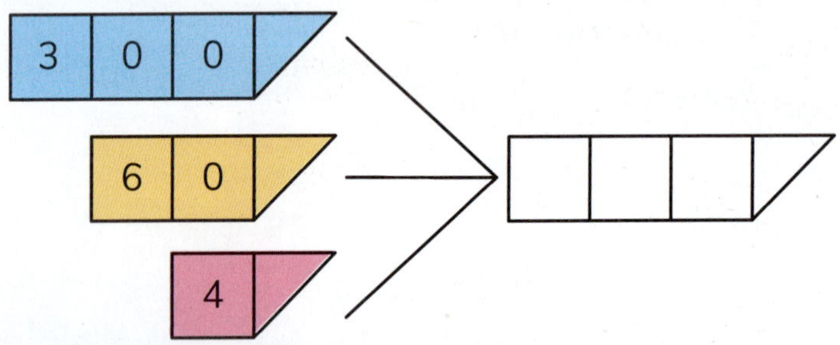

b

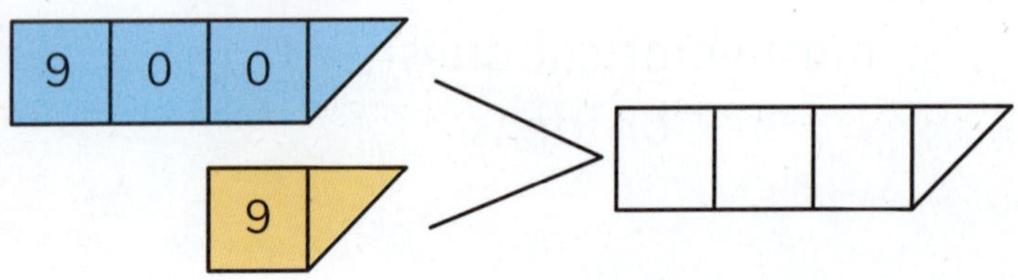

4 Copy and complete these number sentences.

a 562 = ☐ + 60 + ☐

b 305 = 300 + ☐

5 Write the missing numbers.

a 16 × 10 = ☐

b 56 × ☐ = 560

This unit is all about our number system. You will look at linear sequences and non-linear sequences, negative numbers, multiplying and dividing by 10 and 100, and place value.

Imagine you save $2 each week.

Can you write a number sequence for how much you have at the end of each week?

You add the same amount each time, so this is a linear sequence.

The term-to-term rule is 'add 2'.

If you save a different amount each time, the sequence will be non-linear.

One of the main ideas in place value is that the value of a digit depends on its position in the number.

Think about what the digit 7 is worth in $7 and $70.

Do you have enough money to buy the bike?

There are $7 in the bag

The bike costs $70

Think about the numbers 126 and 162.

What is the value of the digit 2 in each number?

1.1 Counting and sequences

We are going to . . .

- count on and back in steps of tens, hundreds and thousands starting from any number
- count back through zero to include negative numbers such as −2
- recognise linear sequences and **non-linear sequences**
- extend sequences and describe the term-to-term rule
- recognise and extend patterns that represent square numbers.

You will continue counting forwards and backwards in steps of constant size and you will start to use negative numbers.

Around the coasts of Antarctica temperatures are between −10 °C and −30 °C.

Try counting back in tens starting at 30 and ending with −30.

difference
linear sequence
negative number
non-linear sequence
rule
sequence
spatial pattern
square number
term
term-to-term rule

Worked example 1

Carlos writes a number sequence.

The first term in his sequence is 8.

He uses the rule 'subtract 2' to work out the next term.

What is the fifth term in his sequence?

$8 \xrightarrow{-2} 6 \xrightarrow{-2} 4 \xrightarrow{-2} 2 \xrightarrow{-2} 0$

Start with 8 and subtract 2 each time until you have five terms.

Answer: The fifth term is 0.

Worked example 2

The numbers in this sequence increase by 50 each time.

$60 \xrightarrow{+50} 110 \xrightarrow{+50} 160 \xrightarrow{+50} \dots$

What is the first number greater than 1000 that is in the sequence?

Explain how you know.

60, 110, 160, 210, 260, . . .	Write down the first few terms. (You could write down all the terms in the sequence, but it would take a long time.)

Answer: The terms all end in 10 or 60
so the first number greater than 1000 is 1010.

Exercise 1.1

1 a Mia counts on in steps of 100.
She starts at 946.
Write the next number she says.

b Kofi counts back in steps of 100.
He starts at 1048.
Write the next number he says.

c Bibi counts on in steps of 1000.
She starts at 1989.
Write the next number she says.

d Pierre counts back in steps of 1000.
He starts at 9999.
Write the next number he says.

e Tara counts back in ones.
She counts 3, 2, 1, 0.
Write the next number she says.

2 Copy and complete this square using the rule 'add 2 across and add 2 down'.

What do you notice about the numbers on the diagonal?
Discuss with your partner.

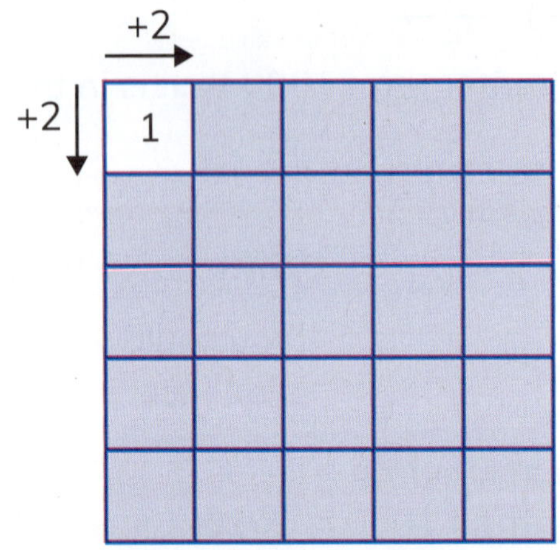

Draw two more 5 by 5 squares and choose a rule using addition.
Predict what the numbers on the diagonal will be before you complete the squares.

3 Choose any two of these three sequences.

How are they similar to each other and how are they different?

2, 4, 6, 8, . . .

2, 5, 8, 11, . . .

3, 5, 7, 9, . . .

4 Look at these sequences.

Which could be the odd one out? Explain your answer.

13, 16, 19, 22, . . .

8, 11, 14, 17, . . .

−5, −2, 1, 4, . . .

9, 12, 15, 18, . . .

16, 19, 22, 25, . . .

Think about your answers to questions 3 and 4.
Are there other possible answers?

5 Use different first terms to make sequences that all have the term-to-term rule 'add 3'. Can you find a sequence for each of the following?

a Where the terms are all multiples of 3.

b Where the terms are not whole numbers.

c Where the terms are all odd.

d Where the terms include both 100 and 127.

6 Abdul makes a number sequence.

The first term of his sequence is 397.

His term-to-term rule is 'subtract 3'.

Abdul says, 'If I keep subtracting 3 from 397 I will eventually reach 0.'

Is he correct?

Explain your answer.

7 Which sequences are linear and which are not?

Write the next term for each sequence. Explain your answers to your partner.

a Add five: 4, 9, 14, . . .

b Subtract four: 20, 16, 12, . . .

c Add one more each time: 2, 3, 5, . . .

d Multiply by three: 2, 6, 18, . . .

e Subtract one less each time: 50, 41, 33, . . .

f Divide by two: 32, 16, 8, . . .

8 Here is a spatial pattern.

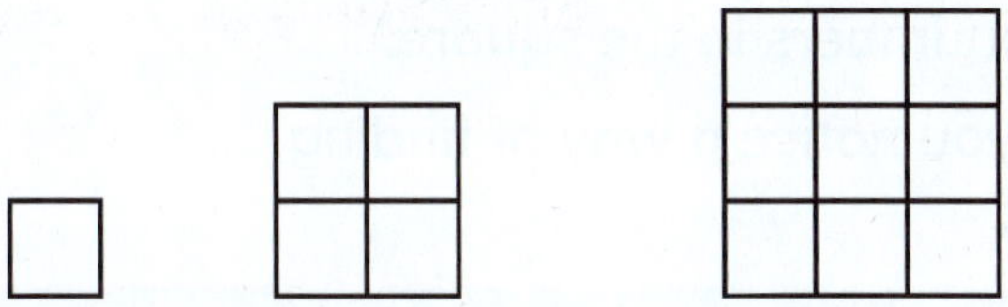

Draw the next term in the pattern.

What number does it represent?

Think like a mathematician

These sets of beads have **consecutive** numbers in the circles.

The numbers add up to the number in the square.

Example:

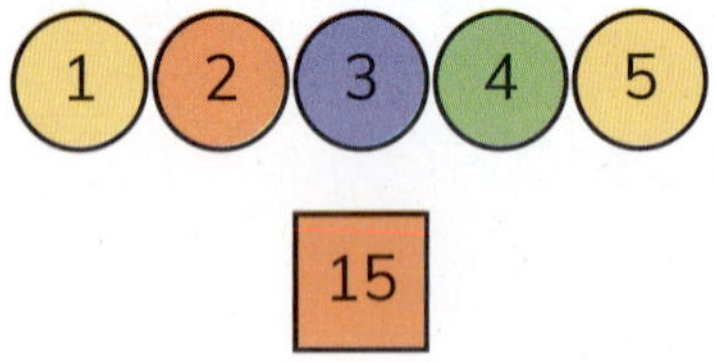

- You will show you are **specialising** when you identify examples that fit the criteria 'The numbers add up to the numbers in the square'.
- You will show you are **generalising** when you notice a way of finding the middle number.

Complete these sets of beads.

a

b

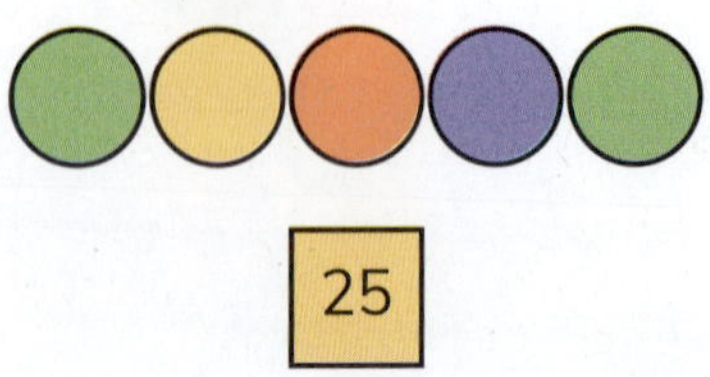

> **Tip**
>
> Consecutive numbers are next to each other.
>
> For example, 3, 4, 5 and 6.

Describe to a partner how to find the middle number of each set of beads.

- You will show you are **specialising** when you identify examples that fit the criteria 'The numbers add up to the numbers in the square.'
- You will show you are **generalising** when you notice a way of finding the middle number.

Look what I can do!

- [ ] I can count on and back in steps of different sizes.
- [ ] I can extend linear sequences and describe the term-to-term rule.
- [ ] I can recognise non-linear sequences.
- [ ] I can extend patterns that represent square numbers.

1.2 More on negative numbers

We are going to . . .

- read and write numbers less than zero, for example −6 is negative six
- understand how negative numbers are used in the real world, for example to describe a very cold temperature or a position below sea level.

In this section, you will use negative numbers in contexts such as temperature or being above or below sea level.

temperature
zero

An iceberg is ice that has broken off a glacier and is now floating. There is much more ice below sea level than there is above sea level.

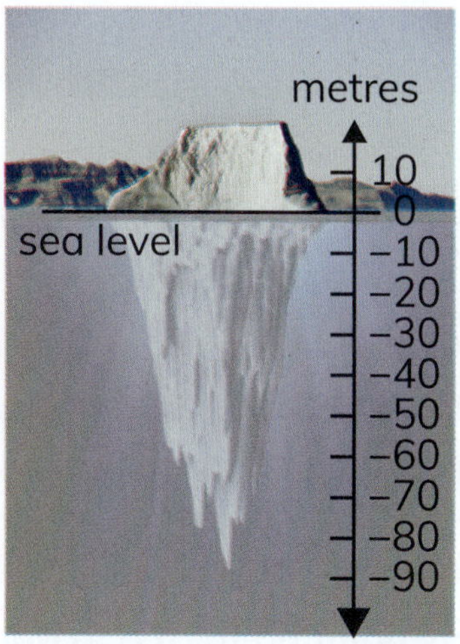

Worked example 3

The temperature in England is 11 °C.

The temperature in Iceland is 15 ° colder.

What is the temperature in Iceland?

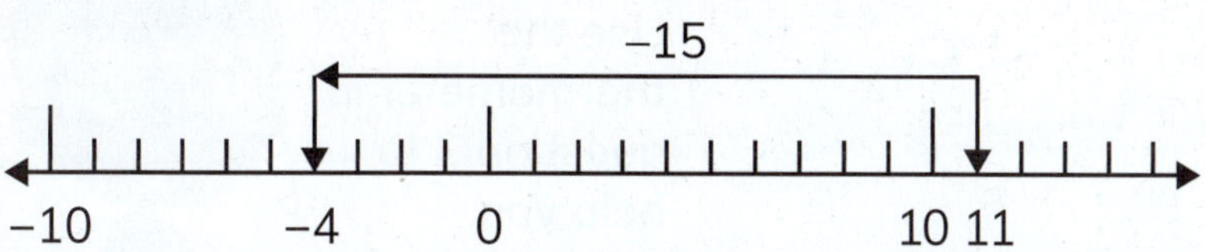

Draw a number line to help.

Start at 11.

The temperature is colder, so you jump back 15 places.

Answer: The temperature in Iceland is −4 °C.

Exercise 1.2

1 Look at the number line.

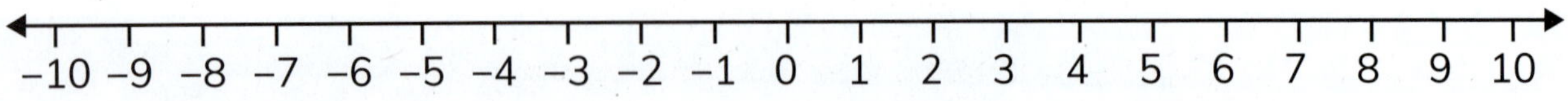

Write where you would land on the number line after these moves.

a start −5 count on 1

b start −2 count back 4

c start −3 count on 3

d start 6 count back 9

2 Here is a number line.

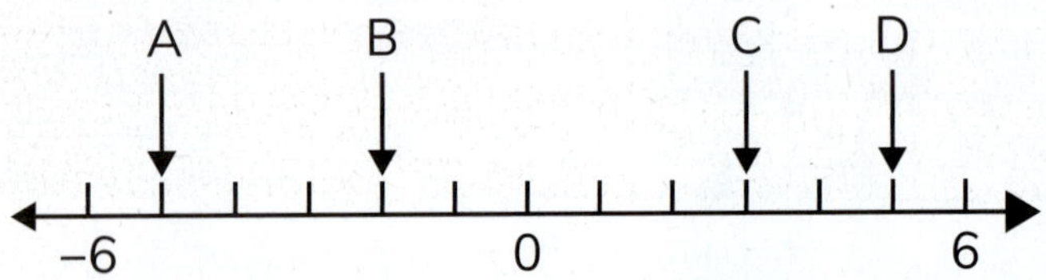

a Which numbers do the arrows A, B, C and D point to?

b Which letter shows the position of a number greater than −4 and less than 0?

3 Look at this thermometer.

What numbers are the arrows pointing to at a, b and c?

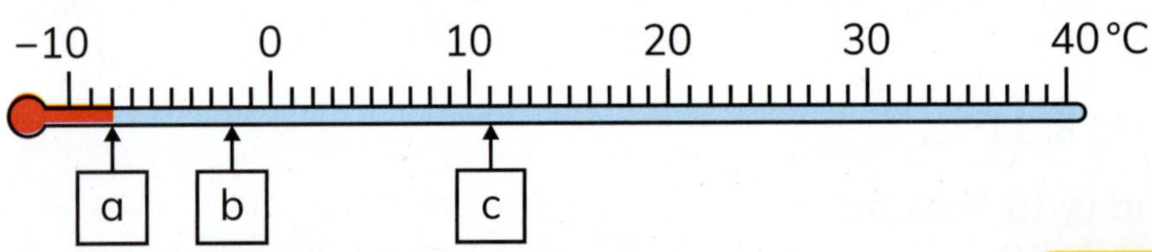

4 Which temperature is the coldest?

−6 °C   0 °C   1 °C   −2 °C

Tip

Use the thermometer in question 3 to help you.

5 The temperature in a town one day was 5 °C.

The temperature dropped by 9 °C overnight.

What was the lowest night-time temperature?

6 The letters on the number line are in the place of numbers.

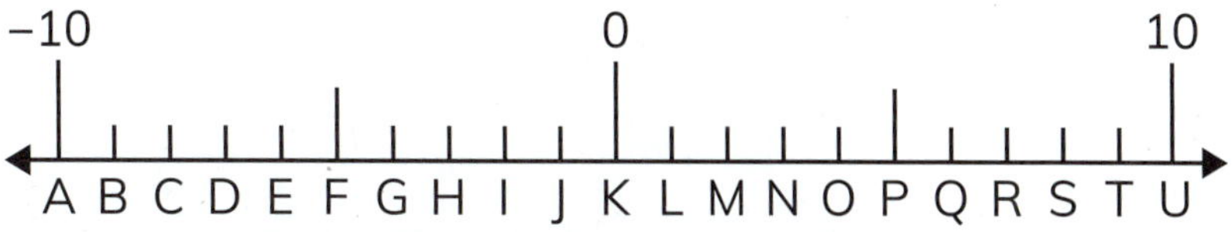

Copy and complete the table to solve the puzzle and find out where emperor penguins live.

−10	3	9	−10	7	−8	9	−2	−8	−10

7 What mistake has Marcus made?

How can you help him correct this mistake?

8 a What temperature is 6 degrees warmer than −4 °C?

b What temperature is 5 degrees less than 1 °C?

c What temperature is 3 degrees warmer than −2 °C?

d What temperature is 3 degrees cooler than 0 °C?

e What temperature is 5 degrees higher than −1 °C?

Number lines are useful for calculating and showing connections between values. Sometimes one is drawn for you, but sometimes you can draw your own to help.

Look at the questions in the exercise and write down how you have used number lines to help you.

Think like a mathematician

The coldest place where people live is Oymyakon in Siberia.

In 1933 the temperature fell to −67 °C.

It was so cold that people's eyelashes froze.

a Investigate the summer and winter temperatures in different places. Order the temperatures you find starting with the coldest.

b Make a poster to show your findings.

c Find examples of temperatures in magazines or on the internet and add them to your poster. You can include maps, pictures and graphs.

Compare your poster to others in your class.

What is similar and what is different?

How could you improve the mathematical content?

How could you improve the presentation?

Look what I can do!

- [ ] I can read and write whole numbers less than zero, for example −6 is negative 6.
- [ ] I can understand how negative numbers are used in the real world, for example to describe a very cold temperature.

1.3 Understanding place value

We are going to . . .

- read and write whole numbers greater than 1000
- say the value of each digit in any whole number and explain how the position of a digit affects its value
- multiply and divide whole numbers by 10 and 100 and understand how the digits move
- compose (put together) and decompose (split) numbers.

In this section, you will work with bigger numbers including thousands, ten thousands and hundred thousands. You will also multiply and divide whole numbers by 10 and 100.

compose
decompose
equivalent
hundred thousand
million
place holder
regroup
ten thousand
thousand

Worked example 4

Look at the number 829.

a What digit is in the tens place?

b What is the value of the 8 in this number?

100s	10s	1s
8	2	9

Use a place value table to help you.

Answer:

a 2

b eight hundreds (or 800)

Remember to write the number of hundreds.

Exercise 1.3

1 a What is the value of the digit 9 in 950 302?

b What is the value of the digit 5?

2 Mia is thinking of a 5-digit whole number.

She says, 'It has a 2 in the ten thousands place and in the tens place.

It has a 5 in the thousands place and in the ones place.

It has a 0 in the hundreds place.'

What number is Mia thinking of?

☐☐☐☐☐

Write your number in words.

3 Decompose these numbers by copying and filling in the missing numbers.

a 805 469 = ☐ + 5000 + ☐ + ☐ + 9

b 689 567 = 600 000 + ☐ + ☐ + 500 + ☐ + ☐

c 508 208 = ☐ + ☐ + ☐ + ☐

Discuss your answers with a partner.

4 Bruno says, 'The largest 5-digit number is 1 less than a hundred thousand.'

Is Bruno correct? Explain your answer.

5 Which number sentence has a different missing number? What is it?

☐ × 100 = 30 000

3 × 100 = ☐

30 000 ÷ 100 = ☐

☐ ÷ 10 = 30

☐ × 100 = 3000

☐ × 10 = 3000

6 Calculate:

a 67 × 10

b 40 ÷ 10

c 3600 ÷ 100

d 415 × 10

e 350 ÷ 10

f 35 × 100

7 If you multiply 606 by 10, what changes and what stays the same?

Discuss your answer with your partner.

Think like a mathematician

Digital sum

The digits in the number 15 total 6 (1 + 5 = 6).

a Find all the whole numbers that have digits with a total of 6.
Do not include zero in any of your numbers.

b What is the largest number?

c What is the smallest number?

You will show you are **specialising** when you find whole numbers that have digits with a total of 6.

Compare your solution with your partner's solution.

Did you get the same answer? Did you use the same method?

Did you find all the 2-digit numbers, then 3-digit numbers and so on?

How could you improve your method?

Look what I can do!

- ☐ I can read and write whole numbers greater than 1000.
- ☐ I can say the value of each digit in any whole number.
- ☐ I can multiply and divide a whole number by 10 and 100.

Check your progress

1 The term-to-term rule for this sequence of numbers is add three each time.

401, 404, 407, 410, 413, 416, 419, . . .

The sequence continues in the same way.

Which of these numbers do not belong to the sequence?

422 428 430 434

2 The numbers in this sequence increase by 50 each time.

$70 \xrightarrow{+50} 120 \xrightarrow{+50} 170 \xrightarrow{+50} \ldots$

What is the first number in the sequence that is greater than 500?

3 Here are three different sequences.

6, 8, 10, 12, . . . 8, 11, 14, 17, . . . 1, 3, 5, 7, . . .

Choose two of the sequences.

In what ways are the two sequences the same?

In what ways are the two sequences different from the third sequence?

4 The temperature in Iceland is −1 °C.

The temperature in Mongolia is 31 °C colder.

What is the temperature in Mongolia?

5 Use digits to write these numbers.

a Three hundred and thirty-five thousand, two hundred and seventy-one.

b One hundred and five thousand and fifty.

c One hundred and twenty thousand, two hundred and two.

6 Write these numbers in words.

a 307 201 b 577 006 c 790 320

7 Martha scored 1646 points in a computer game.

Which of the following is not a correct representation of her score?

A 1000 + 600 + 40 + 6 C 1000 + 606 + 4

B 1000 + 600 + 46 D 1000 + 606 + 40

Continued

8 Which of these numbers is 100 times larger than five hundred and fifty-five?

555 | 5550 | 55 500 | 555 000

9 Copy and complete these number sentences.

a $\square \div 10 = 54$

b $307 \times \square = 3070$

c $\square \times 100 = 6000$

d $3400 \div \square = 34$

10 a What temperature is 5° warmer than −1 °C?

b What temperature is 10° cooler than 0 °C?

Project 1

Deep water

Here is a picture of a bridge spanning part of the sea at an estuary. The scale marked on one of the bridge supports shows the level of the water.
The zero on the scale is at the base of the bridge. At the moment the water is 2 metres below the base of the bridge, shown by the −2 on the scale.

If the water level rose and reached the base of the bridge, how much would it have risen by?

If the water level then rose again and reached the number 2 on the scale, how much more would it have risen by? How much would it have gone up by in total?

The level of the water is checked at midday each day. The picture above shows the water level at midday on Monday, when it is 1 metre below the base of the bridge. There is a flood overnight, and by midday on Tuesday the water level has risen by 2 metres. On Wednesday the flood has finished, and the water level has fallen by 4 metres from where it was on Tuesday.

Where is the water level at midday on Wednesday?
Can you draw a picture to show what this would look like on the scale?

2 Time and timetables

Getting started

1 Here are seven units of time.

seconds | minutes | hours | days | weeks | months | years

Copy and complete each sentence using one of the words.

a We measure our age in _____ .

b I sleep about 8 _____ each day.

c A sports match lasts for 90 _____ .

2 Which of these times are equivalent to the one shown on the clock?

15 minutes past 3 | quarter past 10 | 9:15 | 13 minutes to 3 | quarter past 9

3 Here is part of a bus timetable.

High Street	3.00	4.00
Church Lane	3.05	4.05
Shopping Centre	3.20	4.20
Swimming Pool	3.35	4.35

A bus leaves High Street at 3.00.

What time is the bus at Church Lane?

4 Copy and complete the sentences using one of these words.

minutes | hours | days | weeks | months | years

a April is 3 _____ before July.

b 5:00 is 5 _____ after midnight.

What do you use to tell the time?

Do you use an analogue clock or watch, a digital clock or watch or something else?

The ancient Egyptians measured time using shadows. You can make a simple shadow clock in the playground. Make sure you choose a sunny day!

Do you know of any other timekeeping devices? Try to find out about some.

There are lots of different ways to read and record the time when something happens. In Stage 3, you used only 12-hour times. In this unit, you will learn about the 24-hour clock.

In Stage 3 you used:

- twenty-five to nine
- twenty-five minutes to nine
- 8:35.

Stage 4 introduces you to:

- 8.35 a.m. or 08:35
- 8.35 p.m. or 20:35.

You will also learn more about timetables including those that use the 24-hour clock. You will use timetables to plan journeys and work out how long a journey lasts.

2.1 Time

We are going to . . .

- read and tell the time on digital and analogue clocks
- use a.m., p.m., and 12-hour and 24-hour clock notation with digital and analogue clocks.

a.m.
analogue clock
digital clock
hour
minute
p.m.
second

Where have you seen clocks like these?

An analogue clock has two scales – one from midnight to midday and the other from midday to midnight.

A digital clock shows a time of 13:26 which is 1.26 p.m.

Worked example 1

The clock shows a time in the evening.

a Show the same time on a 24-hour digital clock.

b Write different ways the time could be recorded.

Answer:

a The clock shows 6:50 in the evening.

In 24-hour digital time this is 18:50.

b 6.50 p.m.

Ten to seven in the evening.

Ten minutes to seven in the evening.

When recording time using the 24-hour clock you will always use four digits.

To change an evening time to 24-hour time you have to add 12 to the hours.

$6 + 12 = 18$

You use 'p.m.' to show that the time is in the evening.

Exercise 2.1

1 Copy and complete the following:

a There are ____ days in September.

b There are ____ minutes in 1 hour.

c There are ____ months in a year.

d There are ____ seconds in 1 minute.

2 Write the missing numbers.

a 3 minutes = ☐ seconds

b 5 hours 30 minutes = ☐ minutes

c 7 weeks = ☐ days

d ☐ months = 3 years

e ☐ hours = 2 days 6 hours

f ☐ minutes = $7\frac{1}{2}$ hours

g 300 seconds = ☐ minutes

Check your answers with your partner. Did you get the same answers to question 2? How did you work out the number of minutes in $7\frac{1}{2}$ hours? Did your partner use the same method?

3 Ali went swimming at 5.15 p.m.
Which clock shows the time Ali went swimming?

A B C D

4 Copy and complete the table to show the time using a.m. and p.m.
One has been done for you.

ten past four in the afternoon	4.10 p.m.
quarter past seven in the morning	
quarter to ten at night	
twenty minutes past three in the afternoon	

5 Petra looks at the clock in the classroom. She says, 'It is almost lunchtime.'

Write the time using a.m. or p.m.

6 Chen goes swimming at ten past five in the afternoon.
Which digital clock shows when Chen goes swimming?

7 A wall clock shows this time.

Which two digital clocks could show the same time as the wall clock?

8 Ava converts 9 p.m. to a 24-hour clock time.

Her answer is 19:00.

Ava's answer is wrong.

Correct Ava's answer. Explain what she did wrong.

Think like a mathematician

Digital clocks

Milly dropped her digital clock. When she picked it up she could not tell which way up it was.

a Write in words the two different ways of saying what the time is.

b Write three other times that look the same on a digital clock whichever way up it is.

Use these digital numbers to help you.

You will show you are **specialising** when you find times that look the same on a digital clock whichever way it is up.

Look what I can do!

- ☐ I can read and tell the time on digital and analogue clocks.
- ☐ I can use a.m., p.m., 12-hour and 24-hour clock notation with digital and analogue clocks.

2.2 Timetables and time intervals

We are going to . . .

- read a timetable to solve problems
- choose and use suitable units to calculate time intervals.

It is important to know how to tell the time and be able to read a calendar and a timetable. It can help you to catch a train, bus, plane or boat on time. For example, it is no good arriving at the station just as the train is leaving.

Understanding time and timetables helps you to know if you will get to an important event on time.

calendar
leap year
time interval
timetable

Worked example 2

Here is a coach timetable.

Which coach completes the journey to Corbury in the shorter time?

Anbury	09:09	10:10
Babury	09:24	10:26
Corbury	09:45	10:48

Use a time line.

You can work out the time taken between each stop and add them up.

Or you can work out the time taken between the start and the end.

Compare the times to decide which coach takes the shorter time.

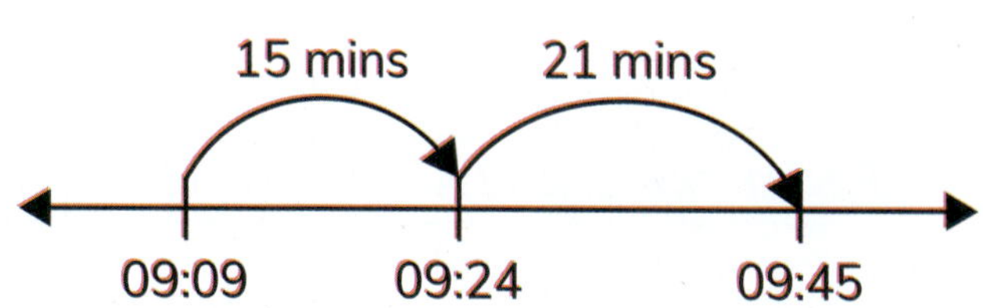

15 mins + 21 mins = 36 mins

The 09:09 coach takes 36 minutes.
The 10:10 coach takes 38 minutes.

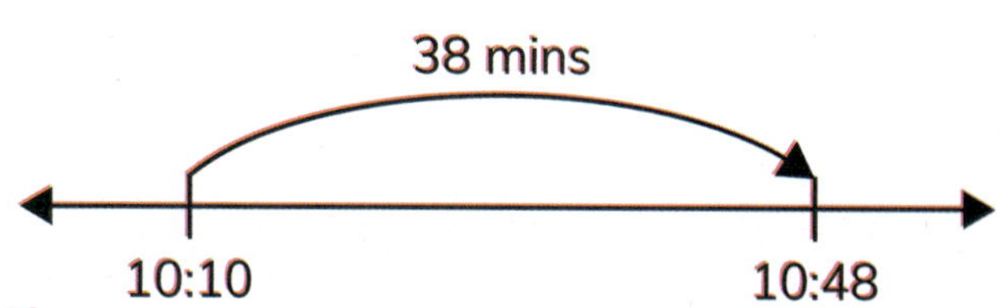

Answer: The 09:09 coach takes the shorter time.

Exercise 2.2

1 Heidi went to her friend's house.
She arrived at 2.00 p.m. and left at 2.45 p.m.
How long was Heidi at her friend's house?

2 The swimming pool opens at 8.00 a.m.
It closes at 6.00 p.m.
How long is the pool open?

3 The time is 9.25 a.m.
Haibo says, 'The time is closer to 09:00 than to 10:00.'
Explain why Haibo is correct.

4 These are the opening times of a museum.

Monday	Closed
Tuesday to Friday	10.30 a.m. to 5.30 p.m.
Saturday	9.00 a.m. to 6.00 p.m.
Sunday	11.00 a.m. to 4.00 p.m.

a How many hours is the museum open on Wednesday?

b Zina arrived at the museum at 3.15 p.m. on Sunday.
How long could she stay before closing time?

5 Here is part of a bus timetable from Dondale to Bodmin.

Dondale	12:12	12:31	12:48	13:02
Knightsbridge	12:21	12:38	12:55	13:11
Bridgetown	12:38	12:52	13:11	13:28
Treham	12:44	13:00	13:17	13:36
Bodmin	13:01	13:17	13:34	13:53

a How many minutes does it take the 13:02 bus from Dondale to reach Bodmin?

b Magda is at Bridgetown at 1 p.m.
What is the earliest time she can reach Treham?
Check your answers with your partner.

6 The Golden Gate Bridge in San Francisco was opened on 27 May 1937.

Jyoti visits the bridge on 27 May 2020.

How many years has the bridge been open?

7 Here is a timetable for Class 4 on Tuesday.

09:00	09:15	09:35	10:35	10:50	11:50	12:35	13:30	14:30	14:45	15:30
Arrival	Assembly	Spanish	Break	Maths	History	Lunch	Science	Break	Art	

a How long does Assembly last?

b How long does morning break last?

c Hassan's favourite lessons are Maths and Science.
How long is spent, in total, in these two lessons?

Questions 4, 5 and 7 use different types of timetable. Which one did you find easiest to use? Why?

Think like a mathematician

a Leila goes swimming each day from Monday 2 December to Friday 6 December.

How many days does she go swimming?

b Ahmed joins a gym club from 1 April to 30 June.

How many months is this?

c Ros works on a project from Wednesday 11 September to Tuesday 8 October.

How many weeks does she work on the project?

Look what I can do!

- [ ] I can read a timetable to solve problems.
- [ ] I can choose and use suitable units to calculate time intervals.

Check your progress

1 Here is a digital clock.

What time is the same as that shown on the clock?

7.07 a.m. | 7.07 p.m. | 5.07 a.m. | 5.07 p.m.

2 Write quarter to twelve in the **morning** as a digital time.

3 Here are five times.

6.45 a.m. | Ten minutes to eight | 15:30 | 9.30 a.m. | quarter past seven

Which time is the 'odd one out'? How do you know?

Continued

4 What are the missing numbers?

a 60 months = □ years

b 72 hours = □ days

c 84 days = □ weeks

5 Bruno leaves school at ten past three. He arrives home at ten to four.

How long does it take him to get home?

6 Use the calendar to answer these questions.

a What day is 13 November?

b What is the date of the first Friday in the month?

c What is the date of the last Saturday of the month?

d The gym club meets on the first and third Wednesday.

What are the dates of the November meetings?

NOVEMBER

S	M	T	W	T	F	S
			1	2	3	4
5	6	7	8	9	10	11
12	13	14	15	16	17	18
19	20	21	22	23	24	25
26	27	28	29	30		

7 The timetable shows the television programmes one morning.

a Gemma turns the television on at 7.45 a.m.

How long does she have to wait for the Weather programme?

b The travel programme lasts 10 minutes.

What time does it finish?

07:30	News
07:55	Weather
08:00	News
08:15	Sport
08:25	Weather
08:30	News
08:45	Travel

8 Use the bus timetable to answer the questions that follow.

Oldcastle	07:09	07:53	11:10	13:12	15:13	18:04	19:10
Diddlington	07:21	08:05	11:22	13:24	15:25	18:16	19:22
Lenford	07:44	08:28	11:45	13:47	15:48	18:39	19:45

a How long does it take to travel from Oldcastle to Diddlington?

b How long does it take to travel from Oldcastle to Lenford?

c What is the latest bus you can catch in Oldcastle if you want to be in Diddlington by 3.30 p.m.?

Project 2

Rolling clock

The picture shows a clock rolling down a slope.

Here are some pictures of different clocks that are on the slope.

What times do they show? How do you know?

A

B

C

D

Here are four more rotated clocks. They show 3 o'clock, 10 minutes past 10, 20 minutes to 4 and half past 11.

1

2

3

4

Which is which?

How do you know?

3 Addition and subtraction of whole numbers

Getting started

You can use any method to answer these questions.
Remember to estimate the size of your answer before you calculate it.

Show all your working.

1 Calculate 42 + 36.

2 Find the difference between 95 and 9.

3 Find the total of 65 and 29.

4 Copy the sorting diagram and write each of these numbers in the correct place.

7 13 12 25 8

	Less than 10	Greater than 10
Even		
Odd		

You add and subtract in your everyday life.

Think about your birthday. Every year you add 1 to your age. This is addition.

Think about a football team. If a player commits a foul they may be given a red card and sent off the field, meaning there is 1 less player on the field. This is subtraction.

Can you think of occasions where you have added or subtracted today? What were you doing?

Look at these 'L shapes'.

Each one is made from an odd number of dots.

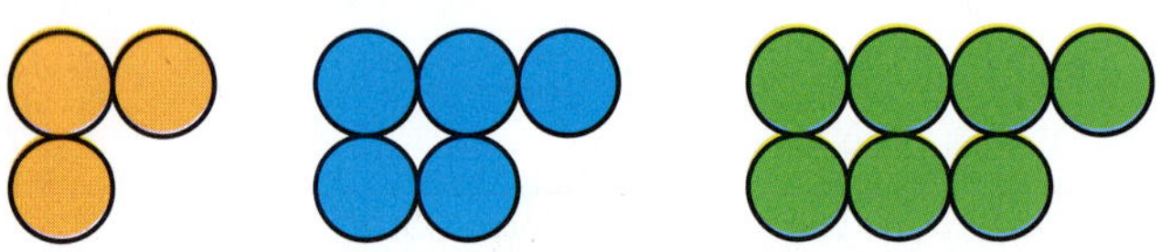

The shapes show us that if we divide an odd number by 2 there is always 'a bit left over'.

Think about what happens when you add and subtract odd and even numbers. Do you end up with odd or even numbers?

In this unit you will also use a symbol to represent a missing number or operation in number sentences.

Can you work out what the square and circle represent?

3 + ☐ = 15   10 ◯ 2 = 20

› 3.1 Using a symbol to represent a missing number or operation

We are going to . . .

- use a symbol to represent a missing number or operation sign in an addition or subtraction calculation.

Many people, both young and old, enjoy solving number puzzles. Very young children start with simple jigsaws, and adults enjoy harder puzzles.

symbol

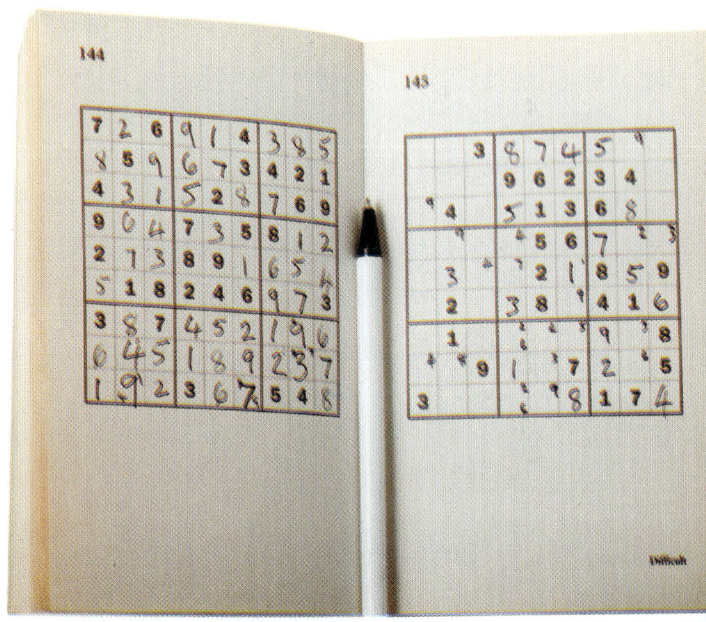

In this unit you will solve missing number puzzles.

You can use a symbol to show a missing number.

For example, 30 – ◯ = 27 or 30 – □ = 27.

Worked example 1

Write the missing number.

650 + □ = 1000

You can read 650 + □ = 1000 as

'I have 650. How many more do I need to make 1000?'

Method 1

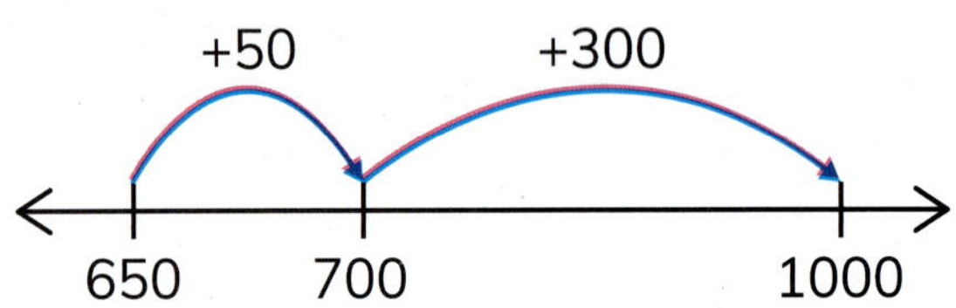

Use a number line to count on from 650.

Remember, the larger the jump the more efficient the method.

Method 2

1000 − 650 = 350

You can rewrite 650 + □ = 1000 as a subtraction: 1000 − 650 = □

Addition and subtraction are inverse operations.

Method 3

650 + 350 = 1000

You can work it out mentally using known facts.

Answer: 350

Exercise 3.1

1 Write the missing numbers.

a 15 + 29 = □

b 35 − 19 = □

c □ − 14 = 8

d □ + 6 = 30

e 12 + □ = 25

f 30 − □ = 16

2 Copy and complete the number sentence.

5□ + □5 = 100

3 Write the missing numbers.

a 1 + 10 + □ = 100

b 57 + □ = 120

c 50 − □ = 31 + 10

4 In this diagram, the numbers on three circles in a straight line add up to 1000.

Copy and complete the diagram.

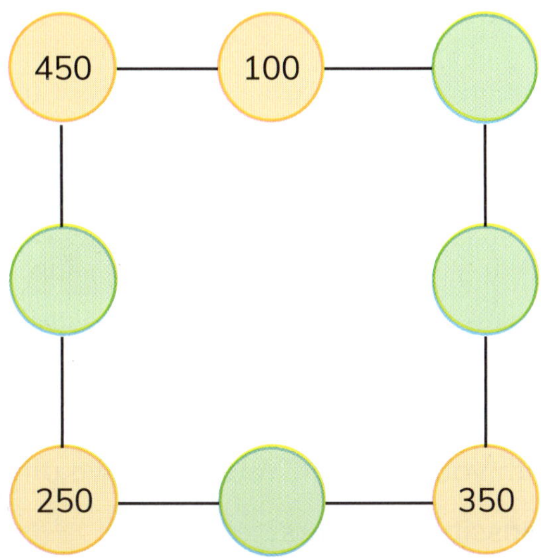

Check your answer with your partner.

In this question, you can choose different starting points.

How did you decide which number to find first?
Did your partner do the same?

Think about your method. Was it the best method?
Did you remember to check your answer?

5 Find the missing operation signs.

a 28 ○ 72 = 100

b 55 = 70 ○ 15

6 In this diagram the rule is:
'Double the number in the square and add the number in the triangle to make the number in the circle'.

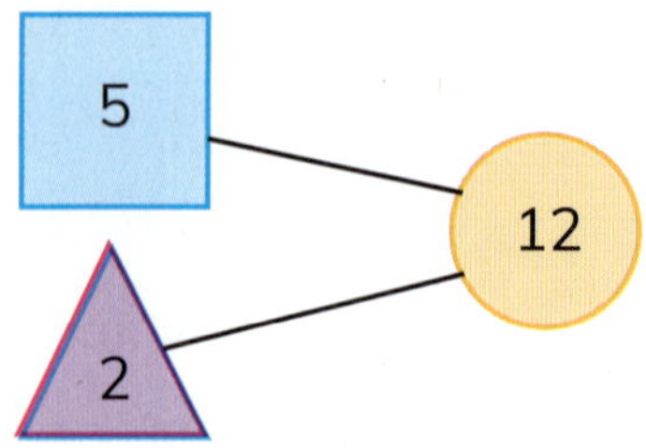

Use the same rule to find these missing numbers.

a

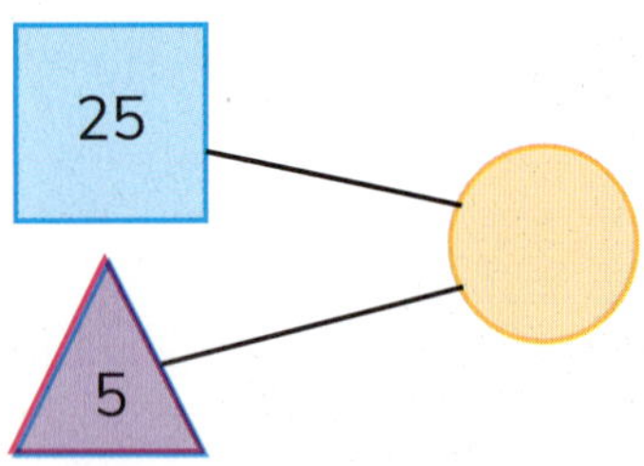

b

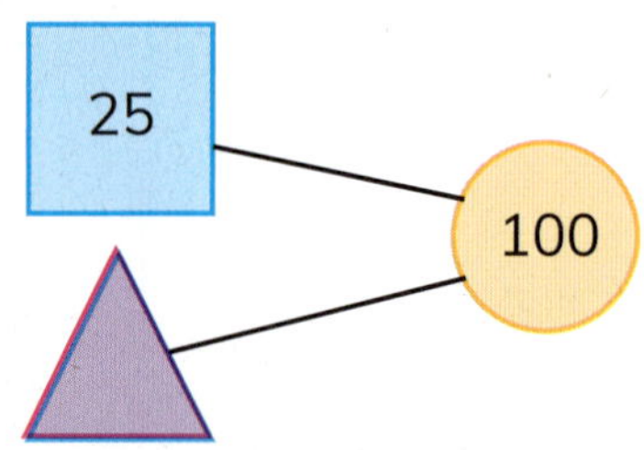

7 □ + △ + ○ = 10

What numbers could □, △ and ○ represent?

Discuss your answer with your partner. You may have different answers.

Can you think of other possible answers?

Think like a mathematician

Use each of the numbers 3, 4, 5, 6 and 7 to complete the cross pattern. The total going across must be the same as the total going down.

You will show you are **specialising** when you find solutions to the problem.

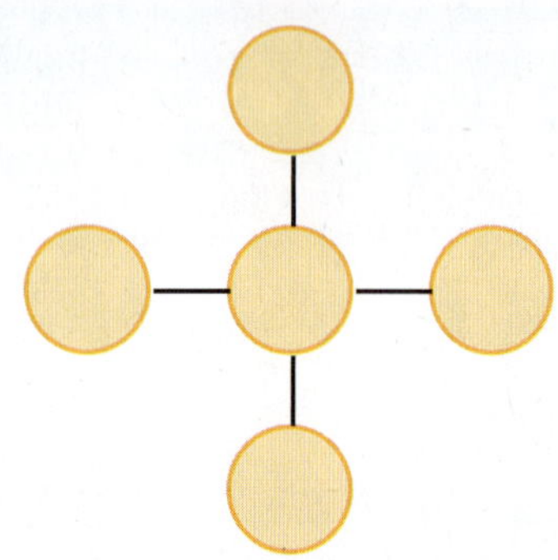

Look what I can do!

- ☐ I can find a missing number represented by a symbol.
- ☐ I can find a missing operation sign represented by a symbol.

3.2 Addition and subtraction of whole numbers

We are going to . . .

- compose (put together) whole numbers
- decompose (split) a whole number into parts
- regroup a number as part of a calculation
- choose an appropriate mental or written calculation to add or subtract whole numbers
- estimate the size of an answer before doing the calculation.

When you go shopping you spend money. You use addition to work out how much to pay. You use subtraction to work out how much change you should get.

In this section, you will estimate and then add and subtract pairs of 2-digit numbers mentally. You will learn about different written methods for addition and subtraction.

compose
decompose
difference
regroup

Worked example 2

Written method of addition

Calculate 235 + 174.

Estimate 200 + 200 = 400	Start with an estimate.
235 = 200 + 30 + 5	
174 = 100 + 70 + 4	Decompose the numbers.
235 + 174 = 300 + 100 + 9	Add the hundreds, tens and ones together.
= 409	Then compose the parts.

Answer: 409

Worked example 3

Written method of subtraction

Calculate:

a 459 – 318 **b** 424 – 179

a 459 – 318

Estimate 500 – 300 = 200	Start with an estimate.
459 = 400 + 50 + 9	Decompose the numbers.
318 = 300 + 10 + 8	
459 – 318 = 100 + 40 + 1	Subtract the hundreds, tens and ones.
= 141	Then compose the parts.

b 424 – 179

Estimate 400 – 200 = 200	Sometimes when you decompose, you need to regroup before you can subtract the hundreds, tens and ones.
424 = 300 + 110 + 14	
179 = 100 + 70 + 9	
424 – 179 = 200 + 40 + 5	$\begin{array}{r} 400 + 20 + 4 \\ - \; 100 + 70 + 9 \\ \hline \end{array} \longrightarrow \begin{array}{r} 300 + 110 + 14 \\ - \; 100 + \;\; 70 + \;\; 9 \\ \hline \end{array}$
= 245	

Answers:

a 141 **b** 245

Think like a mathematician

Addition patterns

You can use any calendar for this investigation.

March						
Su	M	Tu	W	Th	F	Sa
		1	2	3	4	5
6	7	8	9	10	11	12
13	14	15	16	17	18	19
20	21	22	23	24	25	26
27	28	29	30	31		

April						
Su	M	Tu	W	Th	F	Sa
					1	2
3	4	5	6	7	8	9
10	11	12	13	14	15	16
17	18	19	20	21	22	23
24	25	26	27	28	29	30

a Choose a 3 × 3 square on the calendar, for example:

8	9	10
15	16	17
22	23	24

b Add opposite corners.

8	
	24

8 + 24 = 32

	10
22	

10 + 22 = 32

c Investigate other 3 × 3 squares.

d Record your results.

- You will show you are **generalising** when you recognise patterns in your results.
- If you explain your results, you will show you are **convincing**.

Exercise 3.2

1 a Calculate 607 − 391.

 b Find the sum of 376 and 219.

 c What is the difference between 345 and 67?

 d Subtract 385 from 721.

Tip

Remember to estimate before you calculate.

2 Rajiv says, 'If you add 6 to a number ending in 7 you will always get a number ending in 3.'
Is Rajiv correct?
Discuss your answer with a partner and write an explanation.

How did you decide whether Rajiv was correct or not?

How did you explain your answer?

Did you think about showing examples on a diagram like a hundred square or writing a list of examples in a systematic way?

How could you improve your answer?

3 Asif needs 355 chairs for a school concert.
He has 269 chairs already.
How many more chairs does he need?

4 The table shows the mass of some fruit and vegetables.

Fruit or vegetable	Mass
Apple	130 g
Banana	210 g
Carrot	90 g
Potato	240 g

How much do the apple and banana weigh altogether?

5 Pierre had 469 stamps at the beginning of the year.
During the year he collected 137 more stamps.
How many stamps does he have at the end of the year?

Swap with a partner and check their answer.
Have they used the same method as you?
Did they get the same answer?

6 Bashir is thinking of a number.
He says, 'If I subtract 16 from my number, the answer is 95.'
What number is Bashir thinking of?
Discuss your answer with a partner.

7 Aiko says, 'When you add two 2-digit whole numbers together the answer cannot be a 4-digit number.'
Is Aiko correct?
Explain your reasoning.

Look what I can do!

- [ ] I can choose an appropriate mental or written calculation to add or subtract whole numbers.
- [ ] I can estimate the size of an answer before doing the calculation.
- [ ] I can solve problems involving the addition and subtraction of whole numbers.

3.3 Generalising with odd and even numbers

We are going to . . .

- make and test general statements involving addition and subtraction of odd and even numbers.

counter-example
even
generalisation
(general statement)
odd

Each 'L-shape' is made from an odd number of dots.

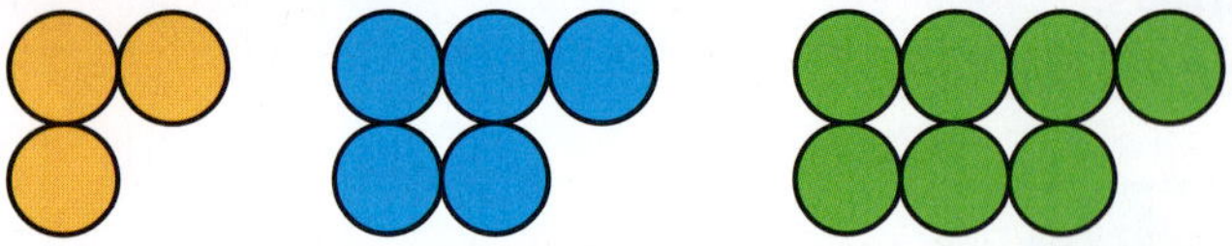

What happens when you put two similar L-shapes together?

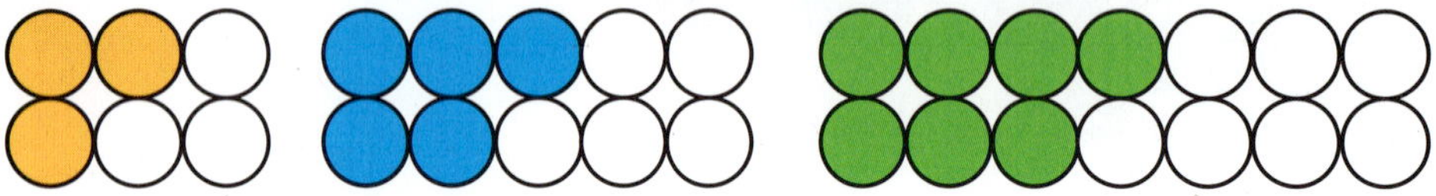

Each rectangle is made from an even number of dots.

3 + 3 = 6

5 + 5 = 10

7 + 7 = 14

In each case odd + odd = even.

A statement like this that uses odd to stand for **any** odd number and even to stand for **any** even number is called a generalisation or general statement. It works for **all** examples.

In this section, you will add and subtract odd and even numbers.

Worked example 4

Paula says, 'I added three odd numbers and my answer was 50.'
Explain why Paula cannot be correct.

1 + 3 + 5 = 9 11 + 23 + 35 = 69 9 and 69 are odd and Paula's answer of 50 is even.	Try some examples of three odd numbers added together.
I know that: odd + odd = even If I add another odd number I get: even + odd = odd	Think about any general statements you know that are always true.

Continued

Answer: Adding three odd numbers always gives an odd answer, so Paula cannot be correct because 50 is even.

You could explain this answer using the general statement:

odd + odd + odd = odd

Exercise 3.3

1 Find three examples that match these general statements.

- The sum of two even numbers is even.
- The sum of three odd numbers is odd.

2 Here are three cards.

odd	even	odd or even

Choose one card to complete this sentence.

When you add two odd numbers together the answer is _____ .

3 Here are six digit cards.

1	2	3	4	5	6

Use three cards to show the difference between two even numbers is even.

□ − □ = □

Think of two other even numbers and show the difference between them. Does this also show that the difference between two even numbers is even?

4 Hassan says, 'Adding two odd numbers always gives an odd number answer.' Give a counter-example to show that Hassan is wrong.

5 Martha says, 'I added three even numbers and my answer was 25.' Explain why Martha cannot be correct. Discuss your answer with a partner.

6 Salem says, 'When you add 5 to any number the answer will be odd.'
Is he correct?
Explain how you know.
Discuss with your partner.

7 Heidi says, 'When you find the difference between two odd numbers the answer is odd.'
Is she correct?
Explain how you know.
Discuss with your partner.

Look back at your answers to questions 5, 6 and 7.

- Did you use the worked example to help you?
- Did you find it helpful to discuss your answers with your partner?
- How can you improve your answers?

Think like a mathematician

Odd lines

a Place the numbers 1 to 9 inside the grid so that each row, column and diagonal add up to an odd number.

b You can extend this investigation to look at the numbers 1 to 16 on a 4 × 4 grid.

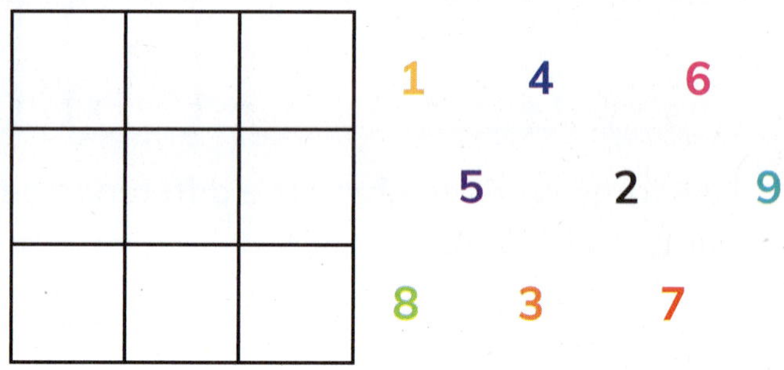

- You will show you are **specialising** when you find solutions to the problem.
- You will show you are **conjecturing** if you make predictions about results on a 4 x 4 grid, based on those for 3 x 3 grid.

Look what I can do!

☐ I can make and test general statements involving addition and subtraction of odd and even numbers.

Check your progress

1 Write the missing number.

100 − □ = 58

2 Write the missing number.

2 + 20 + □ = 100

3 A total of 245 chairs are needed for a school performance.
169 chairs are already in place.
How many chairs need to be put in place?

4 A school library has 387 books.
They are given 79 books.
How many books are in the library now?

5 Here are six digit cards.

1 2 3 4 5 6

Use four of the cards to make this calculation correct.

□□ + □□ = 60

6 Bashir is thinking of a number.
He says, 'If I add 26 to my number, the answer is 95.'
What number is Bashir thinking of?

7 Find three examples to match the statement, 'the sum of three even numbers is even'.

8 Alma says, 'When you add 4 to any number the answer is always an even number.'
Is Alma correct?
Explain how you know.

4 Probability

Getting started

1 Write one of these phrases to describe the chance of each event happening.

It will happen | It might happen | It will not happen

a You will see a monster today.

b You will write something at school today.

c You will flip a coin once and it will land on heads.

2 Sylvester counted the different colour flowers in the garden. These are the flowers.

a Which tally chart shows the flowers Sylvester counted?

A

Colour	Number of flowers
Red	||
Yellow	|||
Blue	𝍸 ||

B

Colour	Number of flowers
Red	||
Yellow	||||
Blue	𝍸 |

C

Colour	Number of flowers
Red	||||
Yellow	||
Blue	𝍸 |

b Which colour flower are you most likely to see in the garden?

c Which colour flower are you least likely to see in the garden?

3 Spinner A

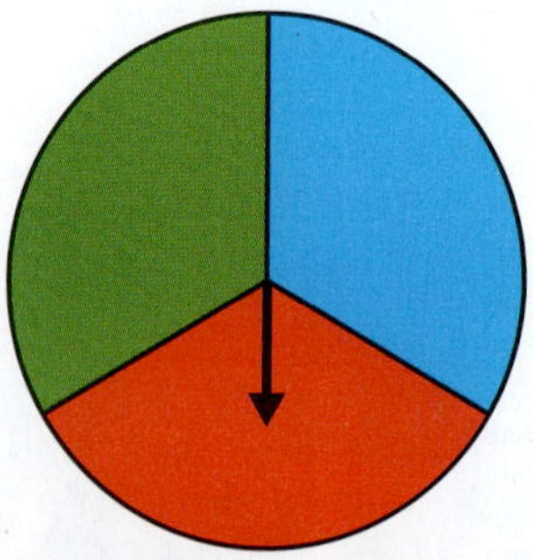

Spinner B

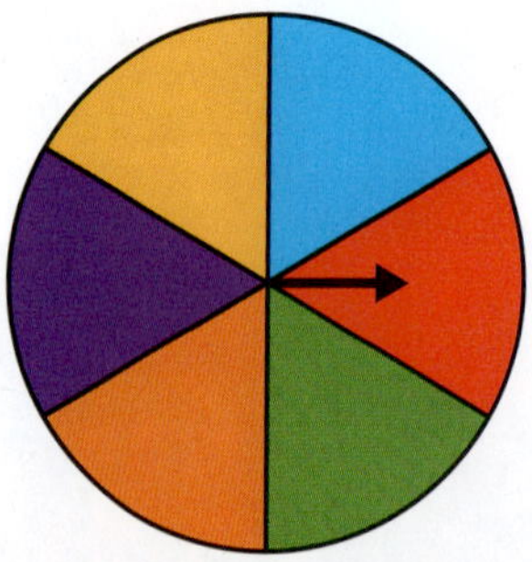

Are you more likely to get a red spin on Spinner A or Spinner B?

Explain why.

Probability and likelihood about understanding the world and the decisions you make every day. It helps you to decide what risks to take. A weather forecast uses probability and likelihood to explain how likely it is to rain.

Which people should take an umbrella? Explain your decisions to your partner.

4.1 Likelihood

We are going to . . .

- use likelihood words to describe the chance of events happening
- use experiments to investigate the chance of events happening.

Likelihood is about how likely something is to happen. Lots of people need to know what event is most likely to happen or what the chance is that something will happen.

Farmers and gardeners need to know about the likelihood of rainfall and sunshine so that they can decide which crops to grow. Leaders need to know what the likely outcomes are in a situation as this will help them make the right decisions.

certain
even chance
good chance
likely
likelihood
maybe
no chance
outcome
poor chance

Worked example 1

What is the likelihood of a dice landing on 5?

Use the language of chance.

Step 1: It is possible for the dice to land on 5, so the likelihood cannot be described as 'no chance'.	Check if the outcome is impossible. An impossible outcome has 'no chance'.
Step 2: The dice could also land on 1, 2, 3, 4 or 6, so the likelihood cannot be described as 'certain'.	Check if the outcome is certain.
Step 3: There are more outcomes that are not 5, so it is unlikely the dice will land on 5.	Are there more outcomes that **are** 5, or more outcomes that are **not** 5?

Answer: There is a **poor chance** that the dice will land on 5.

Exercise 4.1

1 Choose one of these words or phrases to describe the likelihood that each event happens.

No chance	Poor chance	Even chance	Good chance	Certain

a The sun will go down today.

b I will drop a cake and it will fly upwards.

c I will find a four-leaf clover.

d I will be taller in three months.

e I will pick a red apple from this bag without looking.

2 Write an event of your own that matches the likelihood.

a It is certain I will . . .

b There is no chance I will . . .

c There is a poor chance I will . . .

d There is a good chance I will . . .

e Maybe I will . . .

f It is likely that I will . . .

3 A website shows a head or tail on a coin when you press 'Flip the coin'.

Otto pressed the button 20 times. Here are the results.

Copy and complete the table to show Otto's results.

	Total
Heads	
Tails	

4 Sal makes this spinner.

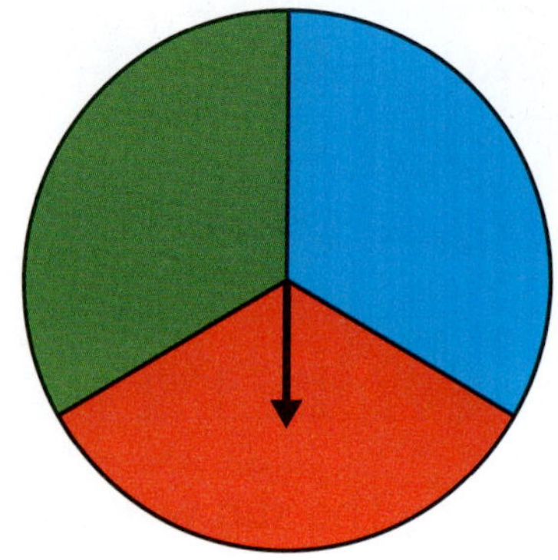

a What is the chance that it will land on red?

b What is the chance that it will land on yellow?

c What is the chance that it will land on a colour?

5 Jess makes a different spinner. She spins it 50 times. These are the results.

Colour	Tally	Total
Red	卌 卌 II	12
Blue	卌 卌 卌	15
Yellow	卌 卌 I	11
Green		0
Purple	卌 卌 II	12

Draw what you think Jess's spinner looks like.

Talk to your partner about your drawing. Try to convince them of the reasons why you think Jess's spinner looks like the spinner you have drawn.

Think like a mathematician

Work with a partner to investigate the results when you roll a dice 50 times.

Together draw a table to record how many of each number you roll.

It could look like this:

Number	Tally	Total
1		
2		
3		
4		
5		
6		

Continued

Think about these questions, then conjecture and discuss them with your partner.

- What do you think the tally chart will look like when you have finished? Why?
- How many 1s do you think you will throw? Why?
- How many 8s do you think you will throw? Why?

Roll the dice 50 times and record the outcomes in your table. Discuss each of these questions and answer them together in sentences using the words 'likely', 'maybe', 'no chance', 'poor chance', 'even chance', 'good chance' or 'certain'.

a What is the chance of rolling a 3?

b What is the chance of rolling a 7?

c What is the chance of rolling an odd number?

d What is the chance of rolling a number less than 10?

Based on your investigation, write a conjecture of your own about chance. Share and discuss your sentence with your partner. Does your partner use the language of chance correctly to show that they understand it?

Think about how you collected the outcomes of your investigation and recorded them in your table.

- Did you record the outcomes quickly? If yes, how? If no, what could you change?
- Did you record the outcomes accurately? If yes, how? If no, what could you change?
- Did you find the totals quickly? If yes, how? If no, what could you change?
- Is your table easy to read? If yes, how? If no, what could you change?

Look what I can do!

- [ ] I can use the correct language to describe the chance of events happening.
- [ ] I can carry out experiments to explore the chance of events happening and I can describe the results.

Check your progress

1 There are ten sweets in the jar. Beth takes a sweet out of the jar without looking.

Are these statements true or false?

a It is certain that Beth will take a red sweet.

b There is no chance that Beth will take a red sweet.

c There is a good chance that Beth will take a yellow sweet.

d There is a poor chance that Beth will take a blue sweet.

e There is a poor chance that Beth will take a green sweet.

2 Everyone in the group flipped a coin ten times.

Copy and complete the sentence:

There is _____ of flipping a tail.

Here are the outcomes.

Copy and complete the table to show how many heads and tails there are.

	Tally	Total
Head		
Tail		

5 Multiplication, multiples and factors

Getting started

1 Copy and complete this multiplication grid.

×	1	5	10	
10	10			
5				
2				
1				2

2 Write the first four multiples of 5.

3 Write the missing number.

$3 \times \square = 9 \times 3$

4 Answer this question without a calculator.

Explain your method.

$39 \times 3 + 39 \times 7$

5 Calculate 19×3.

Show your method.

This unit is all about multiplication, multiplication tables, multiples and factors.

Arrays are helpful for thinking about multiplication facts.

You can spot arrays everywhere in real life when you begin to look around.

Can you think of other examples of arrays?

In this unit, you will learn about factors for the first time.

You can use the array to help find factors.

3 and 5 are factors of 15.

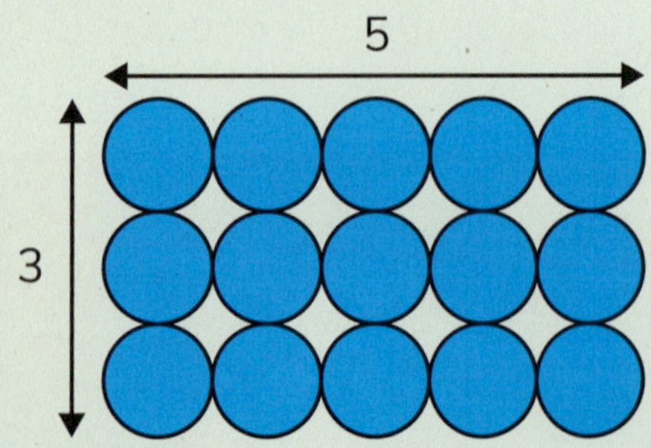

5.1 Tables, multiples and factors

We are going to . . .

- find multiplication facts for all tables
- recognise factors and find factors of numbers
- recognise multiples and find multiples of numbers.

In this section you will extend your knowledge of table facts to include the 7 times table and you will work out multiples and factors of whole numbers.

array
factor
inverse operations
multiple
product

How many people can share this chocolate bar so that everyone has the same number of pieces?

How many pieces do they each get?

The number of people and the number of pieces are factors of 28.

Worked example 1

This bar of chocolate is divided into 24 pieces.

4 and 6 are factors of 24.

Find all the factors of 24.

Method 1

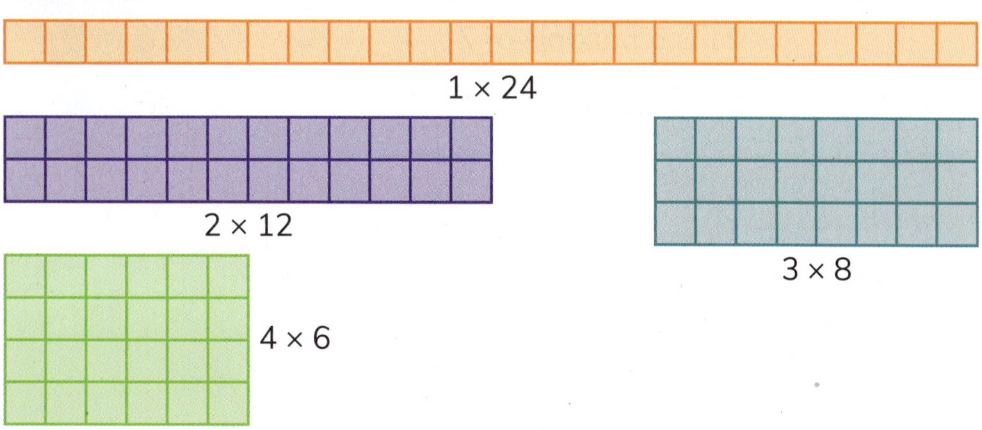

Draw diagrams to show all the ways you can arrange the 24 pieces into rectangles.

Continued

Method 2

Draw a factor bug where each pair of legs has a product of 24.

The legs on the left-hand side show numbers in order starting from 1.

Method 3

1 × 24 = 24

2 × 12 = 24

3 × 8 = 24

4 × 6 = 24

Record all the multiplication facts where the product is 24.

Answer: The factors of 24 are 1, 2, 3, 4, 6, 8, 12, 24

Exercise 5.1

1 Helga is thinking of a 2-digit number.
She says:
It is less than 3 × 6
It is more than 3 × 5
It is not equal to 2 × 8
What is Helga's number?

2 Here is part of a number grid.

21	22	23	24
31	32	33	34
41	42	43	44
51	52	53	54

Which numbers are multiples of 7?

Tip

Remember you can check a division fact using multiplication.

21 ÷ 7 = 3 because 3 × 7 = 21

21 is a multiple of 7

Multiplication and division are inverse operations.

3 Copy and complete this list of factors.

The factors of 32 are 1, ____, ____, ____, ____, 32

4 Bruno says, 'The dates of all the Saturdays this month are 1 less than a multiple of 7.'

S	M	T	W	T	F	S
	1	2	3	4	5	6
7	8	9	10	11	12	13
14	15	16	17	18	19	20
21	22	23	24	25	26	27
28	29	30				

Is Bruno right?
Explain your answer.

5 Sam picks 50 apples.
He packs **all** the apples into boxes.
He puts the same number of apples in each box.
How many boxes does Sam use?
Find different solutions.

6 Here are ten digit cards.

0	1	2	3	4	5	6	7	8	9

Use each card once to make five 2-digit numbers that are multiples of 3.
Ask your partner to check your answers.
Did you both make the same numbers?

7 Copy and complete the calculation so that the answer is a multiple of 8.

57 + ☐ = ☐

Can you find more than one answer?

Look back at your answers to questions 5, 6 and 7.
In questions 5 and 7, what did you do to help you find different answers?
In question 6, how did you make sure you used all the cards?
Think about whether you worked systematically.

8 Copy the Venn diagram and write the numbers in the correct place.

5 6 7 8

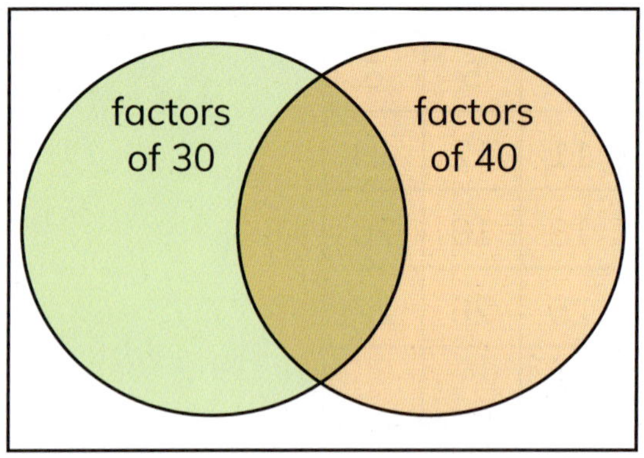

Think like a mathematician

Here are four cards.

3 4 5 6

a Place the cards in a square and multiply across the columns.

4	3
6	5

$4 \times 3 = 12$

$6 \times 5 = 30$

b Move the cards and multiply again.

c How many different products can you find?

- You will show you are **generalising** when you recognise patterns in your results.
- If you explain your results, you will show you are **convincing**.

Tip

The product of 4 and 3 is 12.

The product, 12, is the answer to the multiplication.

Look what I can do!

- ☐ I can find multiplication facts for all tables.
- ☐ I can recognise factors and find factors of numbers.
- ☐ I can recognise multiples and find multiples of numbers.

5.2 Multiplication

We are going to . . .

- group numbers in different ways in multiplication using the associative law
- estimate the answer to multiplying a whole number up to 1000 by a 1-digit number
- multiply a whole number by a 1-digit number.

Do you enjoy eating chocolate? This bar could be split into 24 pieces or into 6 lots of 4 or 4 lots of 6.

associative law
carry

$4 \times 6 = 24$

$6 \times 4 = 24$

In this unit, you will multiply larger numbers by 1-digit numbers. You should always estimate the size of the answer first to check your answer is about right.

Worked example 2

Calculate 18 × 5 using factors.

$18 = 9 \times 2$ — 9 and 2 are factors of 18.

So, $18 \times 5 = 9 \times 2 \times 5$
$= 9 \times 10$
$= 90$

The associative law allows you to multiply numbers in any order, so you can do 2 × 5 first.

Answer: 90

Worked example 3

Calculate 27 × 4.

Use the most efficient method you understand.

Estimate first:

$30 \times 3 = 90$ and $30 \times 4 = 120$

so the answer will be between 90 and 120

Mental method

27×4 → $20 \times 4 = 80$ and $7 \times 4 = 28$

Decompose 27 into 20 and 7.

Multiply 20 by 4.

Multiply 7 by 4.

$27 \times 4 = 80 + 28 = 108$

Add the two answers together.

Grid method

×	20	7
4	80	28

$80 + 28 = 108$

Set out the number in a grid.

You can easily extend this method to multiply larger numbers and to multiply by a 2-digit number.

Continued

Expanded method

	20	+ 7			
		× 4			
	8	0		20 × 4	
	2	8		7 × 4	
1	0	8			
1					

Show the stages of your working.

You do not have to write 20 × 4 and 7 × 4 in your working.

Compact method

	2	7	
		× 4	
1	0	8	
	2		

This is a standard written method involving carrying.

7 × 4 = 28. Write down 8 and carry 2 tens.

20 × 4 = 80. Add on 20 to give 100. Write down 0 and carry 1 hundred.

Answer: 108

Exercise 5.2

1 Magda calculates 14 × 5 using factors.
She spills ink on her work. What number is under the ink blots?

2 Amir and Ben work out 4 × 15.

Amir's method	Ben's method
$4 \times 15 = 4 \times 5 \times 3$	$4 \times 15 = 2 \times 2 \times 15$
$= 20 \times 3$	$= 2 \times 30$
$= 60$	$= 60$

Which method do you like best? Explain why.
Discuss your answer with your partner.
Think of other ways to work out 4 × 15.

3 Work out the following. Estimate your answer first.

a 47 × 5 **b** 29 × 4 **c** 89 × 3 **d** 74 × 6

Compare the methods you used with your partner.
Identify the advantages and disadvantages of each method.

4 Sultan uses the grid method to work out his calculations, but he spills ink on his work.
Copy and complete the calculations.

a 47 × 3 =

×	40	7
3	■	21

■ + 21 = 141

b 93 × 4 =

×	■	3
4	■	12

■ + 12 = 372

c 51 × 5 =

×	50	1
5	■	■

■ + 5 = 255

d 87 × 4 =

×	80	■
4	■	28

■ + 28 = 348

5 Find the product of 56 and 5.

6 Pencils are sold in packs of 5. Each pack costs 95 cents.
Fatima buys 4 packs of pencils. How much does she spend?

7 Use the digits 2, 3 and 5 once to make the multiplication with the greatest product.

□□ × □

Work out the answer.
Compare your answer with your partner.
The person with the larger answer should explain their method.

8 Work out the following. Estimate your answer first.

a 174×4 b 129×7 c 189×3 d 119×8

Compare the methods you used with your partner.
Identify the advantages and disadvantages of each method.

Think about the methods you have used to multiply.
Which one works best for you? Why?

Think like a mathematician

A 3-digit number is multiplied by 3.

There are five different missing digits in the calculation: 1, 2, 6, 7 and 8.

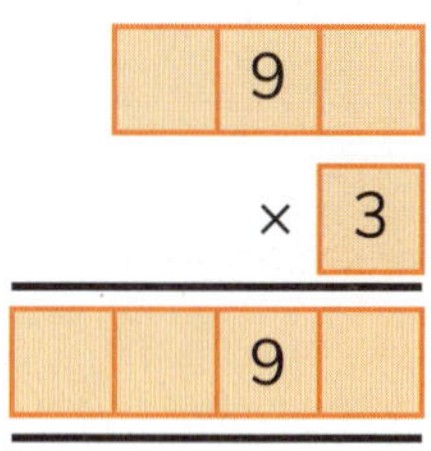

Use these clues to help you complete the calculation.

- The sum of the digits of the 3-digit number is 24.
- The digits in the 3-digit number are consecutive numbers but they are not written in order.
- The answer is between 2000 and 3000.

You will show you are **specialising** when you find solutions to the problem.

Look what I can do!

- [ ] I can group numbers in different ways to help me multiply.
- [ ] I can estimate answers to a calculation before doing the calculation.
- [ ] I can multiply a whole number by a 1-digit number.

Check your progress

1 Here are four digit cards.

5 6 7 8

Use each card once to make this statement correct.

□ × □ = □□

2 Fatima says, 'All multiples of 5 end in 5.'
Is Fatima correct? Explain your answer.

3 Find the product of 800 and 4.

4 42 is the product of two consecutive numbers.

$6 \times 7 = 42$

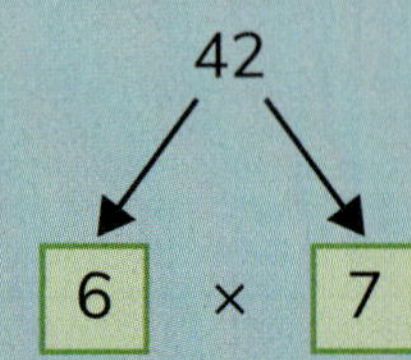

Find the missing pairs of consecutive numbers.

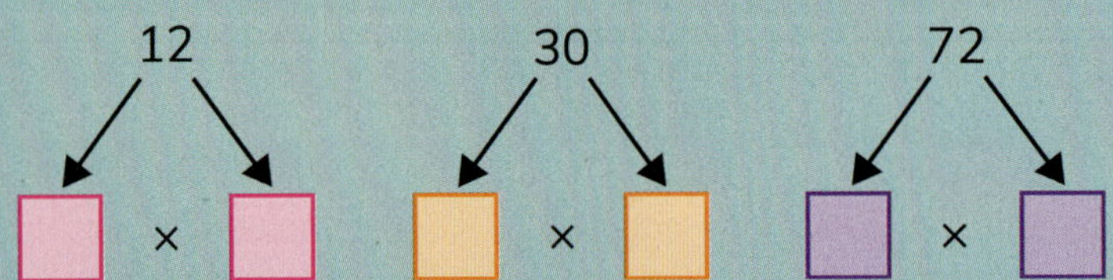

5 Erik and Igor calculate 16 × 2 × 5.
Copy and complete their calculations. Who chose the better method?

Maria and Ingrid calculate 6 × 2 × 15.
Complete their calculations. Who chose the better method?

Continued

6 Here are four digit cards.

3 5 7 0

Use each card **once** to complete these statements.

☐☐ is a multiple of 5 greater than 50.

☐☐ is a multiple of 10 less than 50.

7 Find all the factors of 16.
Find all the factors of 18.
Find all the factors of 20.

What do you notice about the number of factors of 16 compared to the number of factors of 18 and 20?
Why does this happen?

8 Calculate:

a 79×8 b 428×9 c 167×7

9 Here is a number machine.

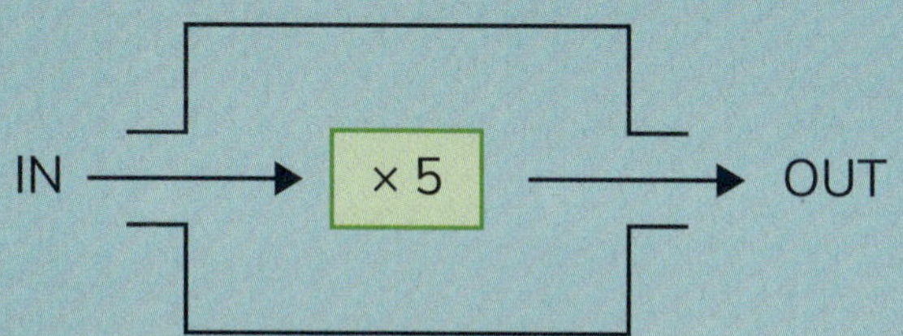

Copy and complete the table.

IN	OUT
123	
345	
567	

Project 3

Square statements

Each of these squares represents a different number from 1 to 10.

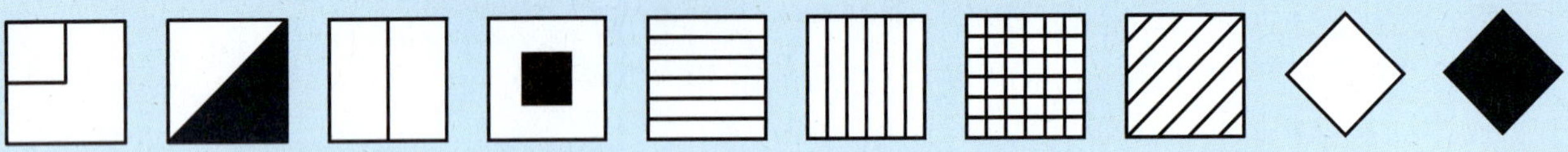

Here are nine statements about these squares. Can you use the statements to work out which number each square stands for?

1 

2  is odd

3 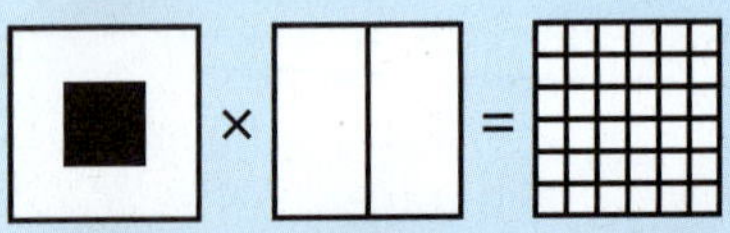

4 

5  and  are factors of 

6 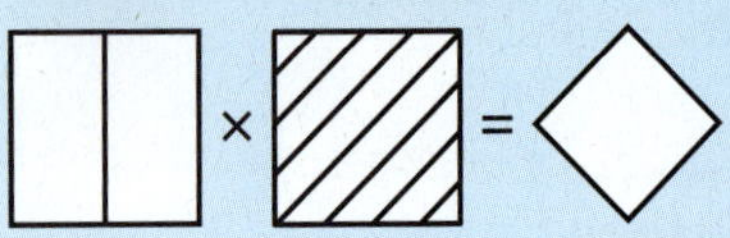

7 The only factors of  are  and 

8  is a multiple of 

9  is the smallest even number

Once you've worked that out, have another look at the statements.

Which ones did you use?
Are there any that aren't helpful? Why?

6 2D shapes

Getting started

1 Write the name of each shape. Use the list of shapes to help you.

triangle | circle | rectangle | hexagon | square | pentagon

a 

b 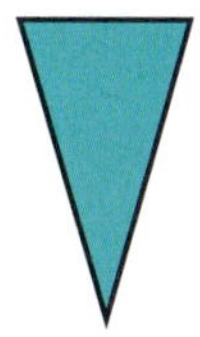

c 

2 Draw a closed shape with five straight sides and five vertices.
What is the name of the shape you have drawn?

3 Which of these shapes is not a hexagon? Explain how you know.

A 

B 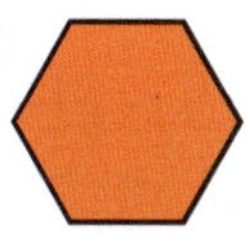

C 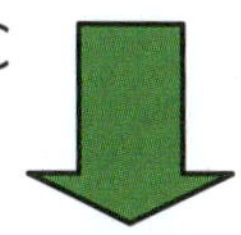

D 

4 Copy the sentence about this pentagon.
Choose the correct word and complete the sentence.

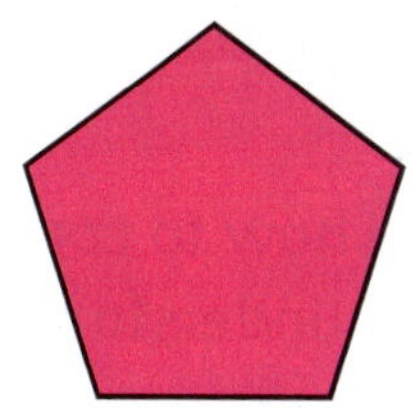

This pentagon is regular / irregular because
it has _____ and _____ .

5 Some of these shapes are symmetrical. For each shape write 'yes' if there is symmetry, or 'no' if there is no symmetry.

a 

b 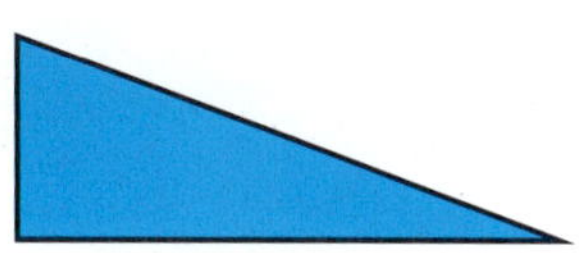

c 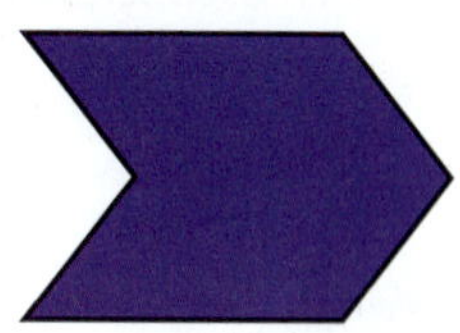

d 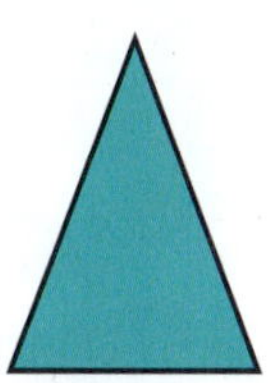

e 

Knowing about 2D shapes and their tessellation and reflective symmetry is useful in art and design for designing floor and wall tile designs, and fabric.

What 2D shapes can you see in this picture?

6.1 2D shapes and tessellation

We are going to . . .

- investigate 2D shapes that can be made by putting two or more shapes together
- develop understanding of the properties of 2D shapes
- explore tessellation of 2D shapes.

Understanding how to combine 2D shapes to make new shapes will help you to understand how shape can be broken down into smaller parts to help you solve problems.

Tessellation is important in many designs.
Which shapes are tessellating in these pictures?

2D shape
parallel
polygon
regular
tessellation

Exercise 6.1

1 Copy and complete each sentence to name the small shapes and name the shape that has been made by putting them together.

a

The four ____ make a ____ .

b

The two ____ make a ____ .

c

The four ____ make ____ .

2 Name a 2D shape that has each of these characteristics.

a At least one right angle.

b At least one curved side.

c At least one pair of parallel sides.

d At least 7 vertices.

e Not a polygon.

Worked example 1

Can this shape by made by putting three triangles together?

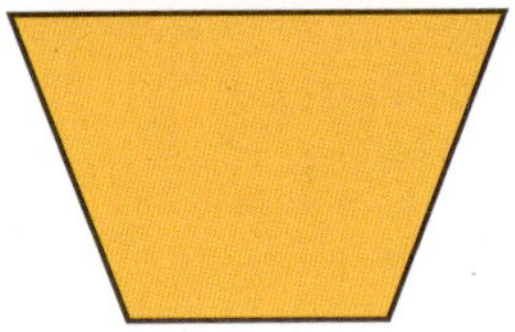

Method 1

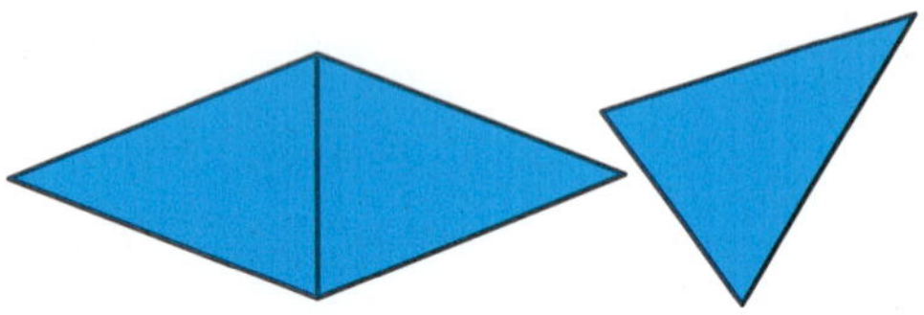

Take three triangles and put them together in different ways to try to make the shape.

Method 2

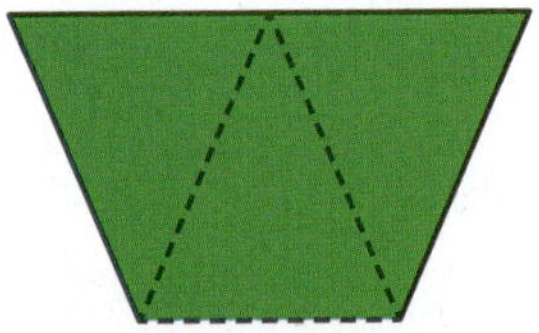

Draw lines on the shape to see if it can be divided into three triangles.

Answer: Yes, the shape can be made with three triangles.

3 Can each shape be made by putting this rectangle and these two triangles together? Answer 'yes' or 'no'.

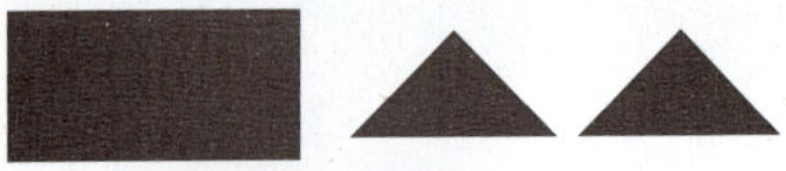

a 

b 

c 

d 

Which method from the worked example do you think is better? Why?

When did you, or might you, use Method 1 and Method 2 to investigate how shapes can go together to make a new shape?

4 Name the shapes in these tessellating tile patterns.

a

b

c

d

5 Make a template by drawing a triangle onto card.
You could trace and copy one of these triangles.

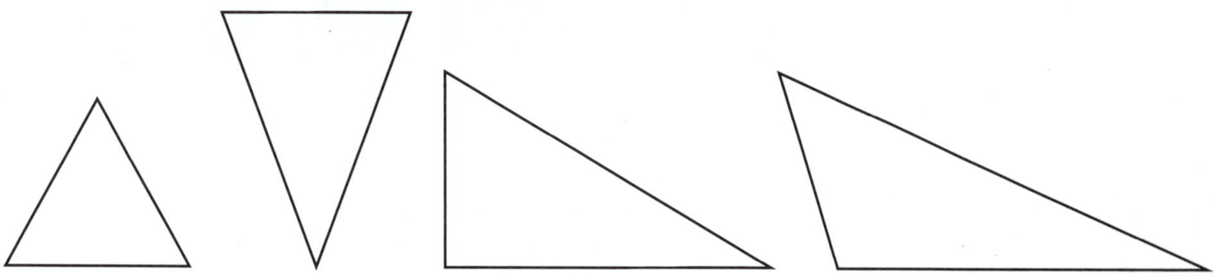

Cut out your template and draw around it ten times to make a tessellating pattern.

Try doing the same with a different triangle.

Do all the triangles tessellate?

Think like a mathematician

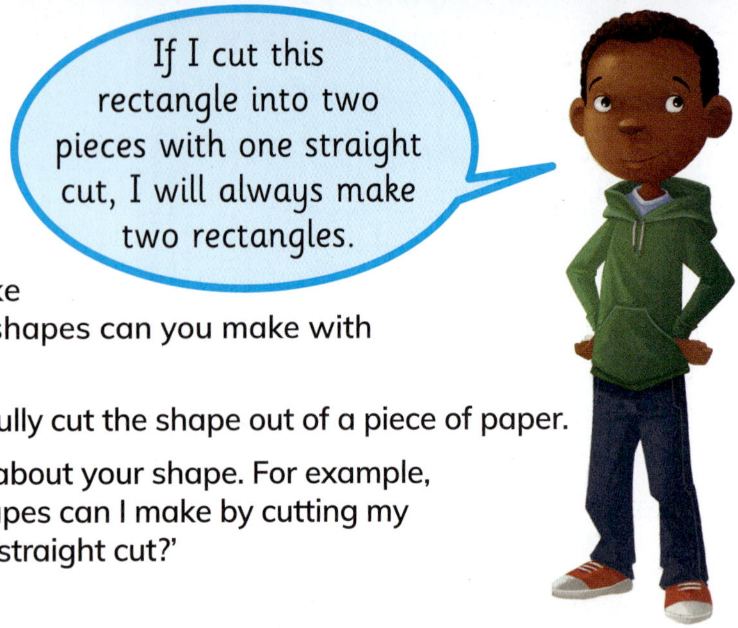

Marcus is not correct.

- **a** Trace and cut out rectangles like Marcus's. What other pairs of shapes can you make with one straight cut?
- **b** Choose a different shape. Carefully cut the shape out of a piece of paper.
- **c** Write a question to investigate about your shape. For example, you could conjecture: 'What shapes can I make by cutting my shape into two pieces with one straight cut?'
- **d** Investigate your question.
- **e** Write a convincing conclusion by copying and completing this sentence:

I found out that . . .

Assess your learning and working in the investigation by answering these questions:

- **a** Did you ask a question that you were able to find the answer to?
- **b** Did you think about how you would find all the possible solutions? Explain your answer.
- **c** Did your investigation give you a better understanding of how two shapes can be put together to make a new shape? Explain your answer.

Look what I can do!

- ☐ I can put two or more 2D shapes together and name the new shape they make.
- ☐ I can name the properties of 2D shapes, such as their number of sides.
- ☐ I can put shapes together to make tessellating patterns, and find out if a shape will tessellate on its own.

6.2 Symmetry

We are going to . . .

- improve our understanding of symmetry in 2D shapes
- find all the lines of symmetry in 2D shapes and patterns.

Symmetrical patterns are usually beautiful and fascinating. You can see symmetry all around you in nature and in art and design. Learning about symmetry helps you to notice similarity, difference and balance, which is important to all parts of mathematics.

horizontal
line of symmetry
symmetry
vertical

Exercise 6.2

1 How many lines of symmetry does each pattern have?

Use a mirror to check for lines of symmetry.

Check for a vertical line, a horizontal line and the two diagonal lines.

a 

b 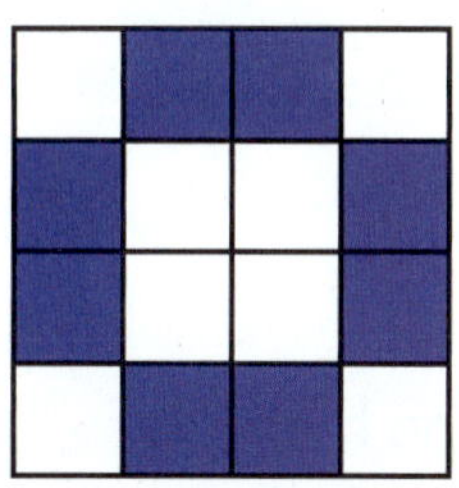

c 

d 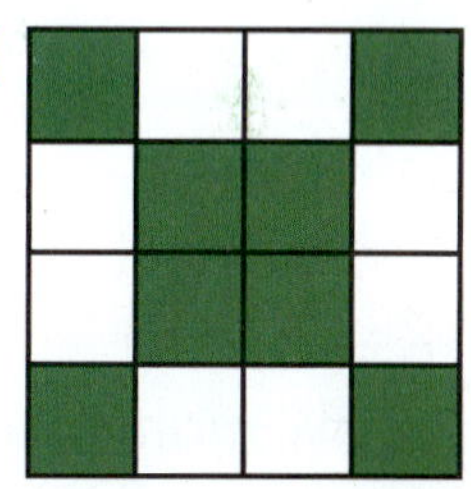

e 

f 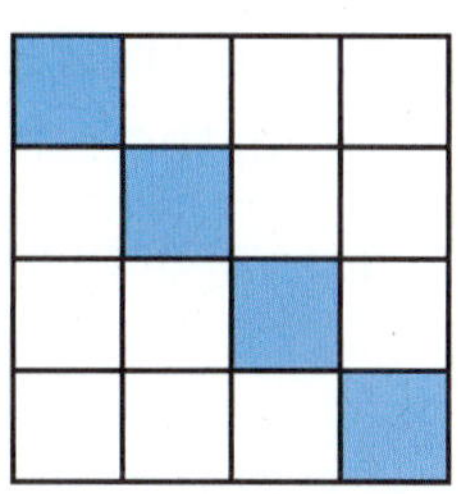

g 

h 

2 How many lines of symmetry does each pattern have?

a 

b 

c 

d 

e 

f 

g 

h 

Reflect on how well you have found all the lines of symmetry in the patterns.

- Which lines of symmetry were easiest to find?
- Which lines of symmetry were hardest to find?
- What will you look for or check to help you find lines of symmetry in the future?

Worked example 2

How many lines of symmetry does this shape have?

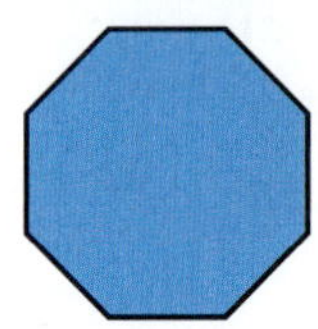

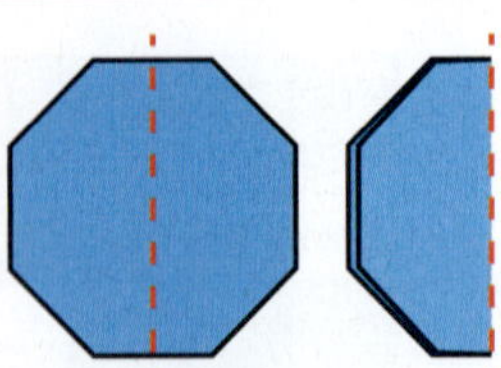

If a shape can be folded in half exactly onto itself along a line, then that is a line of symmetry.

There is a vertical line of symmetry in the shape.

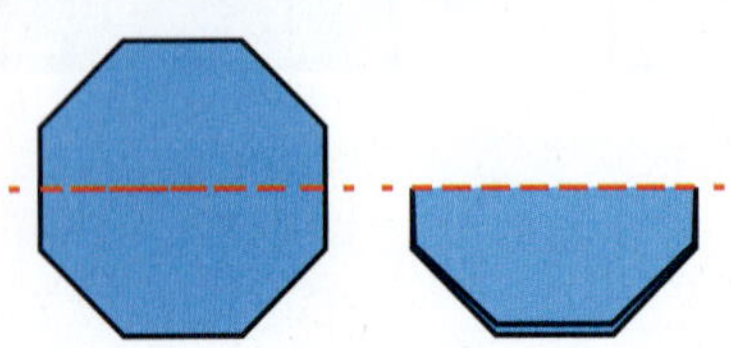

There is a horizontal line of symmetry in the shape.

Continued

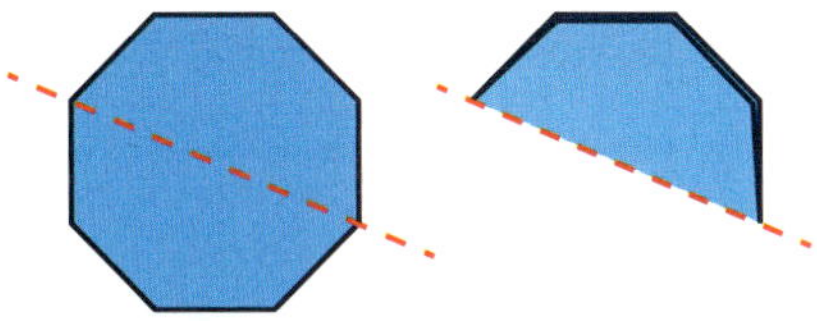

There are also diagonal lines of symmetry.

The lines between these corners are lines of symmetry.

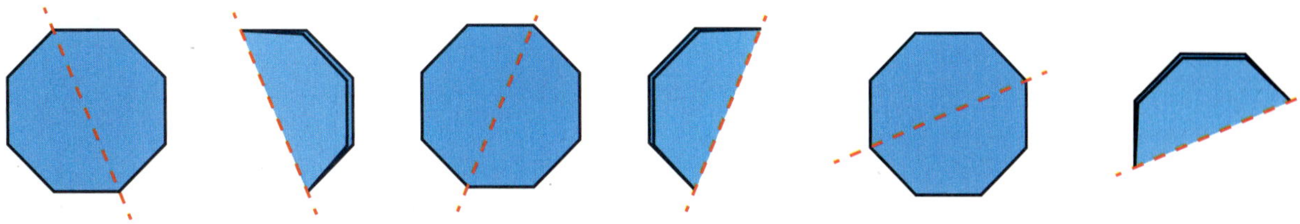

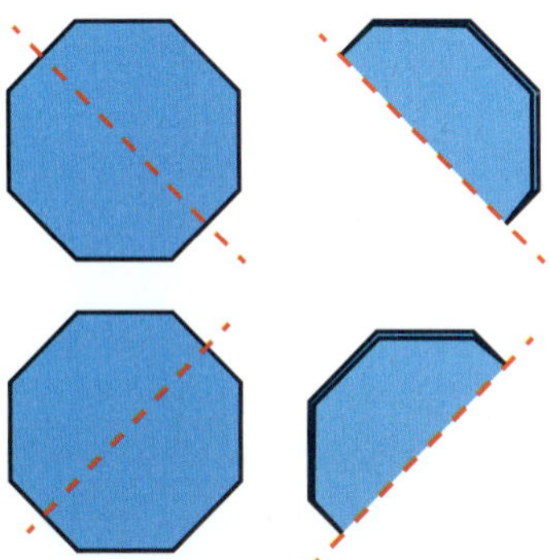

These lines of symmetry go from the centre of one side to the centre of a parallel side.

Tip

Be careful! The line between these corners is not a line of symmetry.

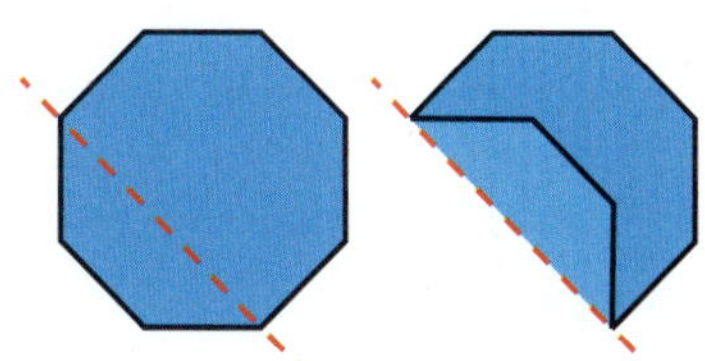

Answer: There are 8 lines of symmetry in the shape.

3 Trace and cut out these shapes.

How many lines of symmetry do the shapes have?

a

b

c

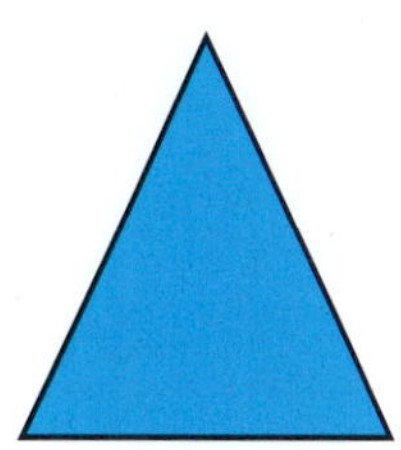

d

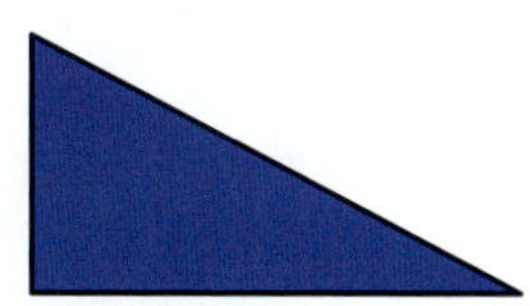

e

f

g

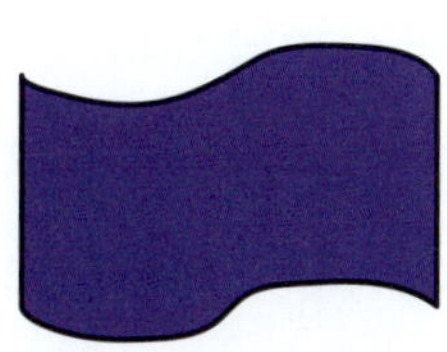

h

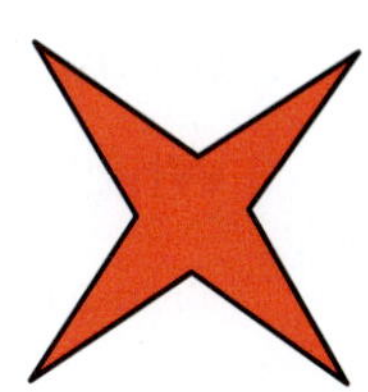

4 A parallelogram is characterised as a 4-sided polygon with two pairs of parallel sides.

Which of these parallelograms have diagonal lines of symmetry? Test your conjectures.

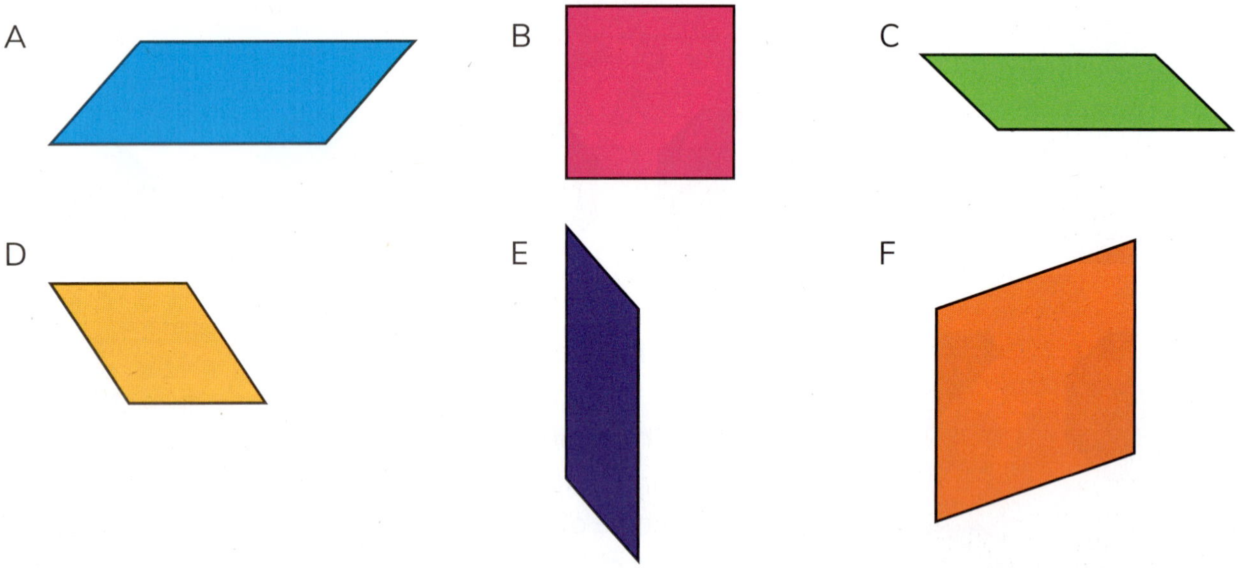

The parallelograms that have lines of symmetry have a special property.

Measure the lengths of the sides of the parallelograms to find out the special property.

Copy and complete the following generalisation:
The parallelograms that have diagonal lines of symmetry all have . . .

5 All of these shapes have four sides.

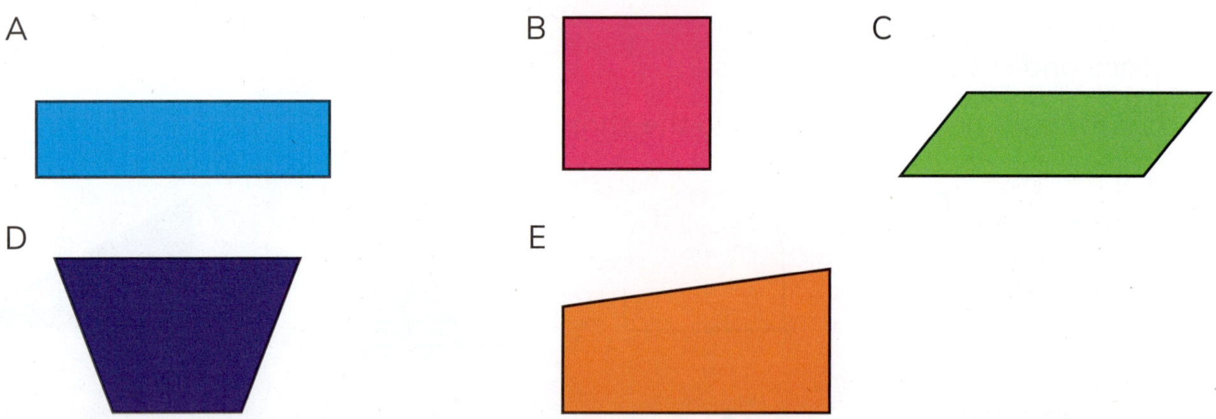

a Do they have the same number of lines of symmetry?

b Which shapes have the fewest lines of symmetry?

c Which shape has the most lines of symmetry?

Think like a mathematician

Investigate the number of lines of symmetry in these regular polygons.

a Trace the shapes and draw on their lines of symmetry.

You could use a mirror or you could fold them to find the lines of symmetry.

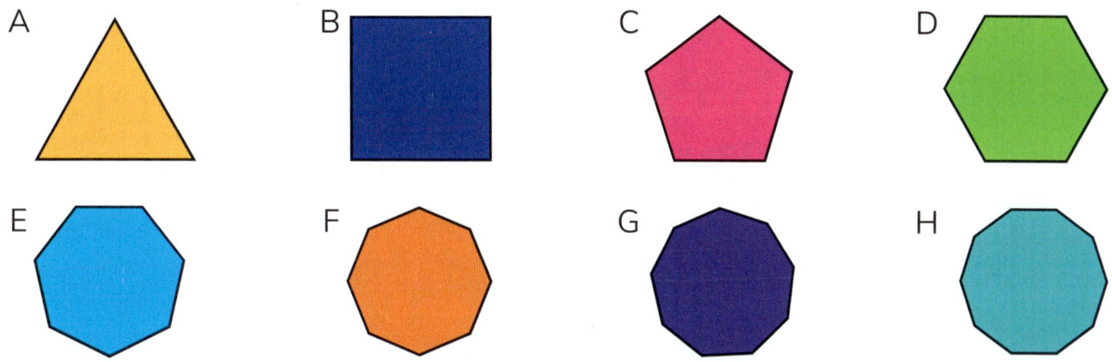

b Copy and complete this table to record the characteristics of each shape.

Shape	Name	Sides	Vertices	Lines of symmetry
A				
B				
C				

Assess how well you have found all the lines of symmetry in shapes.

- Which lines of symmetry were easiest to find?
- Which lines of symmetry were hardest to find?
- What will you look for or check to help you find lines of symmetry in shapes in the future?

Look what I can do!

- [ ] I can find all the lines of symmetry in patterns.
- [ ] I can find all the lines of symmetry in 2D shapes.

Check your progress

1 Copy this shape using tracing paper. Draw straight lines through the shape to divide it into one square and two triangles.

2 Draw three triangles so that together they make a pentagon.

3 Trace this hexagon to make a template.
Show how the hexagon can tessellate.

4 Can these shapes tessellate? Write 'yes', 'no' or 'unsure'.

a a square b a regular triangle c a regular pentagon d a regular hexagon

5 How many lines of symmetry does each picture have?

a 

b 

c 

6 How many lines of symmetry are there in these hexagons?

a 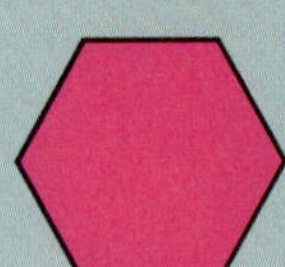

b 

c 

d 

e 

7 How many lines of symmetry does a regular octagon have?

Project 4

Always, sometimes or never true?

Read the five statements below.

- Polygons have straight sides.
- For a regular polygon, the number of sides it has is equal to the number of lines of symmetry.
- A square is a rectangle.
- A quadrilateral has four right angles.
- A triangle has three lines of symmetry.

Decide whether each statement is always true, sometimes true or never true.

How do you know?

7 Fractions

Getting started

The answers to these questions are all **wrong.**

Explain to your partner what the mistake is in each question and how to correct it.

1 Draw a ring around the shapes that have one-third coloured.

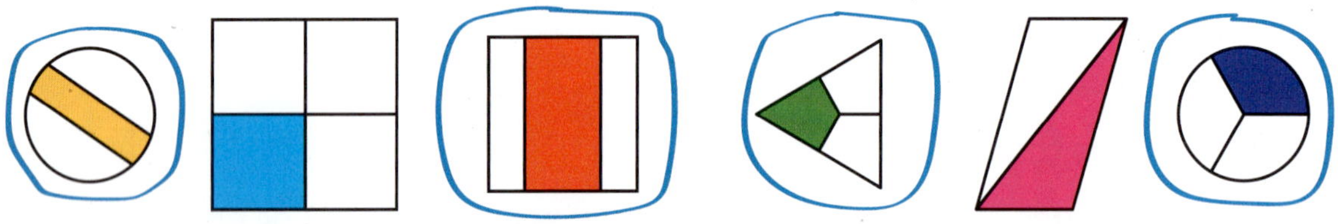

2 What fraction has been shaded in this drawing?

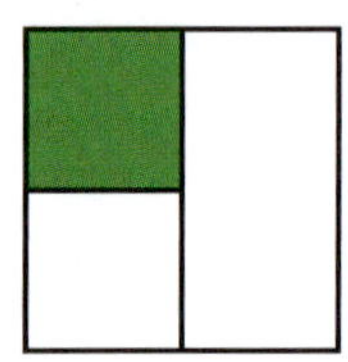

Answer: *a third*

3 Which fraction is larger:

$\frac{1}{6}$ or $\frac{1}{3}$?

Draw the fractions to show which is larger.

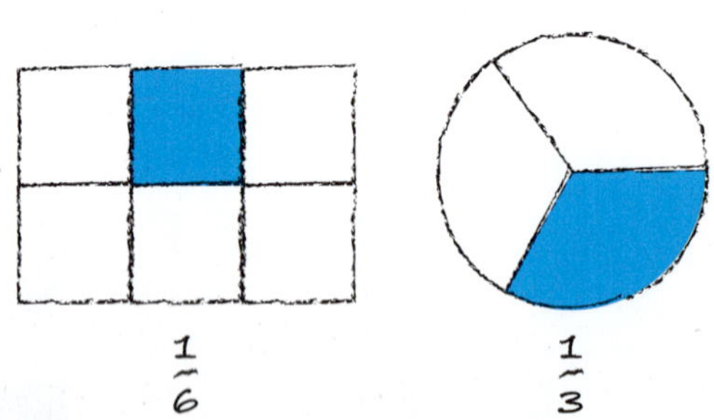

You can see fractions being used all around you in everyday life.

You use fractions when you plan an activity and divide the cost between those taking part.

You also use fractions to calculate the amount you save at the sales. For example, if a jumper usually costs \$20, how much does it cost in a half-price sale?

Mia bought a new mirror in a half-price sale. It cost \$12. How much would it have cost before the sale?

Heidi needs two new pairs of glasses. She pays the full price of \$210 for the first pair.
The shop offers a $\frac{1}{3}$ discount on the second pair.
How can you work out how much Heidi pays for the second pair?

7.1 Understanding fractions

We are going to ...

- show that the more equal parts a whole is divided into, the smaller the fraction is
- learn that a fraction can be represented as a division of the numerator by the denominator.

denominator
fraction
numerator

In this unit you will write fractions with numerators and denominators and learn how to read fractions in words, for example $\frac{3}{4}$ is 'three-quarters'.

You will learn how to divide a shape into fractions. When you divide a shape into lots of the same fraction you must divide the shape into equal parts. Each of these parts must be the same size but the parts can be in different positions.

Worked example 1

Put a cross (×) by the representations of $\frac{2}{5}$ that are not correct. Explain how you know.

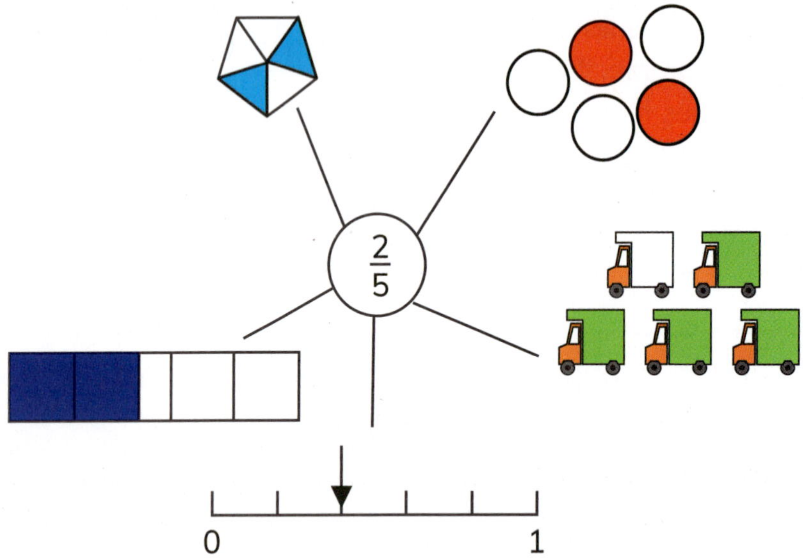

Answer:

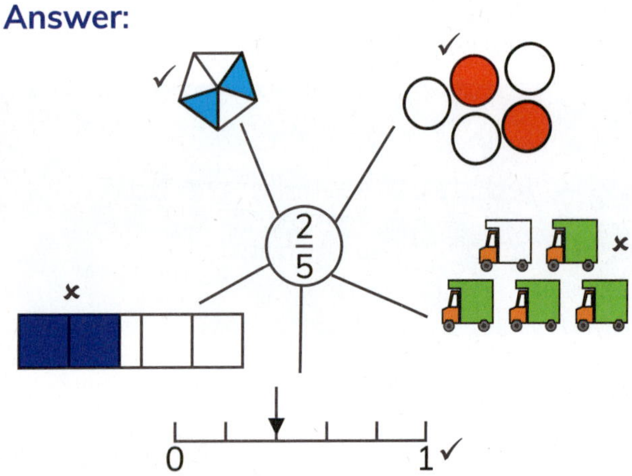

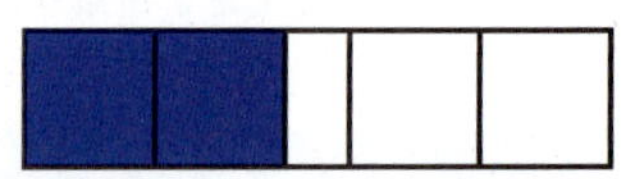

does not show $\frac{2}{5}$ because the parts are not equal in size.

represents one fifth or four fifths.

The other three diagrams are correct:

- The pentagon is divided into 5 equal parts and 2 are shaded.
- There are 5 identical circles and 2 are shaded.
- The number line is divided into fifths and the arrow points at $\frac{2}{5}$.

Exercise 7.1

1 Look at the number wall. It is not complete.

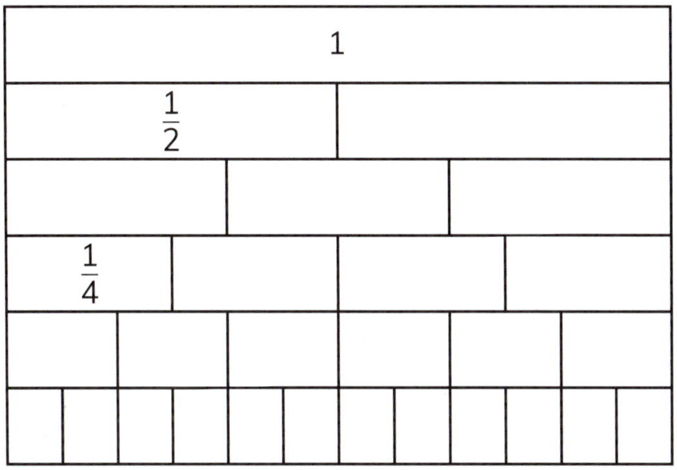

Copy this number sentence and use the number wall to help you complete it.

$\frac{1}{2} > \square > \frac{1}{4} > \square > \frac{1}{12}$

2 Eight people share one cake.
How much of the cake does each person get when they share it equally?

3 Part of a floor is covered with matting.

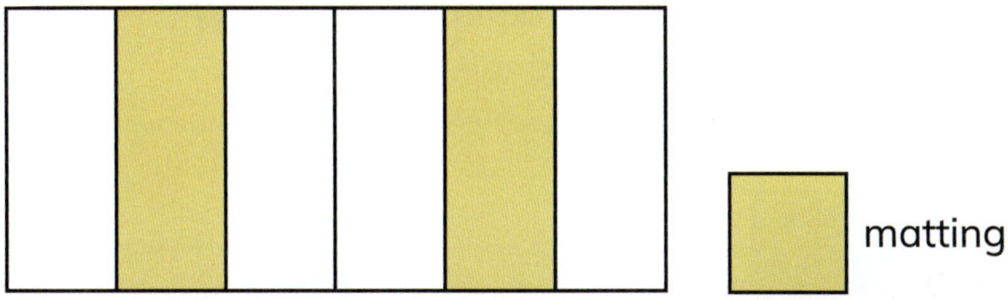

What fraction of the floor is covered with matting?

A $\frac{1}{2}$ B $\frac{1}{3}$ C $\frac{1}{4}$ D $\frac{1}{6}$

Compare your answer with your partner's answer.

There are six rectangles which are equal in area. Two of these rectangles are shaded, but the fraction $\frac{2}{6}$ is not an optional answer.
How did you decide which of the four answers was correct?
Did you agree with your partner?

4 Fatima says, 'The square is divided into four equal parts.'

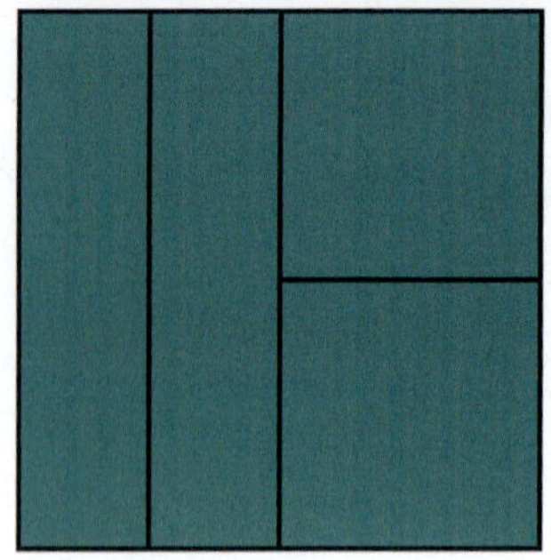

Do you agree with Fatima?
Explain your reasons to your partner, then write them down.

5 Four shapes are divided into parts.

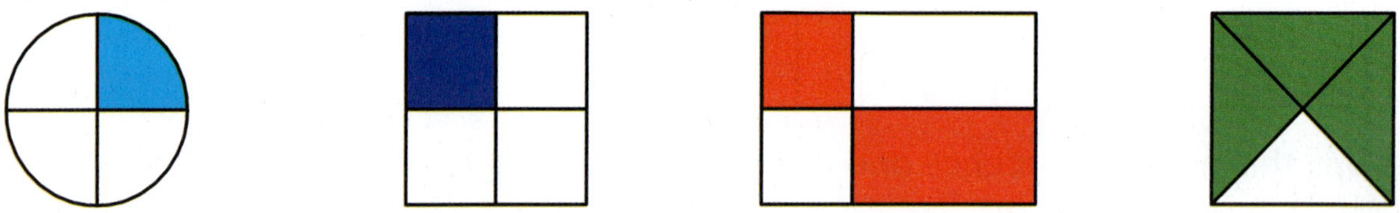

A B C D

Arun chooses a shape.

Which shape is Arun describing?

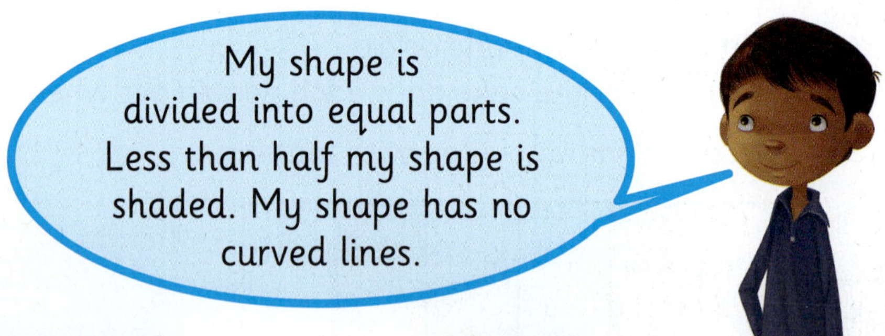

6 Look at these diagrams.

What is the same? What is different?

A B C

7 These diagrams shows four fractions with the same numerator.

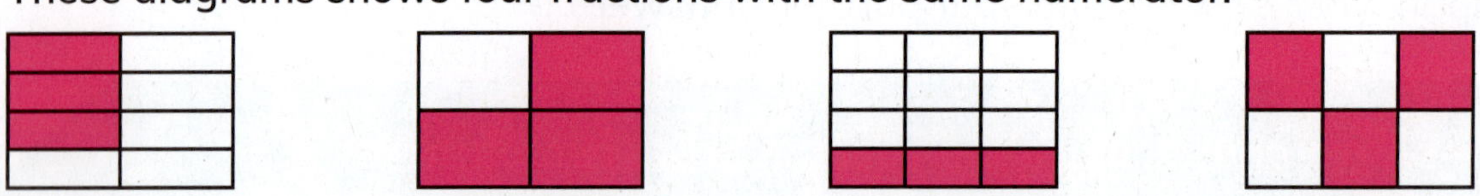

$\frac{3}{8}$ $\frac{3}{4}$ $\frac{3}{12}$ $\frac{3}{6}$

Write the fractions in order of size. Start with the smallest fraction.

Think like a mathematician

Hexagons

This hexagon is divided into four equal parts.
It is divided into quarters.

$1 \div 4 = \frac{1}{4}$

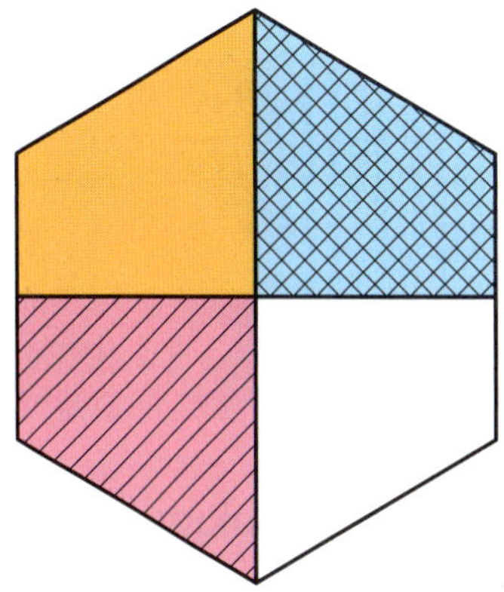

Ask your teacher for a sheet of regular hexagons.

Divide each one into equal parts.
Write each division as a fraction.

Make each hexagon different.

Look what I can do!

- [ ] I can explain that one third is smaller than one half because the whole is divided into three equal parts, not two equal parts.
- [ ] I can show that the more parts a whole is divided into, the smaller the fraction. So, $\frac{1}{5} < \frac{1}{4} < \frac{1}{3} < \frac{1}{2}$.
- [ ] I know that a fraction can be represented as a division of the numerator by the denominator, for example $3 \div 4 = \frac{3}{4}$.

7.2 Fractions as operators

We are going to . . .

- describe a unit fraction as a fraction with a numerator of 1
- use a unit fraction as an operator, for example, find one-fifth of a quantity by dividing by 5 and find one-sixth of a quantity by dividing by 6.

When you are cooking you may need to cook for a smaller number of people than the recipe suggests.

If you want to halve a recipe, you must work out all of the amounts using fractions.

operator
unit fraction

Gingerbread
(Makes about 16)

350 g plain flour
150 g soft brown sugar
80 g butter
2 tsp ground ginger
4 tbsp golden syrup
1 egg

To use this recipe to make eight gingerbread biscuits you would need to halve all of the ingredients.

For example:

$\frac{1}{2}$ of 350 = 175

So you need 175 g of plain flour.

Worked example 2

Safia, Aiko, Lily and Manjit share three chocolate bars equally.

How much chocolate does Aiko get?

$\frac{1}{4}$ of 3 = 3 ÷ 4

There are 3 bars and Aiko is one of four girls, so you find $\frac{1}{4}$ of the 3 bars.

Answer:

Aiko gets $\frac{3}{4}$ bar.

Exercise 7.2

1 What is $\frac{1}{3}$ of \$12?

2 Copy and complete the following.

a 24 ÷ 3 is equivalent to ☐ of 24 b 16 ÷ 8 is equivalent to ☐ of 16

3 a What is one-tenth of 30?

b What is $\frac{1}{5}$ of 45?

c What is one-quarter of 40?

4 Copy and complete these diagrams to find fractions of amounts of money.

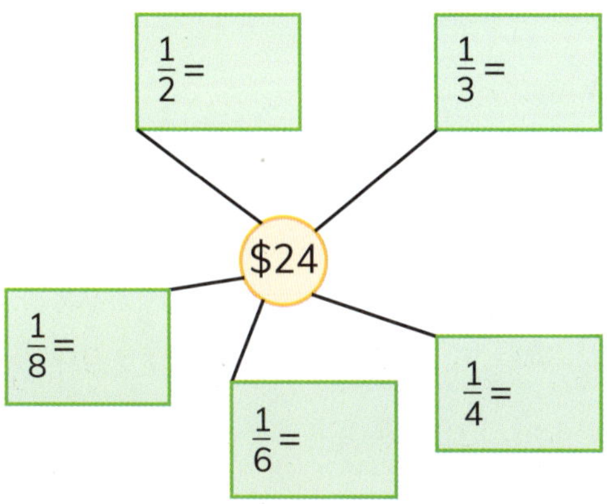

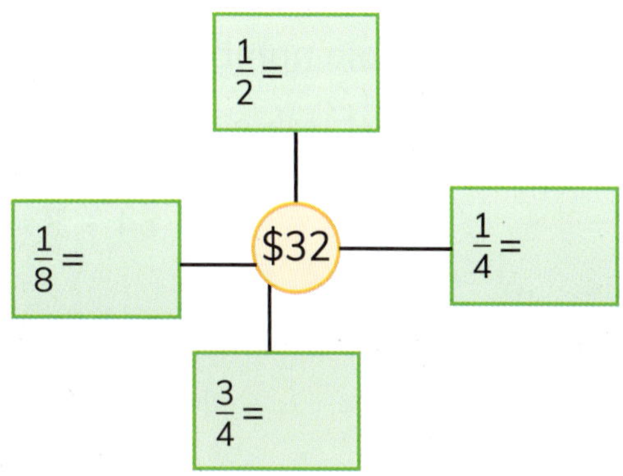

5 Ajay says, 'To find a tenth of a number I divide by 10, and to find a fifth of a number I divide by 5.'
Is he correct?

Explain your reasoning to your partner, then write down your thoughts.

6 Which would you choose: $\frac{1}{3}$ of \$15 or $\frac{1}{4}$ of \$24?
Check your answer with your partner.
Explain how you worked out your answer.

7 Here are some numbers.

10 20 30 40 50 60 70 80

Write one of these numbers in each box to make the fraction sentences correct.

You can use each number **once** only.

$\frac{1}{2}$ of ☐ = ☐ $\frac{1}{4}$ of ☐ = ☐ $\frac{1}{5}$ of ☐ = ☐

Think about the method you used. Did you start by filling in the first two boxes? If you did, was that a sensible decision? How many ways can you fill in the first two boxes?

How many ways can you fill in the last two boxes to find one-fifth of a quantity?

If you were asked another similar question, what would you do differently?

Think like a mathematician

☐ represents a whole number in each calculation.

Investigate the largest value of ☐ in this set of calculations.

$\frac{1}{4}$ of 40 = ☐

$64 \div 8$ = ☐

$\frac{1}{4}$ of ☐ = 4

$\frac{1}{5}$ of 45 = ☐

$\frac{1}{3}$ of ☐ = 9

$24 \div 4$ = ☐

$\frac{1}{3}$ of 21 = ☐

Explain to your partner how you worked out your answer.

You may show you are **convincing** when you explain to your partner how you worked out your answer.

Look what I can do!

- ☐ I can describe a unit fraction as a fraction with a numerator of 1.
- ☐ I can use a unit fraction as an operator. For example, to find one-fifth of a quantity I divide by 5, to find one-sixth of a quantity I divide by 6, and so on.

Check your progress

1 Which shape has $\frac{2}{3}$ shaded?

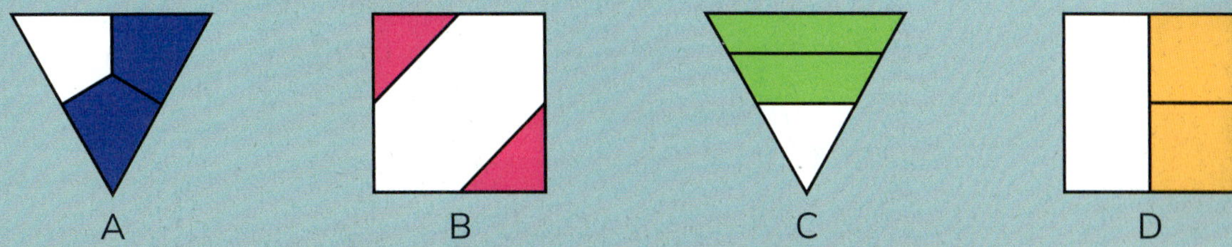

2 Mr Wo divided his garden into six equal parts. He planted beans in the shaded part.

What fraction of the garden does he have left to plant?

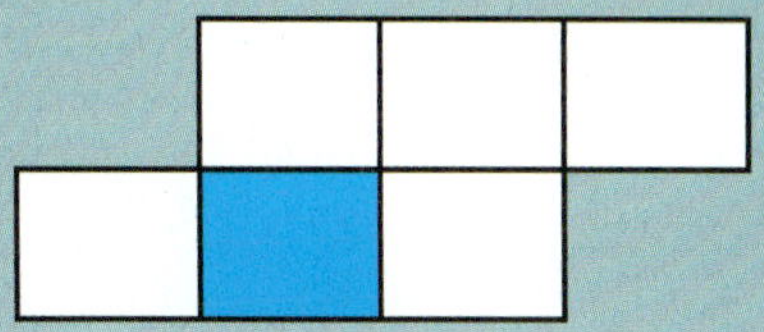

3 Copy the number line and mark each fraction in the correct place.

$\frac{3}{10}$ $\frac{7}{10}$ $\frac{1}{2}$

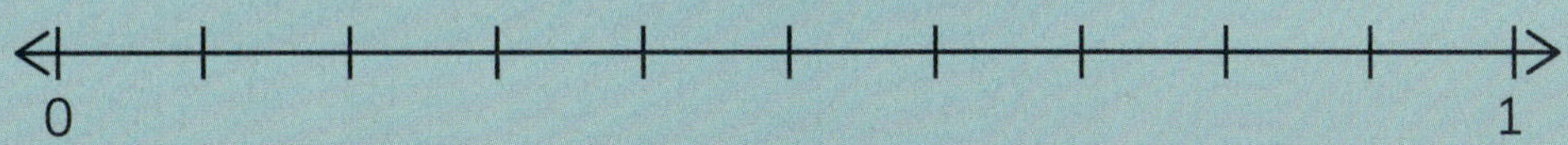

4 Here are four unit fractions.

$\frac{1}{6}$ $\frac{1}{4}$ $\frac{1}{3}$ $\frac{1}{5}$

Place them in order of size starting with the smallest.
Explain how you worked out the order.

5 Copy and complete the following.

For unit fractions, the larger the denominator the ____ the fraction.

To find $\frac{1}{4}$ of a quantity, divide the quantity by ____.

6 The diagram shows 25 circles.
What fraction of the circles are inside the ring?

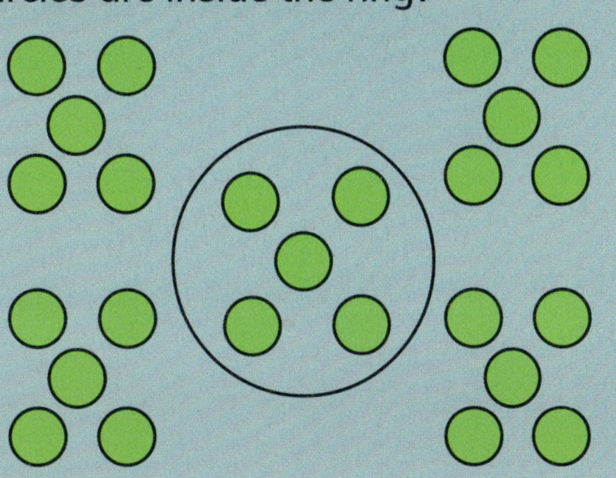

Continued

7 Choose the correct number to answer each calculation.

10 15 20 25 30 35

a $\frac{1}{4}$ of 100 b $\frac{1}{3}$ of 90 c $\frac{1}{2}$ of 30

8 Copy and complete these diagrams to find fractions of 48.

48

$\frac{1}{4}$ of 48 =

$\frac{1}{3}$ of 48 =

$\frac{1}{8}$ of 48 =

$\frac{1}{2}$ of 48 =

9 Jodi says, 'I would rather have $\frac{1}{2}$ of \$30 than $\frac{1}{3}$ of \$60 because $\frac{1}{2}$ is bigger than $\frac{1}{3}$.'

Do you agree with Jodi? Explain your answer.

8 Angles

Getting started

1 Find three angles like this in the room around you.

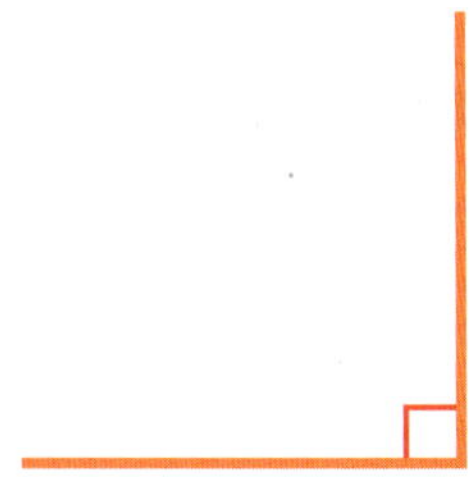

What is this size angle called?

2 Which of these angles are greater than a right angle?

3 How many right angles does each shape have?

a 

b 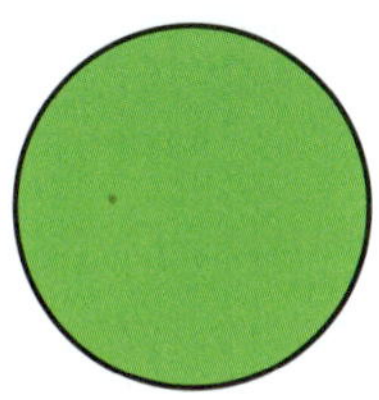

c 

d 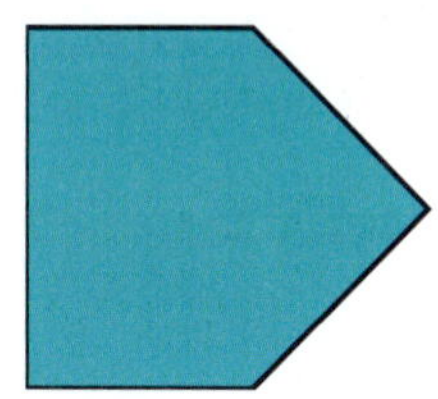

An angle is a measurement of turn.

It can be used to find your way at sea and in designing buildings. Hikers and sailors can use the angle measurements on a compass to help them work out which way to turn. Carpenters use angles to cut wood so that it will fit together correctly in furniture or buildings.

8.1 Comparing angles

We are going to . . .

- compare the sizes of angles.

Talking about different sizes of angles is important.

To make their dance look good these dancers need their feet to all be at the same angle.

How would you explain to the dancers how to change the position of their feet so that they are all the same?

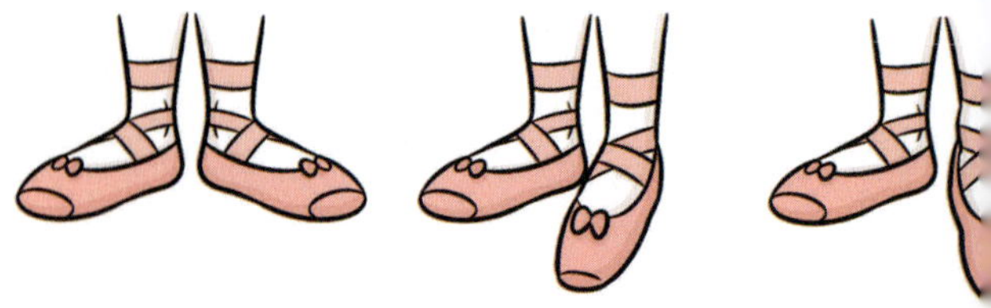

angle compare degrees

Worked example 1

Which of these angles is greater?

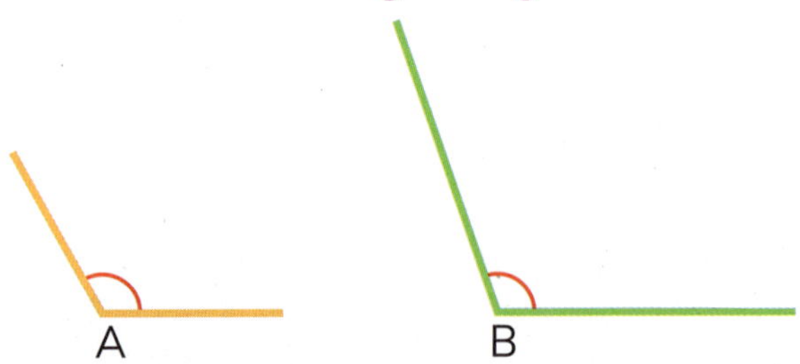

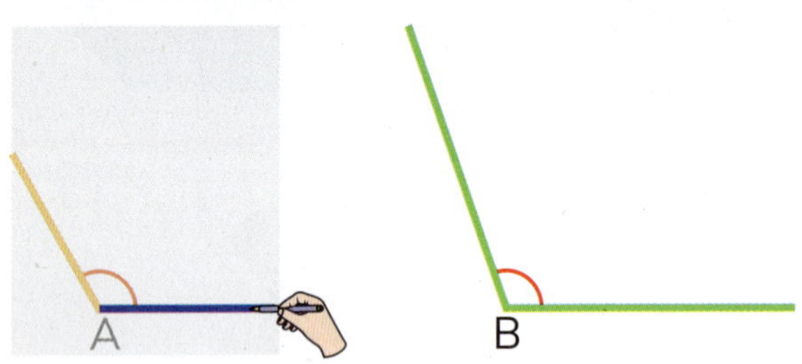

Use tracing paper and a ruler. Trace one of the angles with the tracing paper and a ruler.

Place the traced angle over the other angle to see which angle is greater.

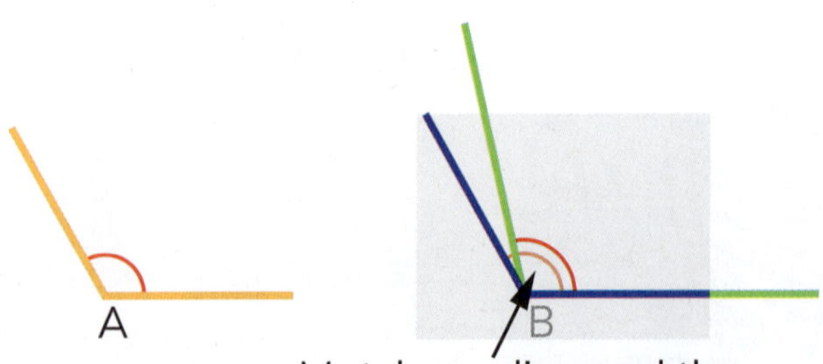

Match one line and the points of the angles

Answer: Angle A is greater than angle B.

Tip

Notice that the length of the lines and the thickness of the lines do not change the angle.

Exercise 8.1

1 Which angle is greater?

a

b

c

2 Are these statements true or false?

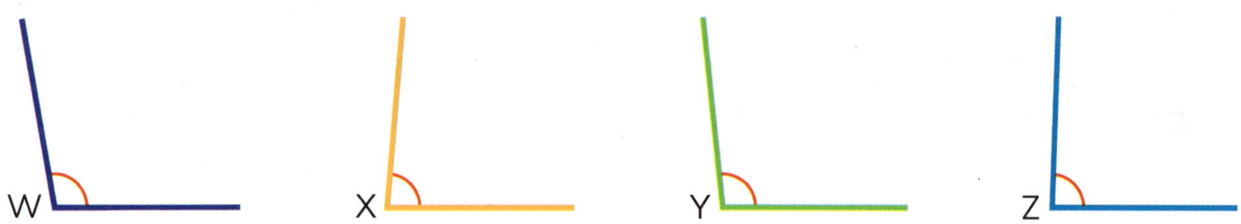

a Angle W is greater than angle X.

b Angle X is less than angle Z.

c Angle Y is less than angle W.

d Angle Z is greater than angle W.

3 Order these angles from smallest to largest.

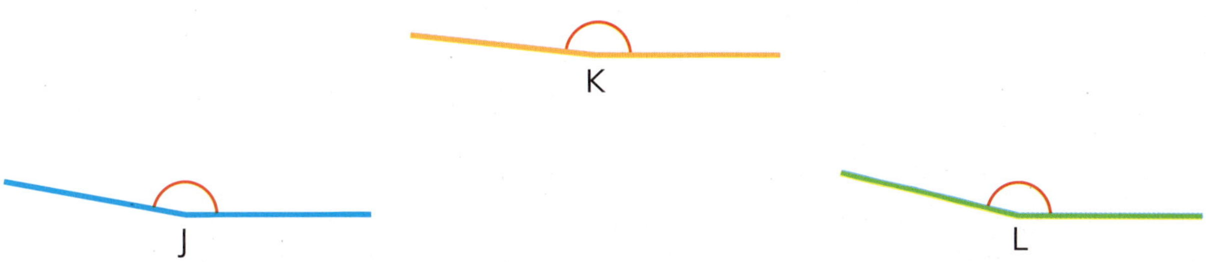

4 Order these angles from smallest to largest.

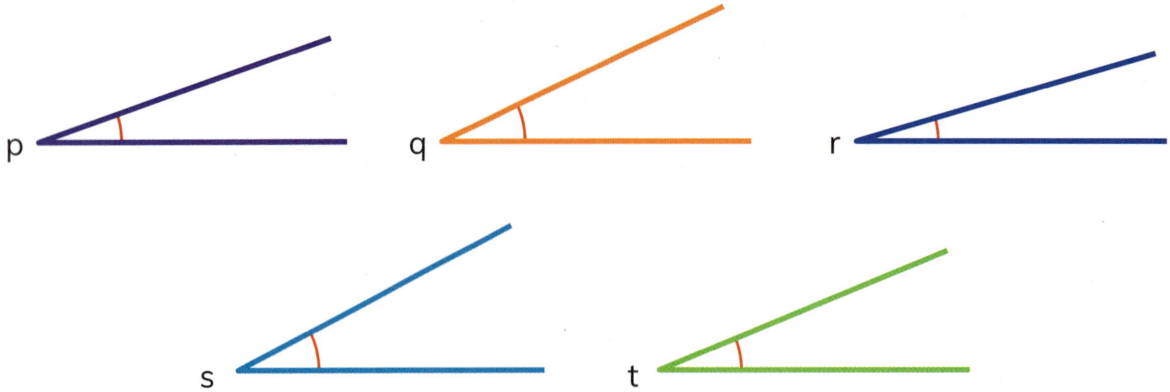

5 Arun has made a mistake.

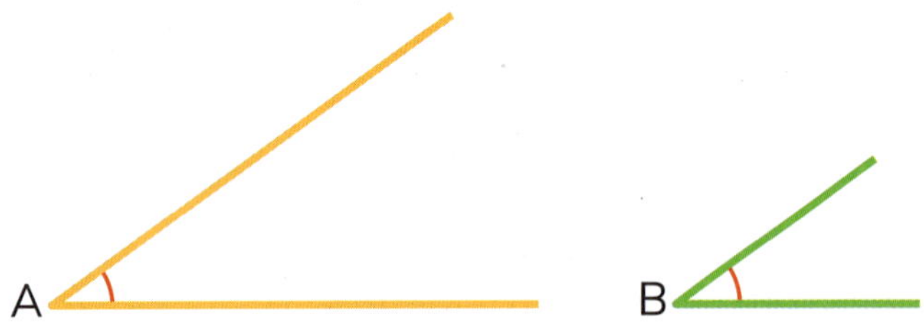

Critique Arun's statement. What is Arun's mistake?

Why do you think Arun made that mistake?

How could you convince Arun that he is wrong?

Think like a mathematician

Clock hands meet at an angle.

At 3 o'clock the hour and minute hands on this clock make a right angle.

a Write the time for the smallest angle you can find between the clock hands.

b Write the time for the largest angle you can find between the clock hands.

c Work with a partner to check your answers. Can you make smaller or larger angles with the clock hands? Critique and improve your answers.

6 A cake is cut into four pieces. Each piece is an angle.

Ask your partner to watch you using tracing paper to compare the four angles.

Decide which is the greatest angle and piece of cake.

Ask your partner to tell you how well they think you compare the angles and what you can improve.

Watch your partner using tracing paper to compare the four angles of cake. Check that they:

- trace the angle using a ruler
- match one line of each angle
- put the corners of the angles together
- only look at the angle, not the width or length of the lines.

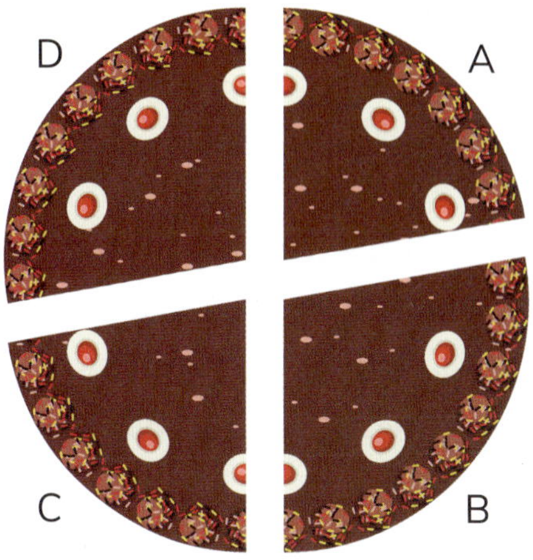

Tell your partner what they are doing well and what they can improve.

With practice, you will sometimes be able to see which angle is greater without using tracing paper.

Look back at the angles in the exercise.

Think about which angles you can tell are greater or less than just by looking at them, and which you would need tracing paper for.

In the future, how can you improve your skill when comparing angles using tracing paper? Copy and complete the sentence.

I can improve how I compare angles by ____.

Look what I can do!

- [ ] I can compare two angles and say which is greatest.
- [ ] I can compare a group of angles and order them from smallest to greatest.

8.2 Acute and obtuse

We are going to . . .

- learn the correct names of different size angles.

It is important to be able to talk about shapes and movements accurately.

In this section you will learn some new words for describing angles. What words do you already know that relate to angles?

acute angle
obtuse angle
right angle

Exercise 8.2

1 Make an angle maker. You will need: card, tracing paper, a ruler, a split pin (or a drawing pin and a small piece of modelling dough).

Trace and copy this diagram carefully onto a piece of card.

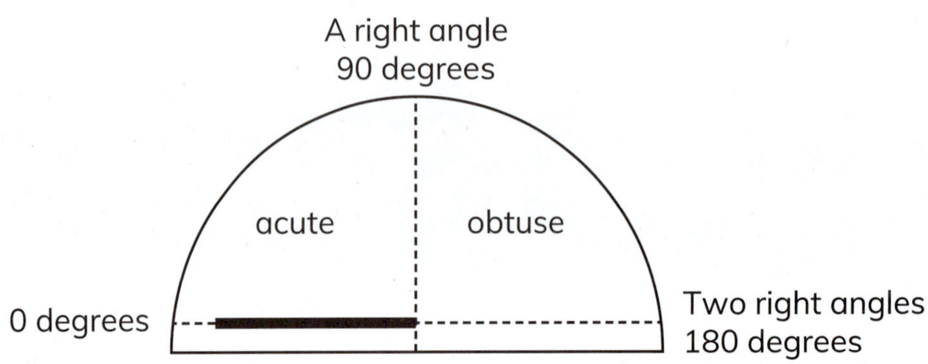

Make a thin rectangle out of card.

Attach the thin rectangle to the diagram with a split pin, or push a drawing pin through the rectangle and diagram into modelling dough.

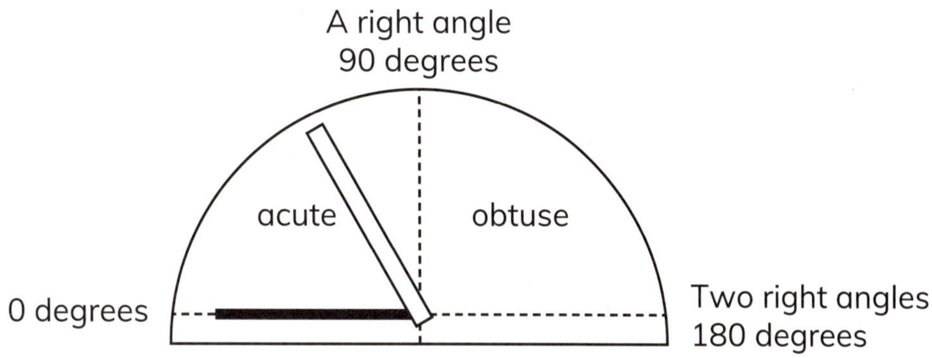

Use your angle maker to make:

- a right angle
- an acute angle
- an obtuse angle.

Worked example 2

Is angle X acute or obtuse?

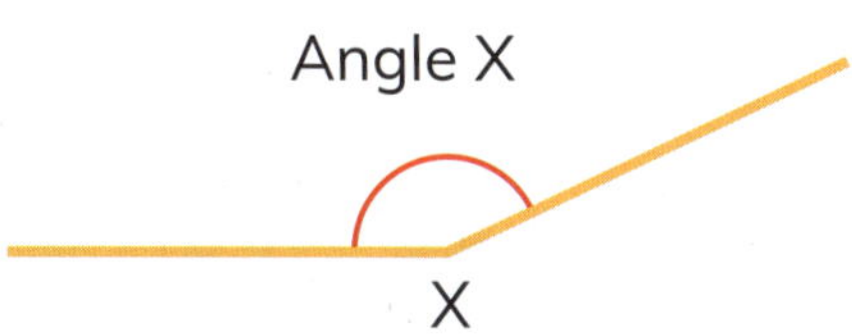

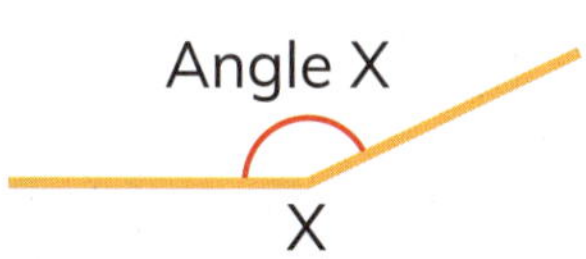

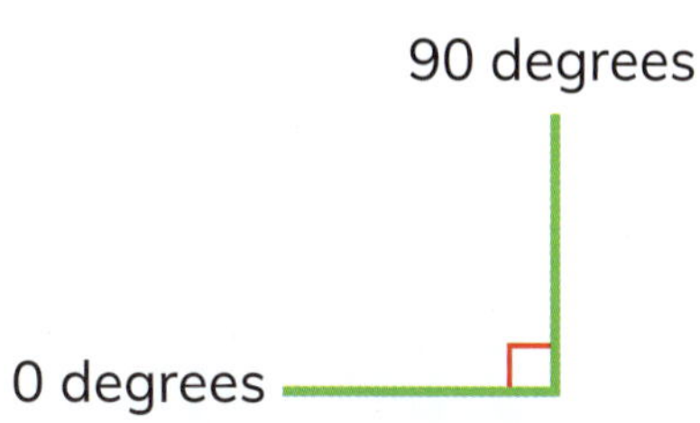

Compare Angle X to a right angle.

An acute angle is less than 90 degrees, it is less than a right angle.

Angle X is greater than a right angle so it cannot be acute.

Compare Angle X to two right angles.

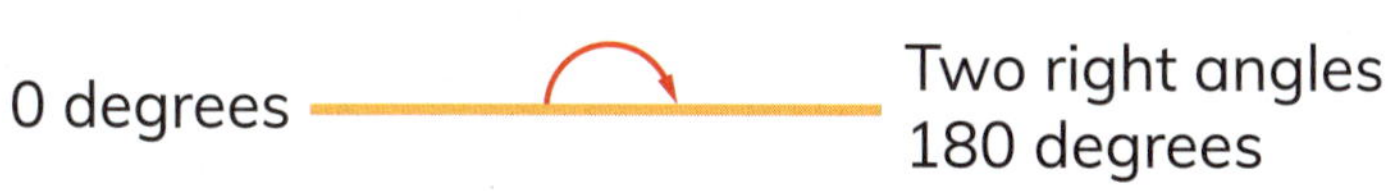

Angle X is less than two right angles.

An obtuse angle is:

- more than 90 degrees (more than a right angle)
- less than 180 degrees (less than two right angles).

Answer: Angle X is obtuse.

2 Write right angle, acute angle or obtuse angle for each angle.

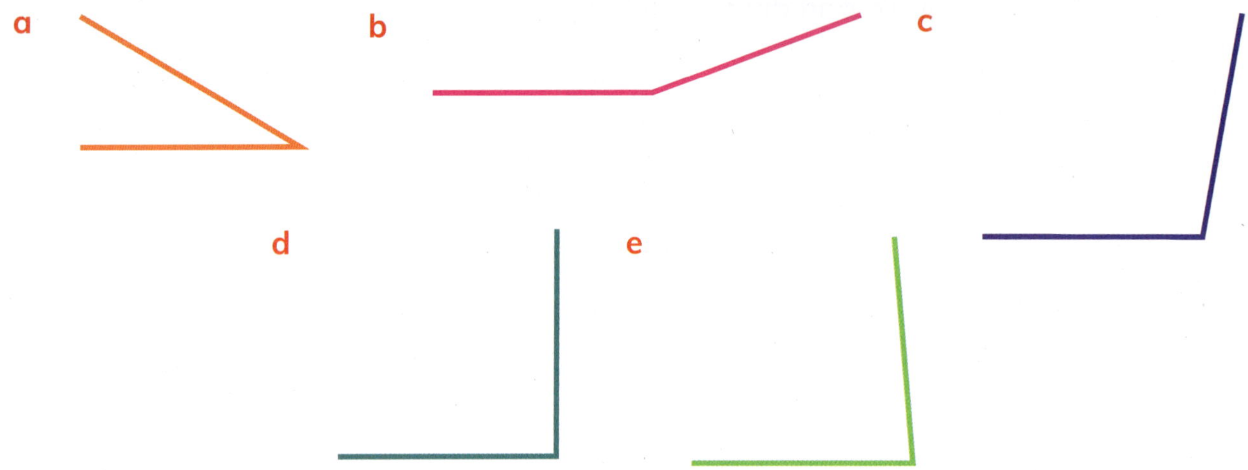

3 a Draw an acute angle.

b Draw an obtuse angle.

4 Copy and complete these sentences.

A right angle is an angle of ____ degrees.

An acute angle is ____ than ____ .

An obtuse angle is ____ than ____ and ____ than ____ .

Think like a mathematician

Maryam has drawn an obtuse angle.

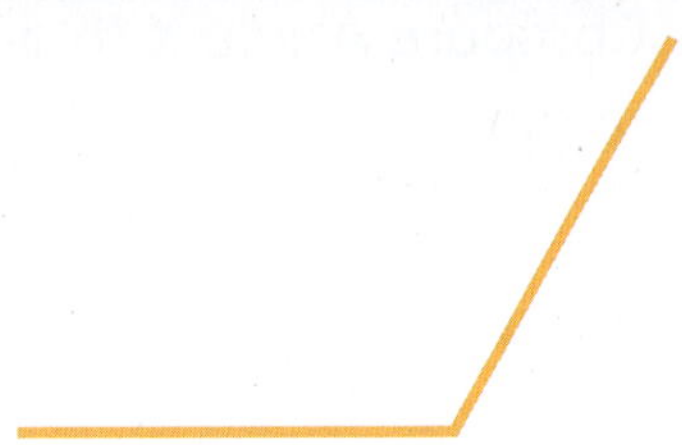

She is drawing a line with a ruler to cut the angle into two angles.

Maryam says, 'If I draw a straight line through an obtuse angle I always get two acute angles.'

Conjecture whether Maryam is correct. Investigate and find out. Then convince your partner of your answer.

How do you remember the angle words **acute** and **obtuse**?

How do you remember which angles are **acute** and which are **obtuse**?

Can you use right angle, acute angle and obtuse angle correctly to classify angles?

What pictures could you draw to help you remember the words acute and obtuse.

Look what I can do!

- [ ] I can use the words right angle, acute angle and obtuse angle to classify angles.

8.3 Estimating angles

We are going to . . .

- estimate the size of an angle.

We can estimate an angle to tell someone how far to turn and what direction to walk in.

Tom is playing a game. He is wearing a blindfold. How would you explain to him how to find the treasure chest, the crown and the necklace?

estimate

Exercise 8.3

1 One right angle is 90 degrees.

  a How many degrees are there in two right angles?

  b How many degrees are there in three right angles?

  c How many degrees are there in four right angles?

2 Stand up. Turn four right angles in the same direction.
Describe what happens to the direction you are facing after turning four right angles.

Worked example 3

You can use this decision tree and diagram to help you estimate the size of angles.

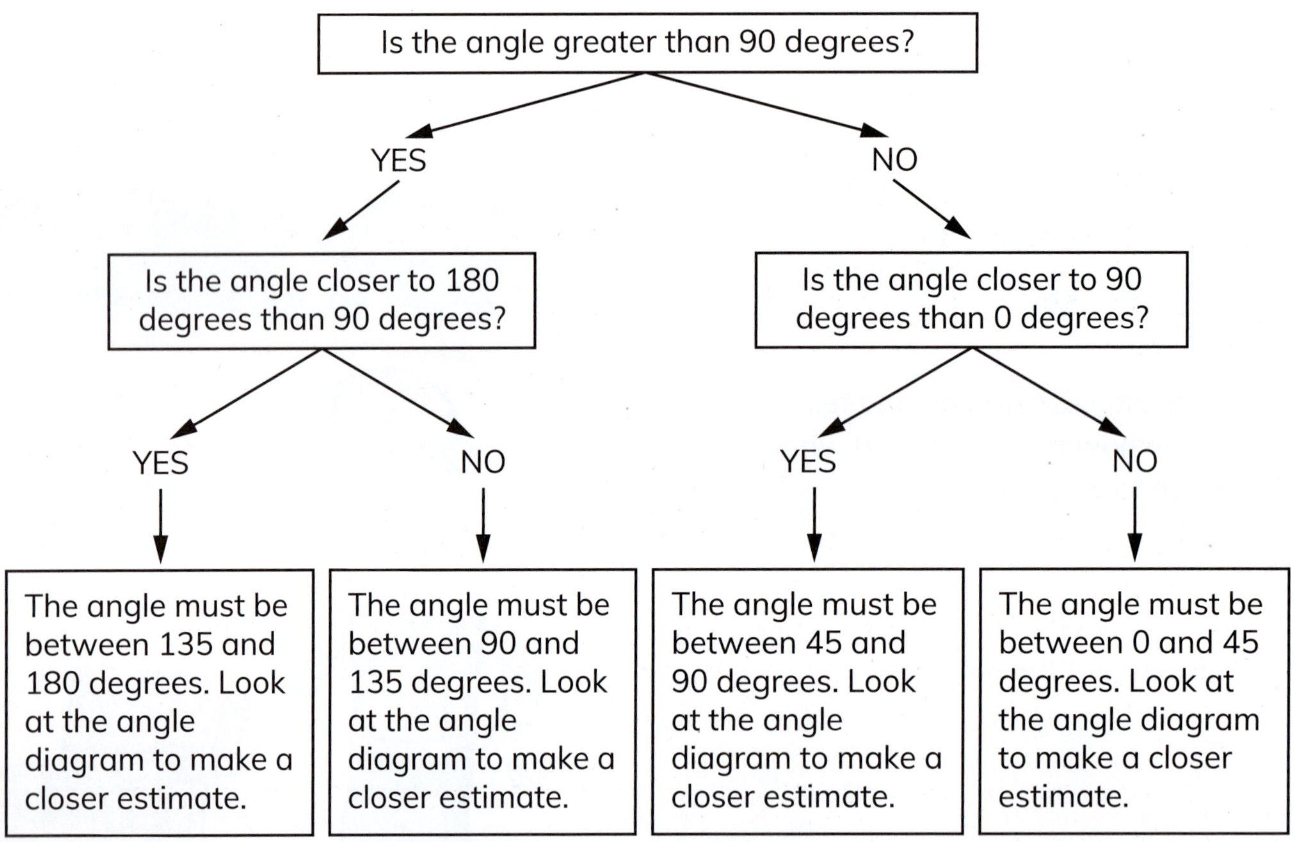

Continued

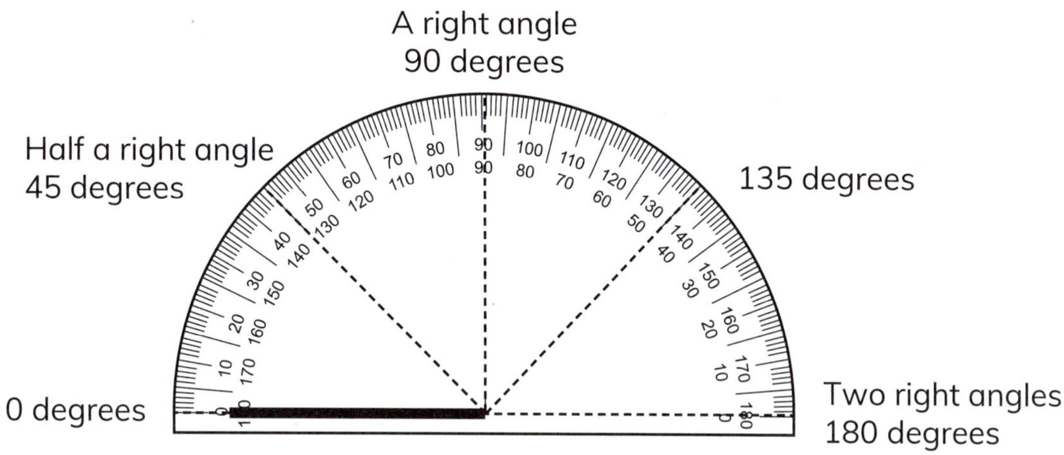

Estimate the size of this angle in degrees.

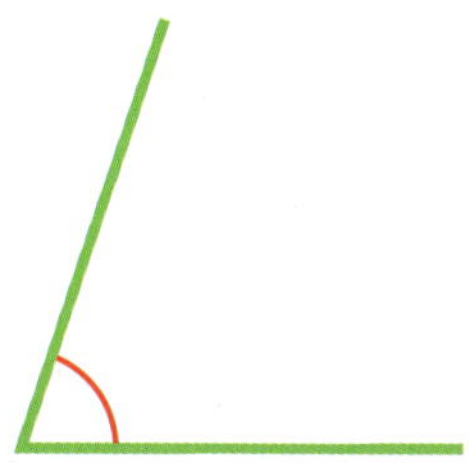

- This angle is less than 90 degrees.
- It is closer to 90 degrees than 0 degrees.
- So, it is between 45 degrees and 90 degrees.

Use the decision tree first.

Looking at the diagram we can estimate that the angle is about 65 degrees.

Then use the diagram to estimate the size of the angle.

Answer: A good estimate would be between 60 degrees and 80 degrees.

(The exact measurement of the angle is 71 degrees.)

3 Estimate the size of these angles in degrees using the decision tree and diagram.

a

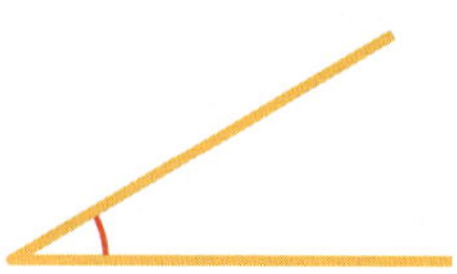

b

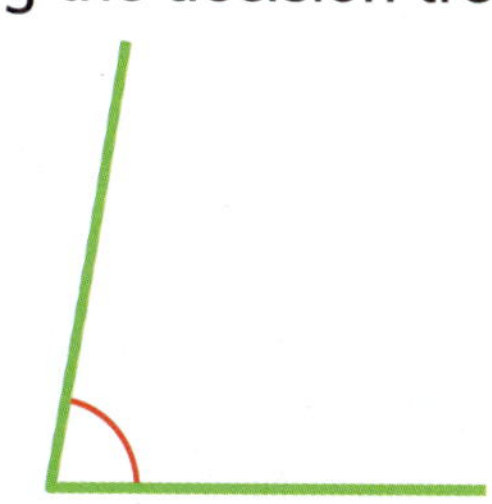

4 Estimate the size of the angle in degrees using the decision tree and diagram.

a 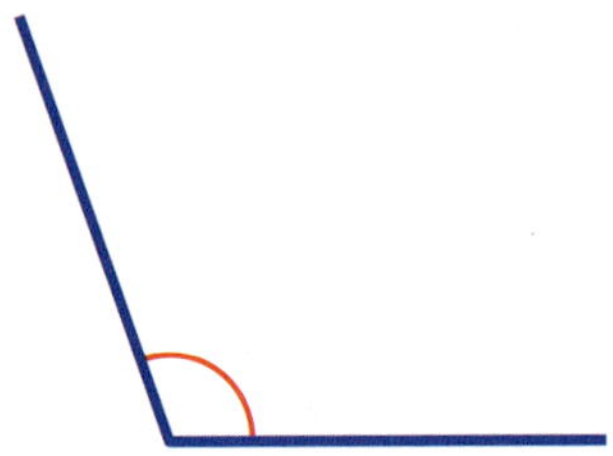

b 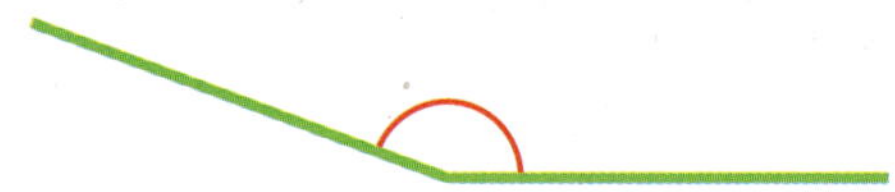

5 What is the best estimate for this angle?

Explain why it is the best estimate.

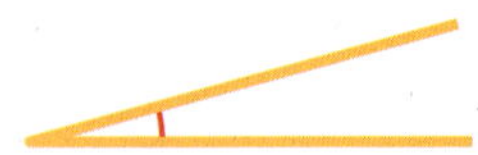

Estimate 95 degrees

Estimate 60 degrees

Estimate 20 degrees

Estimate 38 degrees

Estimate 10 degrees

Compare your answer and explanation with your partner.

Use the decision tree and diagram to decide who has the best explanation.

6 Carly says that she estimates that this angle is 175 degrees.

This is not a good estimate.

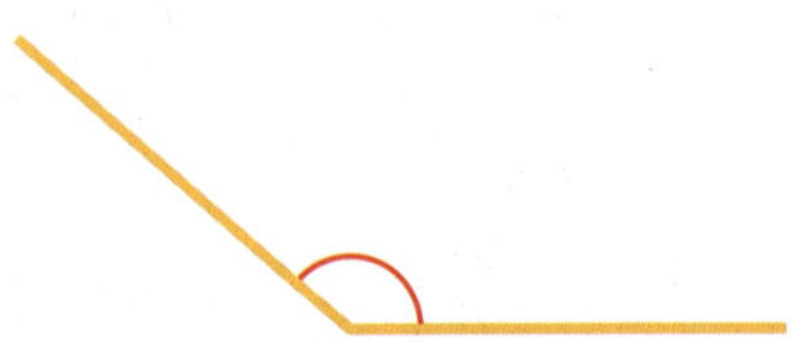

Explain how Carly could improve her estimate.

Look at your explanation for question 6.

Does it include these things?

- Checking if the angle is smaller or greater than 90 degrees.
- Checking if the angle is closer to 0, 90 or 180 degrees.
- Using a diagram of angles to estimate the size of the angle.

How can you improve your skills at estimating the size of angles in degrees?

Think like a mathematician

Work in a small group.

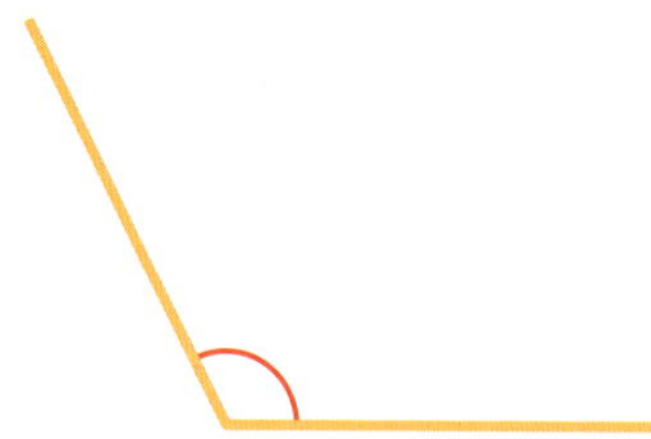

a Each person in the group writes down an estimate for the size of this angle on a small square of paper.

b Write the estimates in order of size.

c Each take a turn to try to convince the others that your estimate is closest to the actual size of the angle.

d Repeat the activity with this angle.

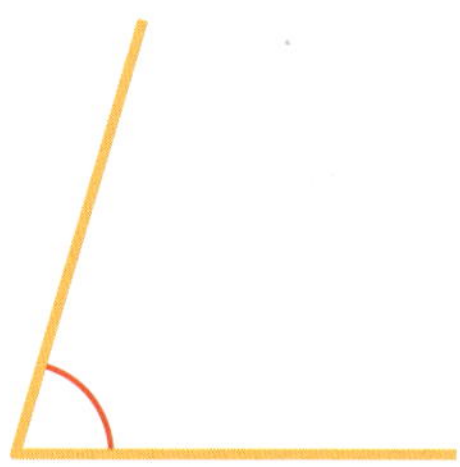

Try to improve your estimate and be better at convincing the others that your estimate is the closest.

Look what I can do!

☐ I can estimate the size of acute and obtuse angles in degrees.

Check your progress

1 Use tracing paper to compare the angles. Which angle is greater?

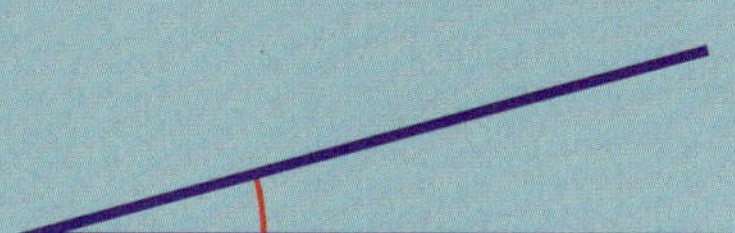

Angle A

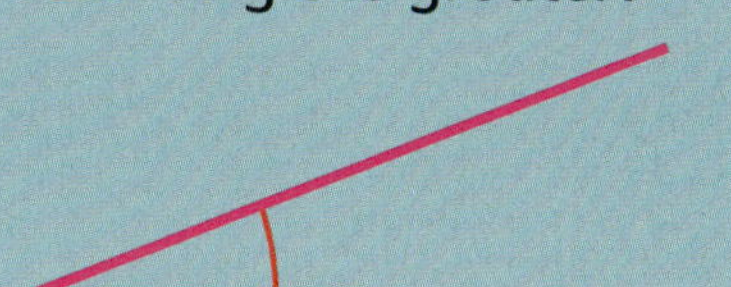

Angle B

Continued

2 Use tracing paper to compare the angles. Order these angles from smallest to greatest.

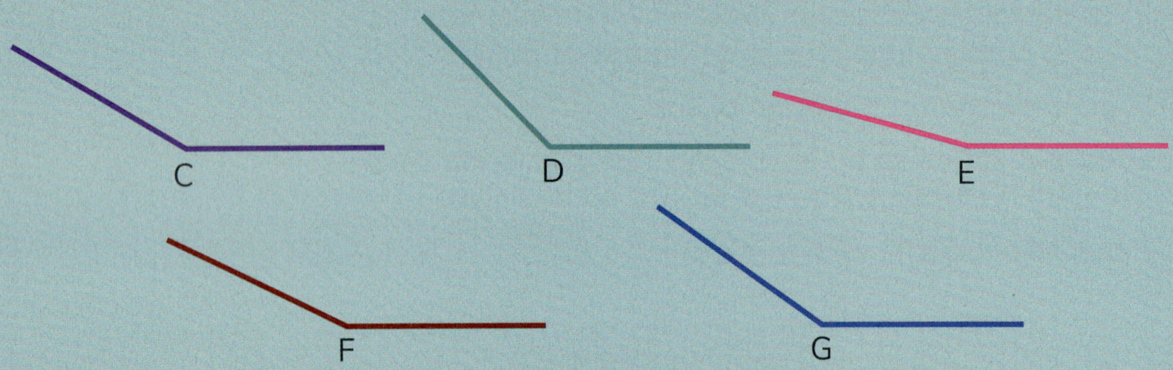

3 How many of the pieces of this cake have an acute angle?

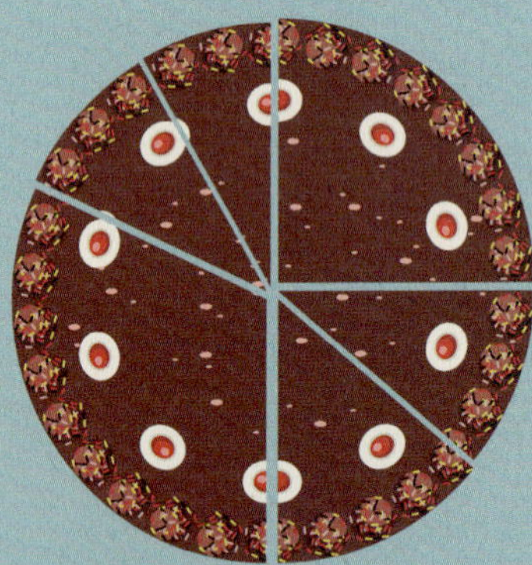

4 How can you tell if an angle is obtuse?

An obtuse angle is ______

5 Estimate the size of this angle in degrees.

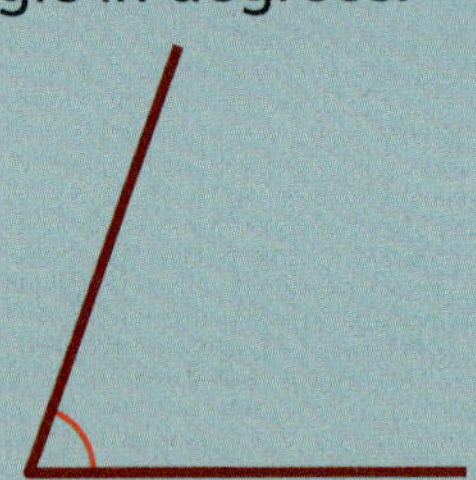

6 Estimate the size of this angle in degrees.

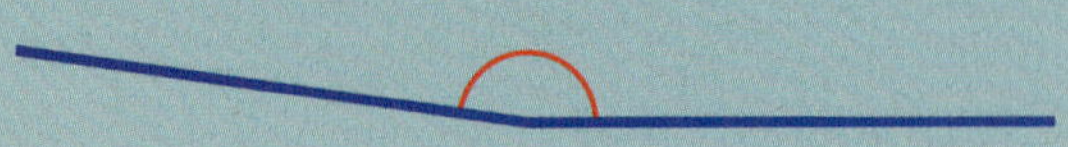

9 Comparing, rounding and dividing

Getting started

1. Which two calculations have an answer 4 remainder 1?

   17 ÷ 4   14 ÷ 3   17 ÷ 5   21 ÷ 4   21 ÷ 5

2. Omar arranges 90 chairs into 5 equal rows.

   How many chairs are in each row?

   Show your working.

3. Write down **all** the numbers from this list that give 150 when rounded to the nearest 10.

   142   145   149   150   153   155   156   159

4. Copy and complete these number sentences using $<$, $>$ or $=$.

   a 216 ◯ 126   b 226 ◯ 216   c 216 ◯ 226

In this unit you will learn about rounding, comparing and ordering numbers.

You can use rounding to estimate answers before you calculate them. This will help you check that your answer is sensible.

> If you need to calculate 92 ÷ 4 you can quickly work out:
>
> 80 ÷ 4 = 20 and 100 ÷ 4 = 25
>
> What does this tell you about the answer to 92 ÷ 4?

This set of Russian dolls are arranged in order according to their size. The order is from shortest to tallest.

What about these numbers?
How are they arranged?
500, 505, 550, 555

You will also learn about division.

When you share food fairly at meal times you are dividing. Division is splitting into equal parts or groups.

9.1 Rounding, ordering and comparing whole numbers

We are going to . . .

- round whole numbers to the nearest 10, 100, 1000, 10 000 or 100 000
- write lists of whole numbers in order, starting with either the smallest or the biggest number
- compare whole numbers using the signs =, < and >.

compare
order
round
round to the nearest

Rounding makes it easier to describe and understand numbers. It is easier to understand 'the distance from Jakarta to New York is roughly 16 000 kilometres' than 'the distance is 16 167 kilometres'.

Worked example 1

Here are four digit cards.

5	6	7	2

Use the cards to write all the 4-digit numbers that are greater than 7000.

Put the numbers you made in order of size, starting with the smallest number.

Place 7 in the thousands place.

7			

Use the other three digits to make as many different numbers as possible.

You are **specialising** when you choose examples and check they meet the criteria.

If you are **systematic**, the numbers may already be in order. If not, rewrite them in order from smallest to largest.

Answer: 7256, 7265, 7526, 7562, 7625, 7652

Exercise 9.1

1 Round these numbers to the nearest 10 000.

a 45 678 b 24 055 c 50 505

2 Round these numbers to the nearest 100 000.

a 147 950 b 865 507 c 157 846

3 At a fundraising event, 5206 people dressed up as children's book characters to raise money for a children's hospital.

a Round 5206 to the nearest 1000. b Round 5206 to the nearest 100.

c Round 5206 to the nearest 10.

4 A number rounded to the nearest 10 is 340.

Find all the possible numbers it could be.

It is harder to work out the original number from a rounded number than it is to round a number. Think about how you solved this problem then discuss your method with your partner.

5 a Round 5495 to the nearest 10.

b Round 5495 to the nearest 100.

c Round 5495 to the nearest 1000.

d Round your answer to (a) to the nearest 100, then round that answer to the nearest 1000.

e Compare your answers to (c) and (d).
Discuss what you notice with your partner.

6 Copy and complete this number sentence using <, > or =.

645 123 ◯ 645 213

7 The table shows the heights of mountains on five different continents.

Mountain	Continent	Height (in metres)
Kilimanjaro	Africa	5895
Everest	Asia	8848
Kosciuszko	Australia	2228
McKinley	North America	6194
Aconcagua	South America	6962

a Write the heights in order starting with the smallest.

b Round each height to the nearest hundred metres.

Think like a mathematician

Here are five numbers:

5505 5455 5045 5500 5050

a Match each of these numbers to the correct letter A, B, C, D or E using the table.

	Number rounded to the:		
	nearest 10	nearest 100	nearest 1000
A	5500	5500	6000
B	5050	5100	5000
C	5050	5000	5000
D	5460	5500	5000
E	5510	5500	6000

When numbers B and C are rounded to the nearest 10, they are the same number (5050). When they are rounded to the nearest 1000, numbers B and C are 5000. But when rounded to the nearest 100 they are different (5000 and 5100).

b Find other numbers that round to 5050 to the nearest 10 and 5000 to the nearest 1000.

c Round each of your numbers to the nearest 100.

Look what I can do!

- [ ] I can write a list of whole numbers in order starting with the smallest or largest number.
- [ ] I can compare whole numbers using the signs =, < or >.
- [ ] I can round whole numbers to the nearest 10, 100, 1000, 10 000 or 100 000.

9.2 Division of 2-digit numbers

We are going to . . .

- estimate the size of an answer when a number up to 100 is divided by a 1-digit number
- divide a number up to 100 by a 1-digit number
- decide whether to round up or round down after division to give the answer to a problem.

Think about when you use division in your everyday life.

For example, to help organise a party for 45 people, you may need a paper plate for each person. If paper plates come in packs of 8, how many packs do you need?

You need to develop strategies to divide 45 by 8 and then make sense of your answer.

division divisor remainder
round up / round down

Worked example 2

Work out 75 ÷ 4

Start with an estimate:

75 rounds to 80 and 80 ÷ 4 = 20 so the answer will be a bit less than 20.

Method 1 – using a number line

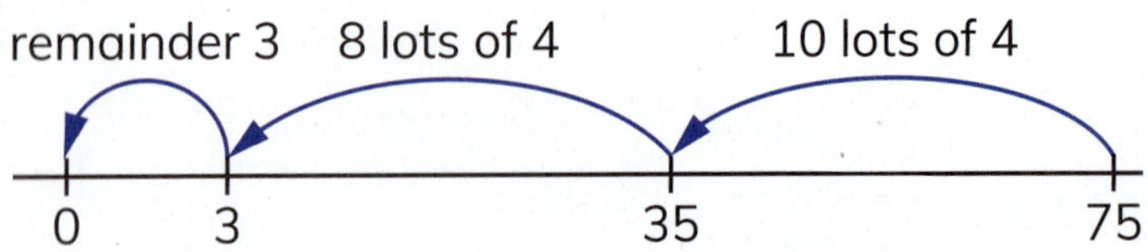

Count back along a number line, first in a group of 10 fours, then a group of 8 fours.

75 ÷ 4 = 18 r3

Continued

Method 2 – repeated subtraction

Subtract using a group of 10 fours, then a group of 8 fours.

75	
− 40	10 lots of 4
35	
− 32	8 lots of 4
3	18 lots of 4 3 left over

Answer: 75 ÷ 4 = 18 r3

Exercise 9.2

Remember to estimate before you calculate an answer.

1. How many weeks are equivalent to 35 days?
2. A shop sells cards in packs of 6.

   Magda buys some of these packs.

   She buys 30 cards.

   How many packs does Magda buy?
3. Complete these calculations.

   a 98 ÷ 7 b 64 ÷ 4 c 96 ÷ 8 d 84 ÷ 6

Think about how you worked out these answers. Did you remember to estimate and check? Did your partner use the same method? Which method do you think is the most efficient?

4. Two sets of calculations which have different properties are mixed together.

   20 ÷ 3 23 ÷ 3 25 ÷ 3 14 ÷ 3 7 ÷ 3

   a Sort the calculations into two sets.

   b Write one more example for each set.

5 60 people go for a walk.

They need to cross a lake by boat.

Each boat can take 9 people.

What is the **least** number of boats needed to take all of the people across the lake?

6 27 apricots are put in bags.

Each bag holds 6 apricots.

How many **full** bags are there?

Discuss with your partner how you decide whether to **round up** or **round down** in questions 5 and 6.

7 Zac and Sarah calculated 75 ÷ 5.
Zac used repeated subtraction and Sarah used a number line.

75	
− 50	10 x 5
25	
− 25	5 x 5
00	
	15 x 5

Answer 15

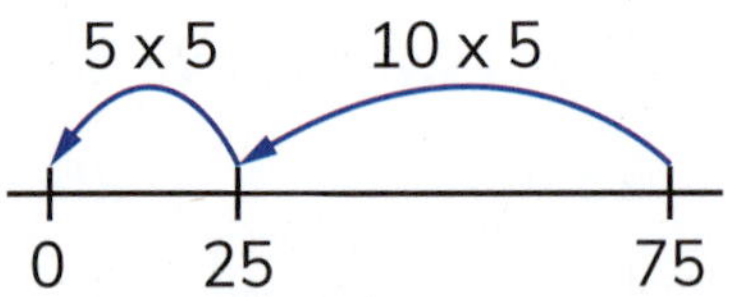

Answer 15

Whose method do you prefer? Explain your reason.

Think like a mathematician

Each of these numbers gives a remainder of 1 when it is divided by 4.

17 81 49

a Investigate other numbers that have a remainder of 1 when divided by 4. Put the numbers in order and look at the pattern of the ones digits, for example 5, 9, 13.

What do you notice about the pattern?

b What about other remainders? You could choose numbers that have a remainder of 2 or 3 when divided by 4, or numbers that have a remainder of 1 when divided by 5.

Write about the patterns you find.

- You will show you are **specialising** when you find solutions to the problem.
- You will show you are **generalising** when you recognise patterns in your results.
- If you explain your results, you will show you are **convincing**.

Look what I can do!

- [ ] I can estimate the size of an answer to a division.
- [ ] I can divide a number up to 100 by a 1-digit number.
- [ ] I can interpret a remainder to give a sensible answer to a question in context.

Check your progress

1 The table shows the length of the railway network in five countries.

Country	Length of network in kilometres
Japan	16 976
Brazil	32 622
Canada	48 150
Italy	16 787
United States	150 966

a Write the lengths in order of size starting with the shortest.

b Round each length to the nearest thousand kilometres.

2 Here are four numbers.

23 34 43 54

Divide each number by 6.

Which number leaves a remainder of 1?

3 If 6160 < □ < 6170 which even numbers could □ be?

4 Here are some divisions.

$72 \div 9$ $24 \div 3$ $40 \div 5$ $42 \div 6$ $64 \div 8$

Find the odd one out.

Explain why it is the odd one out.

5 Melons cost $2 each.

How many melons can you buy for $23?

Project 5

Arranging chairs

Mr Peters is setting up the school hall for some children to watch a film. He is arranging chairs into rows with the same number of chairs in each row.

He arranges the chairs into five rows and discovers that he has four chairs left over.

He collects the chairs back in and tries again. He arranges the chairs into three rows, but this time he has two chairs left over.

Finally he tries rearranging the chairs into just two rows, but he ends up with one chair left over.

How many chairs might Mr Peters have had altogether? How do you know?

10 Collecting and recording data

Getting started

1 These are the sizes of the children's shoes in Class 4.

34, 30, 32, 34, 34, 31, 33, 36, 36, 34,

32, 35, 36, 37, 34, 31, 35, 34, 33, 35

a Copy and complete this tally chart to show how many children have each shoe size.

Shoe size	Tally	Total
30	I	1
31	II	2
32		
33		
34		
35		
36		
37		

b How many children have size 34 shoes?

2 a What size shoes do the children in your class wear?

Copy and complete the tally chart about children in your class.

Shoe size	Tally	Total

b Write two sentences about the shoe sizes of the children in your class. Use the data in your table.

Collecting and recording data can help us to find out the answers to some questions and make decisions.

Sofia is going to make cakes for the school fair. How can she find out what flavour of cakes people might like to buy at the fair?

Sofia can collect and record data about the flavours of cakes that people like. What questions do you think Sofia should ask so that she collects useful data?

10.1 How to collect and record data

We are going to . . .

- plan an investigation to answer a statistical question and consider what data to collect
- conduct investigations to answer statistical questions
- use a dot plot to record data.

To collect useful information to answer a question you need to plan an investigation. You also need to plan how to record the data so that it is easy to read and use.

Leaders and business people need to collect and record data to answer questions in order to make good decisions.

data
dot plot
statistical question

Exercise 10.1

1 Alice wants to answer the question:

How many star jumps can we do in 1 minute?

She uses four friends to investigate the answer.

She asks her friends to do star jumps for one minute.

She uses a stopwatch and paper to record the results.

She records the results in this table.

Name	Number of star jumps
Ben	30
Cerys	24
David	27
Eli	32

a What was the greatest number of star jumps done in a minute?

b Who did the least number of star jumps?

c What was the total number of star jumps for Alice's friends?

2 You are going to plan an investigation to answer the question:

How many multiples of 4 can we write in two minutes?

Copy and complete these sentences to describe how you will collect and record the information.

- The people I will use are ____ .
- I will ask the people to ____ .
- The equipment I will need is ____ .
- I will record the data using ____ .

Carry out your investigation. Record your results.

a What was the least number of multiples of 4 written?

b Who wrote the most multiples of 4?

c How many multiples of 4 were written in total?

3 Write your own question to investigate.

How many ____ can we do in 5 minutes?

Copy and complete these sentences to describe how you will collect and record the information.

- The people I will use are ____ .
- I will ask the people to ____ .
- The equipment I will need is ____ .
- I will record the data using ____ .

Carry out your investigation. Record your results.

a What was the highest number of ____?

b Who did the least ____?

c How many ____ were done in total?

Worked example 1

This data shows how many pets each person has.

0, 1, 3, 1, 1, 0, 2, 4, 1, 2, 2, 0, 0

Show the data using a dot plot.

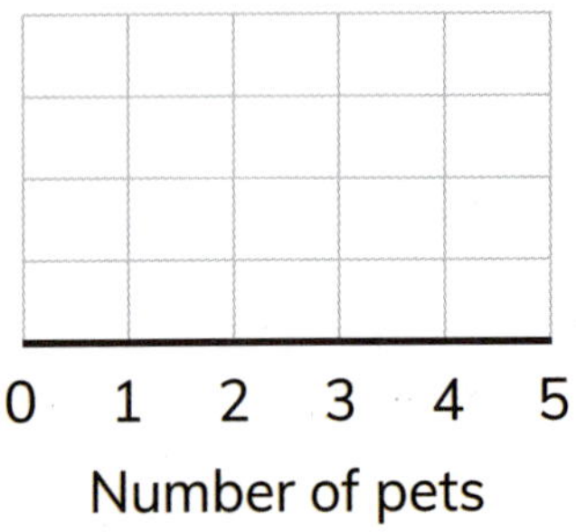

Draw an axis long enough to show all the numbers in the set of data. Label the axis.

It is best to use squared paper to make it easier to space the dots evenly.

Draw one dot above the number on the axis for each time the number appears in the data.

For example there are four 0s so show four dots above 0.

Answer:

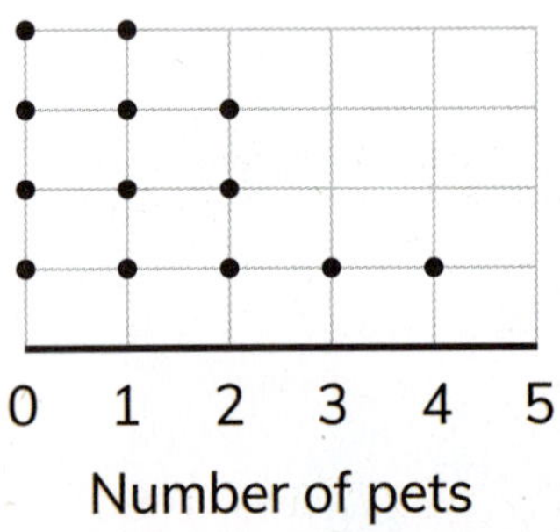

4 Record this data about the number of books read this month in a dot plot.

Number of books read by learners in Class 4:

1, 1, 3, 4, 4, 2, 2, 4, 1, 5, 3, 4, 2, 3, 3, 5, 4, 4, 3, 4

Copy this axis. Remember to label the axis.

Draw one dot above the number on the axis for each time the number appears in the data.

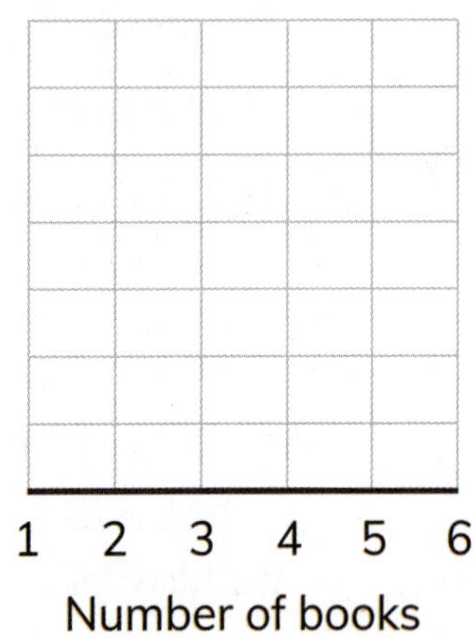

5 These are the scores Class 4 got in their spelling test.

10 5 8 9 10 10 9 3 10 6

6 8 9 10 6 10 9 10 9 10

Record the scores in a dot plot.

6 This dot plot shows how many hours of sport learners in Class 4 do each week.

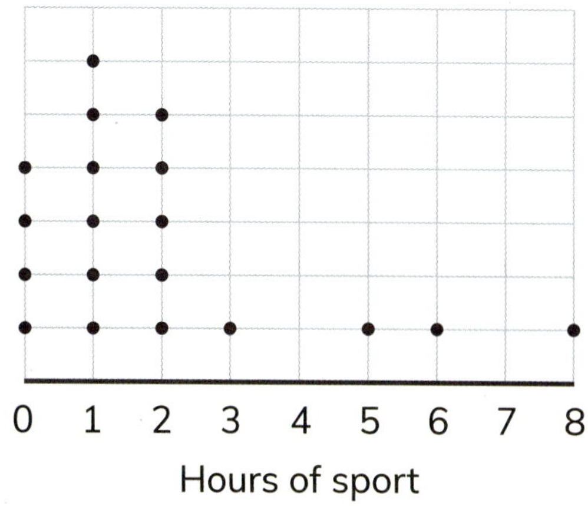

a How many people do 0 hours of sport each week?

b How many people do 4 hours of sport each week?

c How many people do more than 2 hours of sport each week?

d Write a sentence of your own describing the data in the dot plot.

The dot plot shows that ____.

Look back at your dot plots in questions 4 to 6.

- Have you labelled the axis each time?
- Are the numbers clear and evenly spaced?
- Are the dots evenly spaced?
- Is it easy to see how many dots there are for each number?
- Is it easy to compare how many dots there are for different numbers?

Copy and complete this sentence:

To improve my drawing of dot plots I will ____.

Think like a mathematician

a Start critiquing tally charts and dot plots by writing about their differences and similarities.

b Talk about your list with a partner.

c Do you prefer recording data with a tally chart or a dot plot? Why?

7 Here are pages from two children's story books.

Book 1

Book 2

a Which of these two storybooks do you think is easier to read?

b What data could you count, measure or sort on the pages to show which book is easier to read?

c Discuss your ideas with a partner.

d Collect data to compare the two books.

e Display the data in a table, graph or chart.

f What is the same about the two books.

g What is different about the two books.

h Find two books in your classroom and collect data from them to show which is easier to read.

8 With a partner choose your own question to investigate.

Examples:

How many ____ can people do in ____ minutes?

How many ____ do people do in one week?

Copy and complete these sentences.

- The people I will use are ____ .
- I will ask the people to ____ .
- The equipment I need is ____ .

Collect the data.

Record the data in a dot plot.

Write three sentences about the data in your dot plot.

Look what I can do!

- [ ] I can plan an investigation to answer a statistical question and consider what data to collect.
- [ ] I can carry out an investigation to answer a statistical question.
- [ ] I can use a dot plot to record data.

Check your progress

1 Leroy investigated the question:

How many biscuits are in one bag of biscuits?

He counted the biscuits in 15 bags and recorded the results in a dot plot.

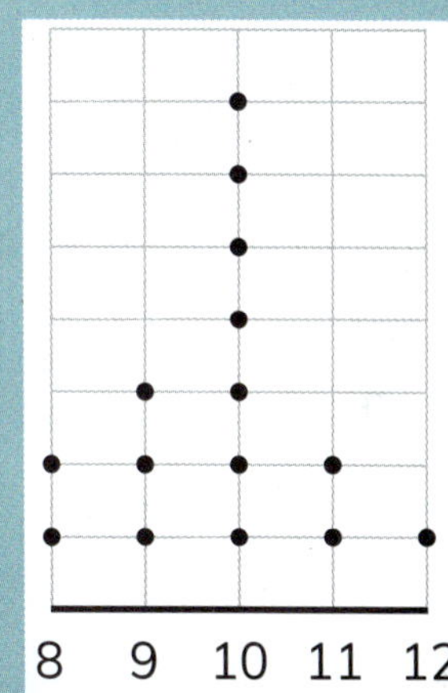

a How should Leroy label the axis?

b How many bags had 9 biscuits?

c How many bags had more than 10 biscuits?

2 Leroy counted the biscuits in another 15 bags.
This is how many biscuits there were in each bag.

10, 9, 10, 10, 8, 11, 9, 9, 12, 10, 10, 10, 7, 10, 10

Draw a dot plot to show the data.

3 How would you investigate the question:

How many times can people write their full name in one minute?

a Copy and complete these sentences:

- The people I would use are _____ .
- I would ask the people to _____ .
- The equipment I would need is _____ .

b Draw a table that you could use to collect the data.

11 Fractions and percentages

Getting started

1 Put these fractions in order starting with the smallest.

$\frac{7}{8}$ $\frac{3}{8}$ $\frac{1}{8}$ $\frac{5}{8}$

2 Use one of the signs < or > to copy and complete this number sentence.

$\frac{3}{5}$ □ $\frac{1}{5}$

3 Here is a number line.

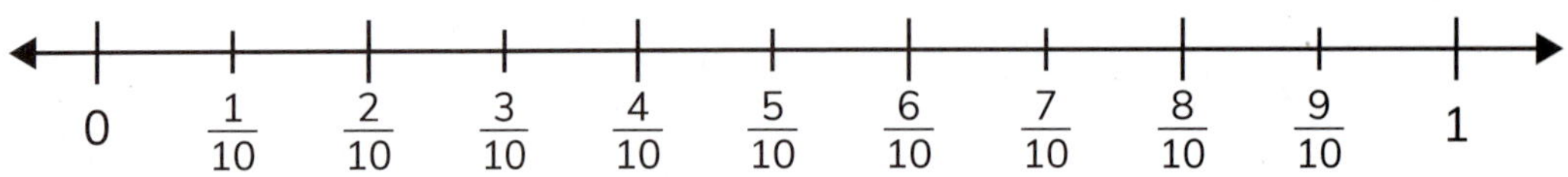

Which fraction is equivalent to $\frac{3}{5}$?

4 Which shapes show a fraction equivalent to $\frac{1}{2}$?

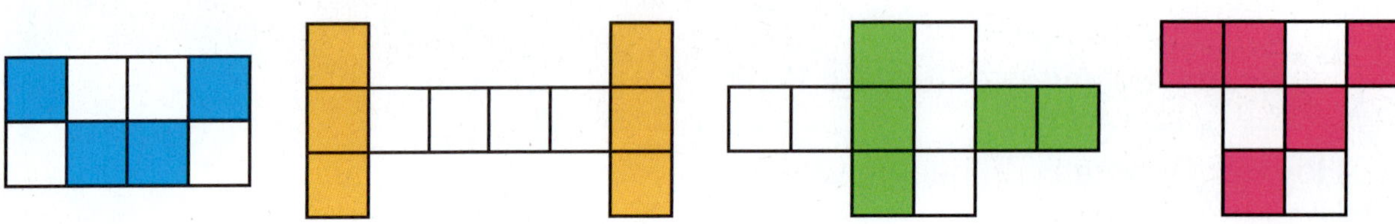

A B C D

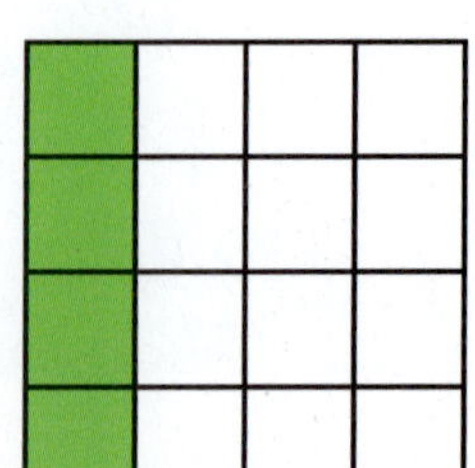

Look at this shape.

4 out of 16 squares are coloured. That is $\frac{4}{16}$.

1 out of 4 columns is coloured. That is $\frac{1}{4}$.

$\frac{1}{4}$ and $\frac{4}{16}$ are equivalent fractions.

Can you think of any other pairs of equivalent fractions?

You will learn more about equivalent fractions in this unit and how to compare different fractions.

You will also learn about percentages for the first time.

You may have seen the percentage symbol (%) in shop windows.

Where else have you seen or heard about percentages?

11.1 Equivalence, comparing and ordering fractions

We are going to . . .

- recognise proper fractions as fractions less than a whole
- recognise when fractions are equivalent
- compare and order fractions.

In Stages 2 and 3, you worked with equivalent fractions for halves, quarters, fifths and tenths. In this unit, you will work with some other proper fractions.

$\frac{3}{6}$ and $\frac{1}{2}$ are equal in value. They are equivalent fractions.

Be careful though. Is $\frac{3}{6}$ of Pie A equal to $\frac{1}{2}$ of Pie B?

Pie A

Pie B

equivalent fraction
proper fraction

Worked example 1

Write this set of fractions in order starting with the smallest fraction.

$\frac{1}{2}, \frac{5}{8}, \frac{3}{8}, \frac{3}{4}$

$\frac{1}{2} = \frac{4}{8}, \frac{5}{8}, \frac{3}{8}, \frac{3}{4} = \frac{6}{8}$ Find equivalent fractions with the same denominator.

Answer:

$\frac{3}{8}, \frac{1}{2}, \frac{5}{8}, \frac{3}{4}$ Write the fractions in order of size.

Tip

You can find equivalence in different ways.

Dividing rectangles:

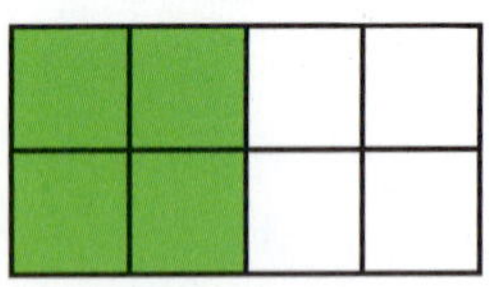

$\frac{1}{2} = \frac{4}{8}$

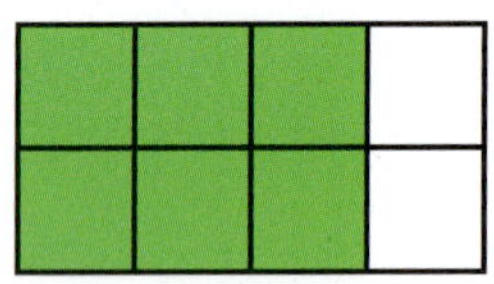

$\frac{3}{4} = \frac{6}{8}$

Using a number line:

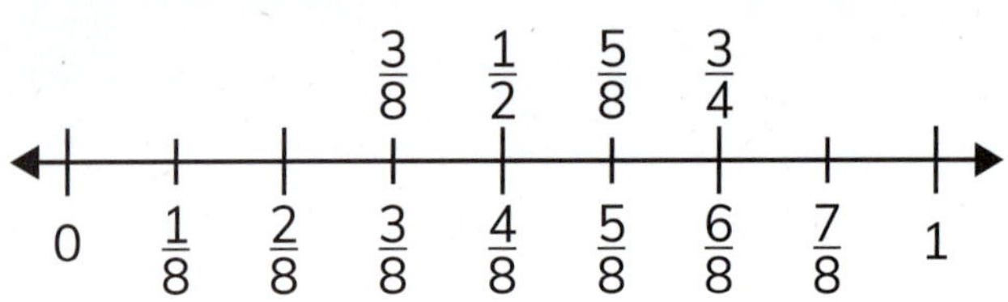

Using a fraction wall:

<table>
<tr><td colspan="8">1</td></tr>
<tr><td colspan="4">$\frac{1}{2}$</td><td colspan="4">$\frac{1}{2}$</td></tr>
<tr><td colspan="2">$\frac{1}{4}$</td><td colspan="2">$\frac{1}{4}$</td><td colspan="2">$\frac{1}{4}$</td><td colspan="2">$\frac{1}{4}$</td></tr>
<tr><td>$\frac{1}{8}$</td><td>$\frac{1}{8}$</td><td>$\frac{1}{8}$</td><td>$\frac{1}{8}$</td><td>$\frac{1}{8}$</td><td>$\frac{1}{8}$</td><td>$\frac{1}{8}$</td><td>$\frac{1}{8}$</td></tr>
</table>

Exercise 11.1

1 These diagrams show equivalent fractions.

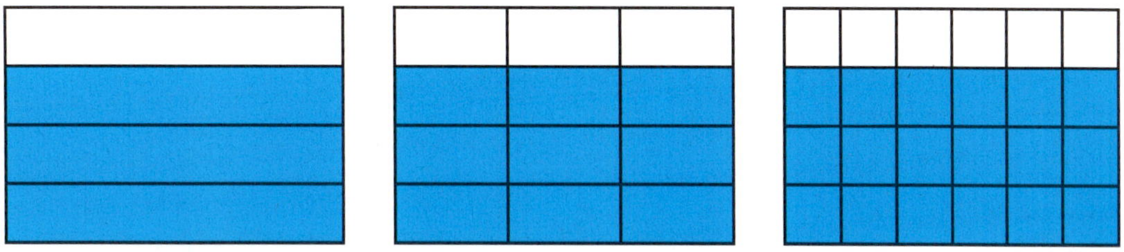

Copy and complete the following:

$\frac{1}{4} = \frac{\square}{\square} = \frac{\square}{\square}$ $\quad$ $\frac{3}{4} = \frac{\square}{\square} = \frac{\square}{\square}$

2 Find four pairs of equivalent fractions in the table.

Which fraction is not used?

$\frac{8}{10}$	$\frac{7}{10}$	$\frac{3}{10}$
$\frac{1}{2}$	$\frac{4}{5}$	$\frac{4}{10}$
$\frac{5}{10}$	$\frac{35}{50}$	$\frac{30}{100}$

3 Which is the odd one out? Explain your answer.

$\frac{3}{4}$ $\quad$ $\frac{9}{12}$ $\quad$ $\frac{4}{6}$

Compare your answer with your partner's answer.

- Did you choose the same fraction and give the same reason?
- Is there more than one answer?

4 Alana makes a fraction using two number cards.

Alana says, 'My fraction is equivalent to $\frac{1}{2}$.

One of the $\frac{\square}{\square}$ number cards is 6.'

What fractions could Alana make?

5 Use the number line as a guide to help you order these fractions.
Start with the smallest fraction.

$\frac{1}{2}$ $\frac{3}{8}$ $\frac{3}{4}$ $\frac{5}{8}$ $\frac{7}{8}$ $\frac{1}{4}$

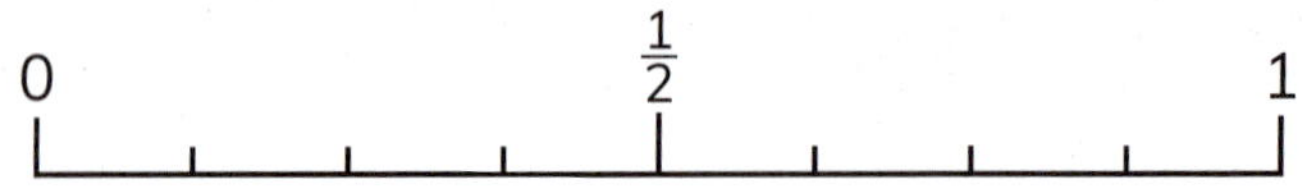

6 Here are three fraction cards.

$\frac{3}{8}$ $\frac{1}{4}$ $\frac{5}{16}$

Use the cards to make this number sentence correct.

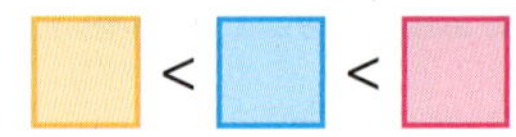

7 Raphael says that $\frac{3}{8} > \frac{3}{4}$ because $8 > 4$.

Do you agree with him?

Explain your decision.

Think about the different strategies you can use to help you find equivalent fractions (diagrams, number lines and number walls).

- Which strategies do you use?
- Does it depend on the fractions you are using?
- Can you find a different strategy to try in the future?

Think like a mathematician

Make as many different pairs of equivalent fractions as you can using the numbers 1 to 10.

Tip

Try using number cards, for example:

$\frac{1}{2} = \frac{2}{4}$ $\frac{1}{2} = \frac{3}{6}$

You will show you are **specialising** when you find solutions to the problem.

Look what I can do!

- ☐ I can recognise proper fractions as fractions less than a whole.
- ☐ I can find equivalent fractions.
- ☐ I can use my knowledge of equivalent fractions to compare and order fractions.

11.2 Percentages

We are going to . . .

- use a percentage as the number of parts in each hundred, for example 10% is 10 out of 100
- use the percentage symbol (%).

You will find many examples of percentages in everyday life.

Percentages are sometimes used on food labels.

Each grilled burger (94g) contains

Energy 924 kJ 220 kcal	Fat 13 g	Saturates 5.9 g	Sugars 0.8 g	Salt 0.7 g
11%	19%	30%	<1%	12%

of an adult's reference intake

Look out for percentage signs next time you go shopping. They are often used when a shop has a sale.

percent percentage

Percentage and percent mean the number of parts out of a hundred. The symbol is %. For example, this diagram shows 25 out of 100 squares shaded which is 25%.

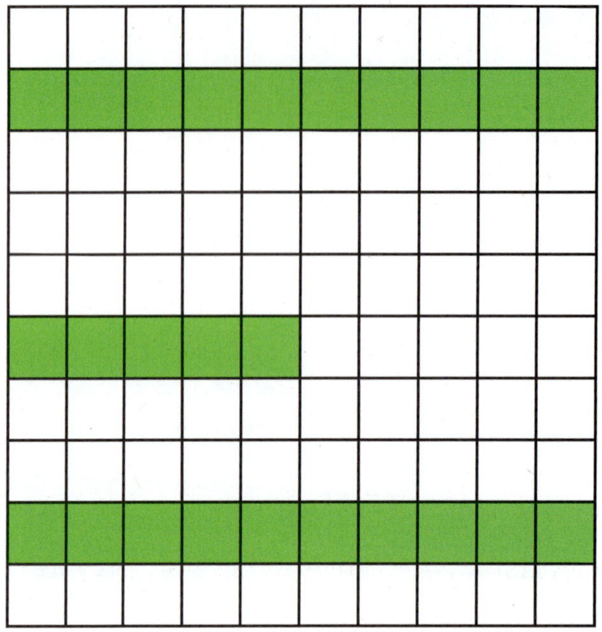

Worked example 2

Here is a diagram of a label inside a dress.

Amy spilled a drink on the label.

What percentage of the dress was silk?

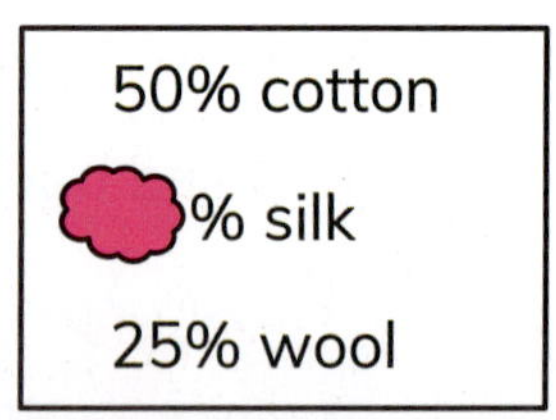

% of silk = 100 – 50 – 25

= 25

100% represents the whole.

Answer: 25% of the dress was silk.

Tip

You could also work this out by adding the amount of cotton and wool together first:

50 + 25 = 75

100 – 75 = 25

Exercise 11.2

1

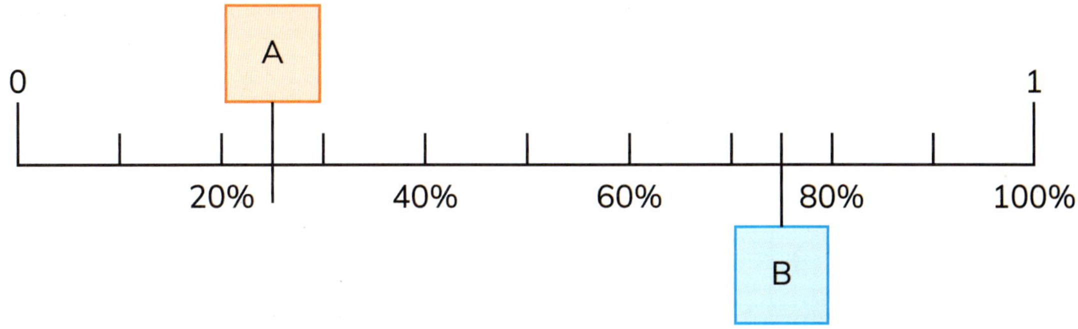

a Write the fraction marked as A.

b Write the percentage marked as B.

2 Write these fractions as percentages.

a $\frac{3}{4}$ **b** $\frac{1}{4}$ **c** $\frac{1}{2}$

3 A team won 25% and drew 25% of the games they played.

What percentage of games did the team lose?

4 Look at the diagram, then write the missing numbers.

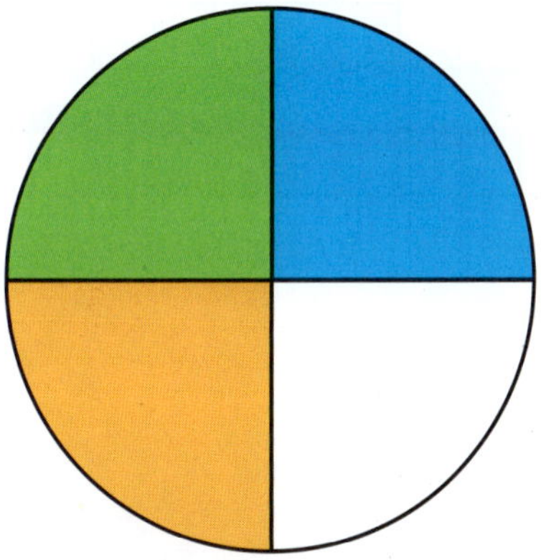

a $\frac{1}{4}$ of the diagram is white. $\frac{1}{4}$ = ______%

b $\frac{3}{4}$ of the diagram is coloured. $\frac{3}{4}$ = ______%

5 What percentage of each diagram is coloured?

a

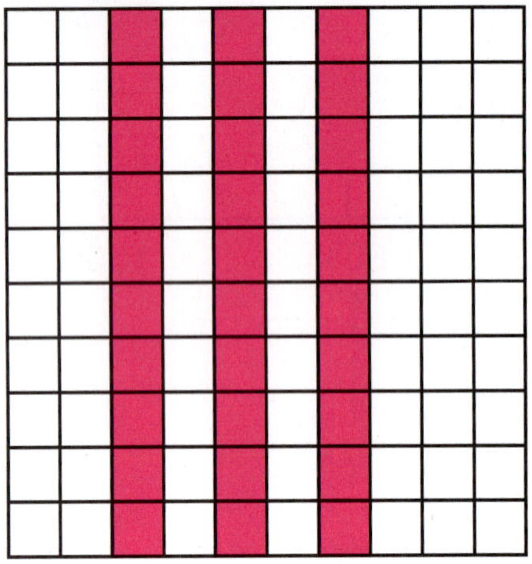

b

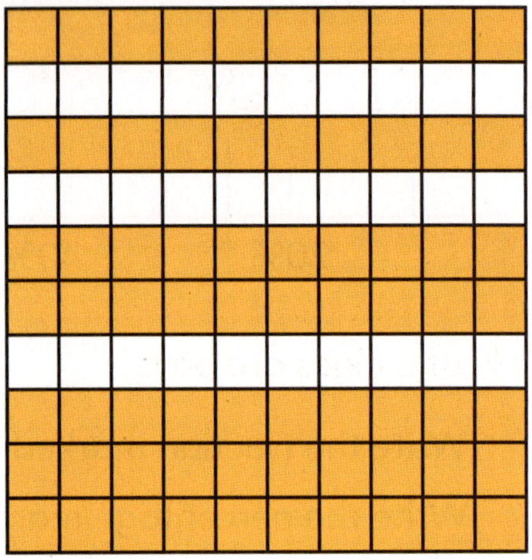

c

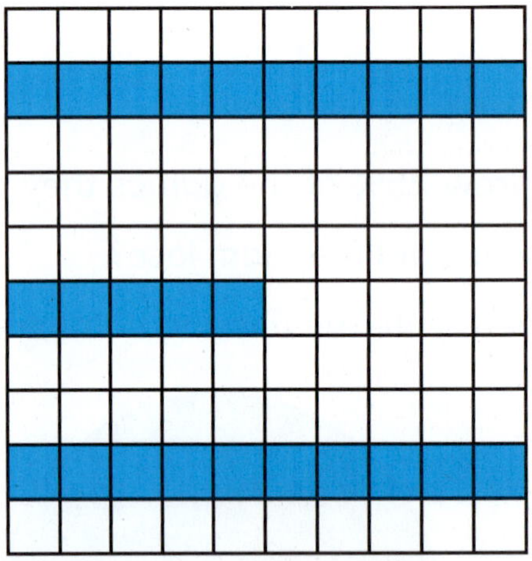

6

a What percentage of the 100 squares is covered by the robot face?

b Write this percentage as a fraction.

7 Copy the table and write these percentages in the correct column.

35%   50%   74%   14%   85%   8%   80%

Smaller than $\frac{1}{4}$	Bigger than $\frac{1}{4}$ but smaller than $\frac{3}{4}$	Bigger than $\frac{3}{4}$

8 55% of a class are boys.

What percentage of the class are girls?

9 Alana draws a pattern of triangles.

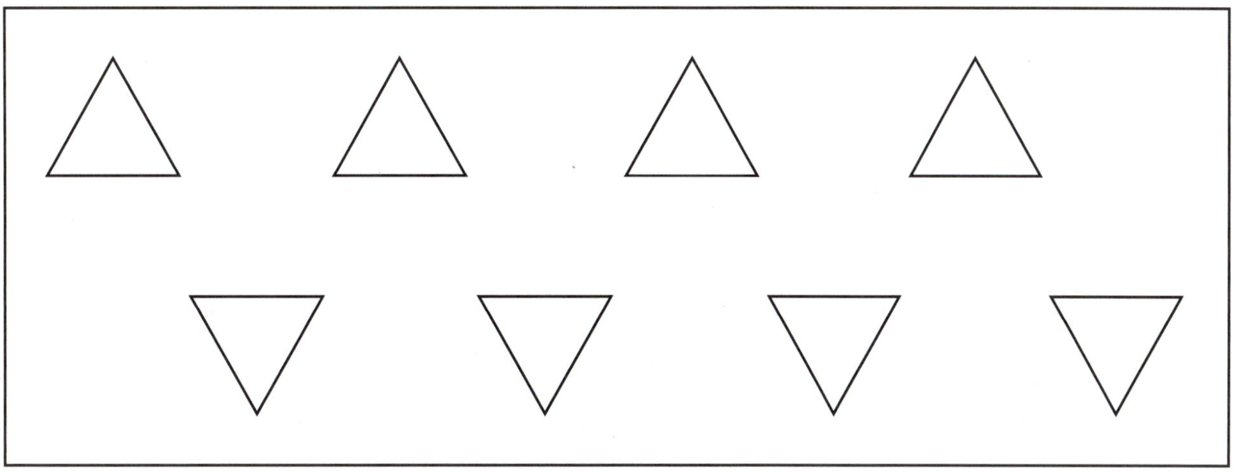

She decides to colour 25% of the triangles.

How many triangles does she colour?

Look what I can do!

- ☐ I can understand a percentage as the number of parts in each hundred, for example 1% is 1 out of 100.
- ☐ I can use the percentage symbol (%) correctly.

Check your progress

1 Use the number wall to help you place $\frac{5}{6}$, $\frac{3}{4}$ and $\frac{2}{3}$ in the number sentence.

$\square < \square < \square$

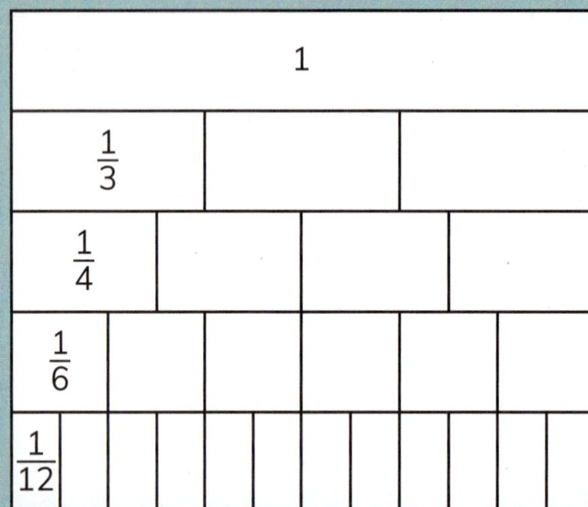

2 Which is the biggest fraction?

$\frac{1}{5}$ $\frac{1}{3}$ $\frac{1}{4}$ $\frac{1}{6}$

3 Sort these diagrams into two different sets.

A B C D E

Explain how you sorted them.

4 Look at these diagrams.

Complete the fractions.

$\frac{1}{5} = \frac{\square}{10} = \frac{3}{\square} = \frac{\square}{20}$

Continued

5 Which is the odd one out in this collection of four fractions?
Explain your answer.

$\frac{30}{100}$ $\frac{3}{10}$ $\frac{6}{20}$ $\frac{3}{9}$

6 Copy and complete these sentences.

a 15 out of 100 is the same as ____%.

b ____ out of 100 is the same as 30%.

7 What percentage of each diagram is shaded?

a

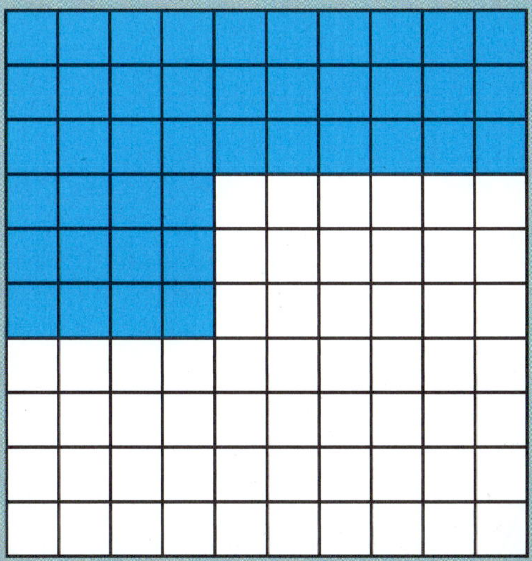

b

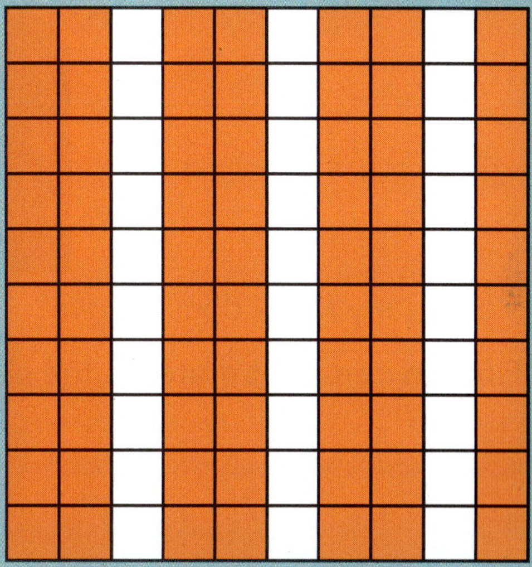

8 Here is a question from a survey.

Imagine you are in a time machine.

Choose whether to go back in time, forward in time or stay the same.

Here are the results of the survey.

Go back in time	48%
Go forward in time	50%
Stay the same	?

What percentage of people chose to stay the same?

12 Investigating 3D shapes and nets

Getting started

1 Find an item that matches the shape in this picture.

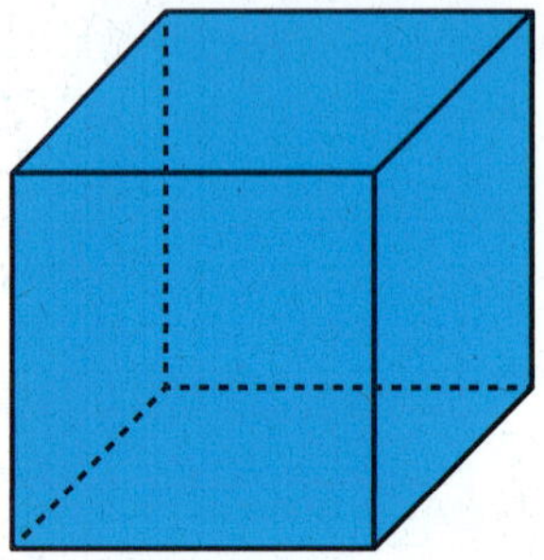

How many faces does it have?

2 Find an item that matches the shape in this picture.

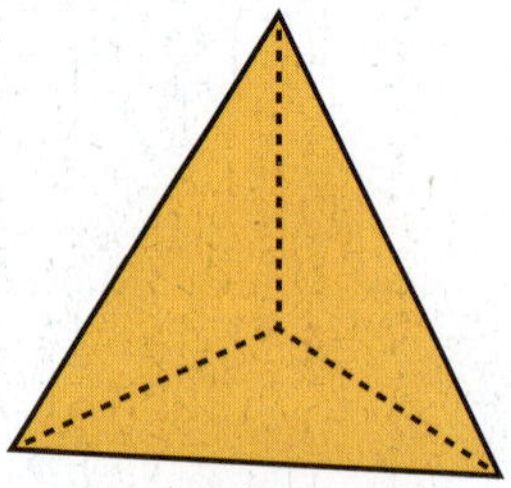

a Put one finger on each of its vertices.
How many vertices does it have?

b How many edges does it have?

3 Match the picture to the shape name.

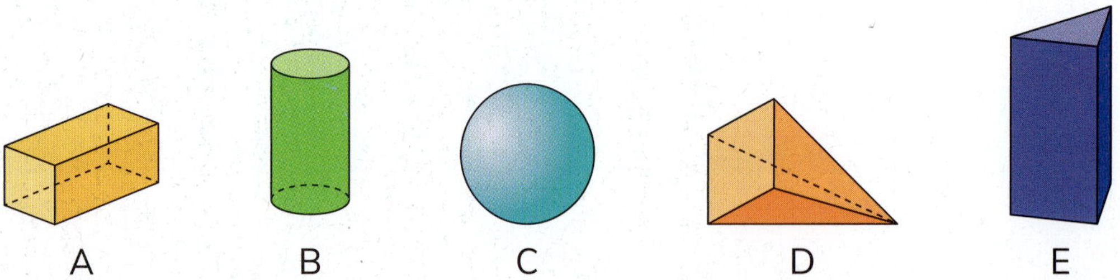

cylinder sphere cuboid triangular prism square-based pyramid

Learning about 3D shapes and how they are constructed is useful for designing and making any solid object or container. Some jobs where knowledge of 3D shapes is important are: artists working in three dimensions, packaging designers and architects.

Try making a model of a building out of different shape blocks. Draw a picture of your model as if it were a building.

12.1 The properties of 3D shapes

We are going to . . .

- identify and describe 2D faces of 3D shapes
- describe the properties of 3D shapes.

This section will help you to become more familiar with the properties of 3D shapes. You will practise using the vocabulary you need to describe shapes. This will help you to talk about 3D shapes clearly with other people.

cone
edge / edges
face / faces
prism
pyramid
vertex / vertices

What words do you already know that describe the shapes in this model?

Worked example 1

Count and name the 2D faces of a square-based pyramid.

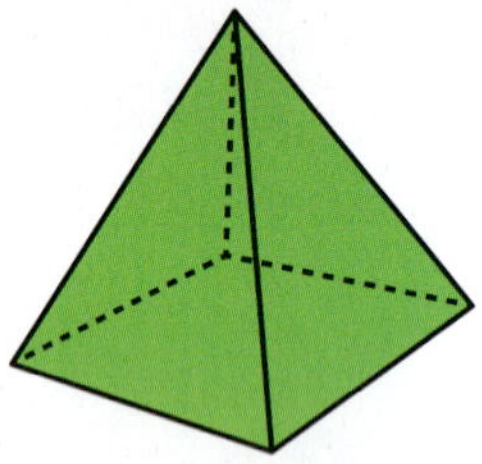

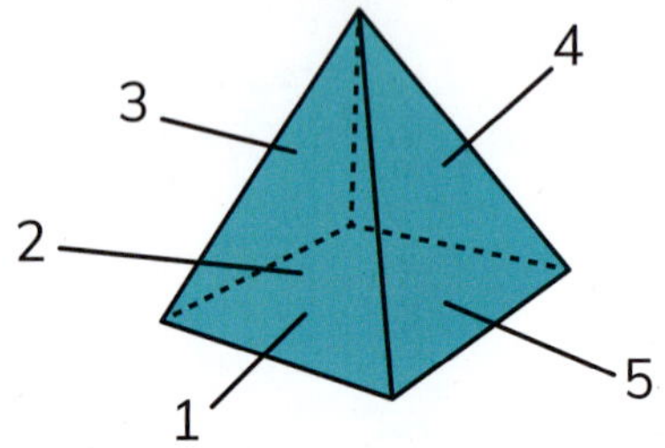

First count the faces.

1 Square
2 Triangle
3 Triangle
4 Triangle
5 Triangle

Next list the faces.

Answer: There are 4 triangular faces and 1 square face.

Exercise 12.1

1 Copy and complete the sentences to show the number of triangular and rectangular faces.

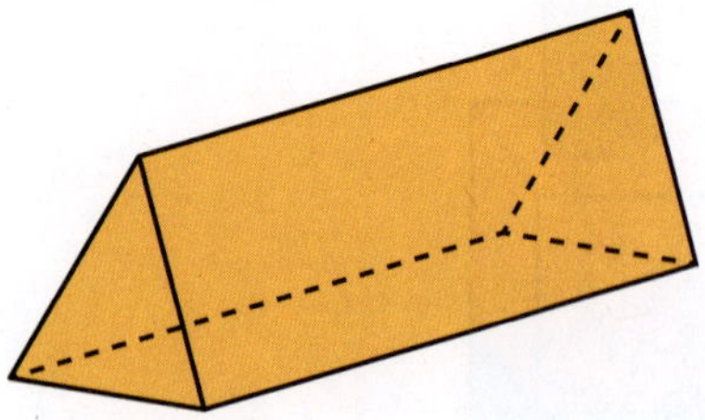

a A triangular prism has ____ rectangular faces and ____ triangular faces.

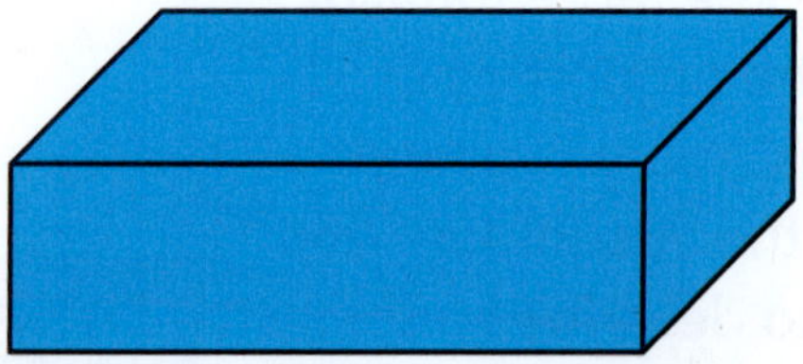

b A cuboid has ____ rectangular faces and ____ triangular faces.

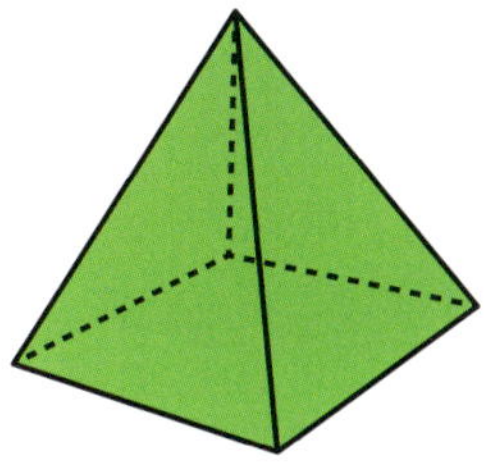

c A square-based pyramid has _____ rectangular faces and _____ triangular faces.

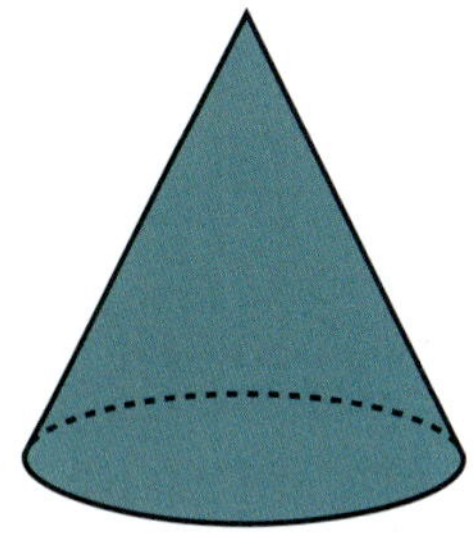

d A cone has _____ rectangular faces and _____ triangular faces.

2 This is a pentagonal prism.

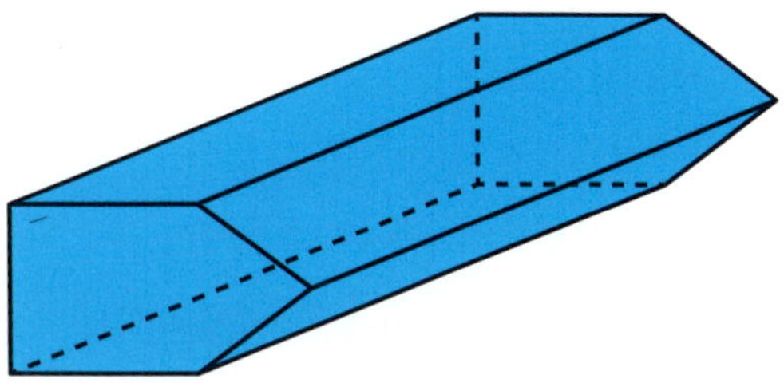

a How many faces does it have?

b What shape faces does it have?

3 A hexagonal pyramid has 7 faces. Write the shape of each face.

4 This is a model of a square-based pyramid. Max has used straws to make the edges. He has used modelling clay to join the edges at the vertices.

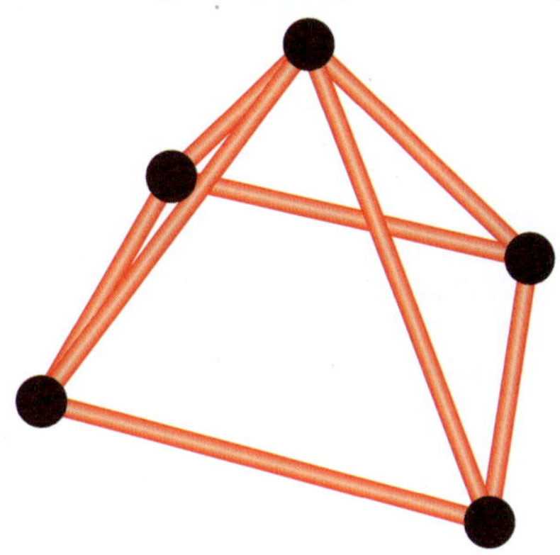

a How many straws has he used?

b How many pieces of modelling clay has he used?

c How many straws would Max need to make a model of a cuboid?

d How many pieces of modelling clay would Max need to make a model of a cuboid?

5

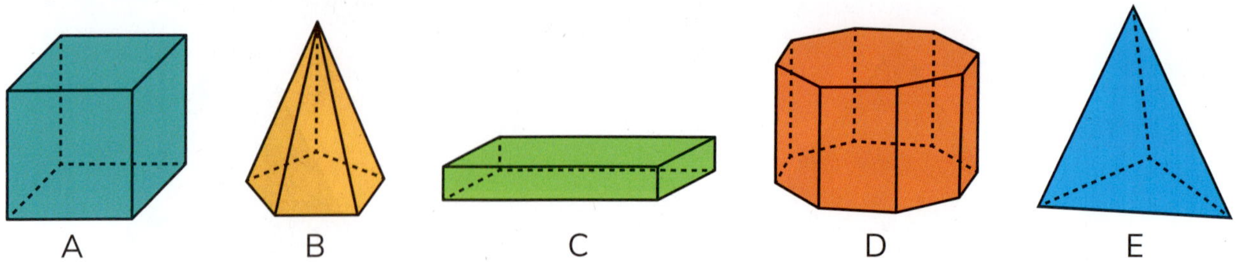

a Choose two of these shapes. Classify the shapes by writing a property that the shapes have in common.

Look at the whole set of shapes.
Use these questions to classify the shapes.

b Which of the shapes has at least one triangular face?

c Which of the shapes has more than 6 vertices?

d Which of the shapes have fewer than 12 edges?

Tip

You could compare the faces, edges or vertices.

face | edge | vertex

How do you remember which word goes with each part of the shape?

Think about how you will remember the meanings of these words in the future.

Try to explain what you do, or will do, for each word.

6 Describe this shape in sentences.

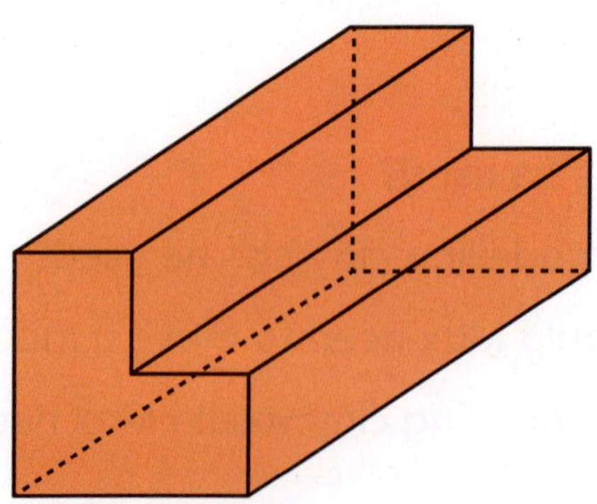

Read your sentences and assess your skills.

- Did you describe the shapes of the faces?
- Did you write how many edges and vertices the shape has?

7 Cubes are special types of cuboids.

a If a cuboid is also a cube what is the fewest number of square faces it can have?

b How many faces can it have that are not squares?

c If a cuboid is not a cube what is the greatest number of square faces that it can have?

d Write two sentences to describe how cubes and cuboids are similar and different.

Think like a mathematician

Use up to 12 straight straws and some modelling clay.

a Specialise by investigating which 3D shapes you can make with exactly 1, 2, 3, 4, 5, 6 or more straws. What number of straws will make a shape? Generalise by writing what number of straws will not make a shape and why.

b You must be able to name each shape. Record the shapes you find by drawing or photographing them. Write the name of the shape and how many straws were needed.

Look what I can do!

- [ ] I can identify and describe 2D faces of 3D shapes.
- [ ] I can describe the properties of 3D shapes using words like 'edges', 'faces' and 'vertices'.

12.2 Nets of 3D shapes

We are going to . . .

- match nets to the 3D shapes they make.

net
tetrahedron

A net of a 3D shape is what it looks like if it is opened out flat.

Imagine you have a box made out of card.

If you cut along the edges you can open it up to make a flat shape.
This flat shape is called a net.

The net can be folded up again to make a box.

Nets are used in cardboard packaging.
The net is drawn onto card, cut out and folded up to make a box.

In this section you will learn about the nets of 3D shapes.

Exercise 12.2

1 Attif has cut and unfolded a box of cereal so that it makes a flat shape.

  a What shape was the box?

  b How many faces did the shape have?

  c What shape are the faces?

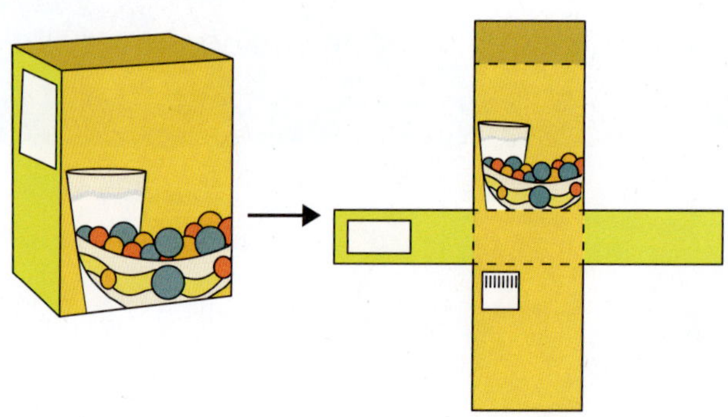

2 Sara has cut and unfolded a packet of sweets so that it makes a flat shape.

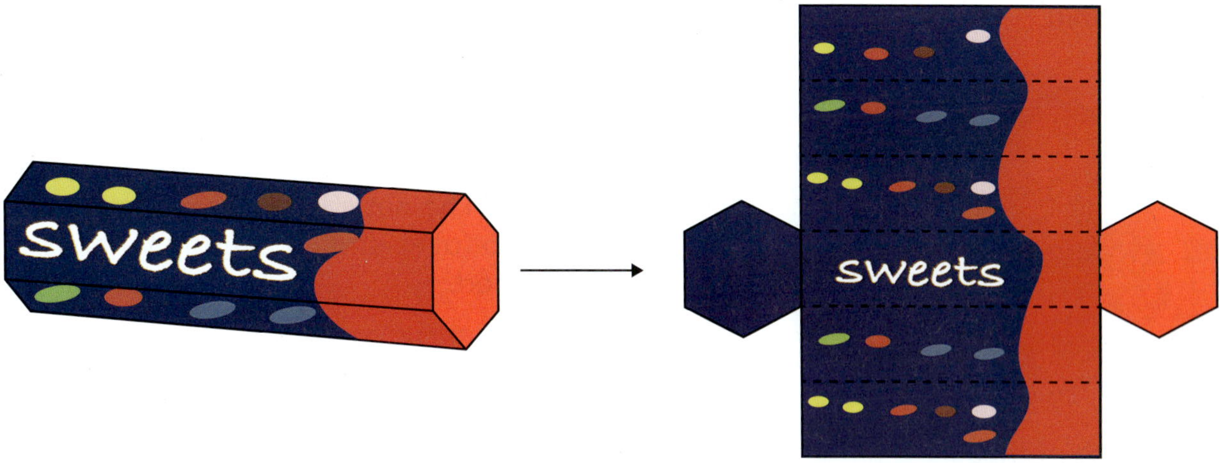

a What shape was the packet?

b How many faces did the shape have?

c What shape are the faces?

Worked example 2

Identify the net of a square-based pyramid.

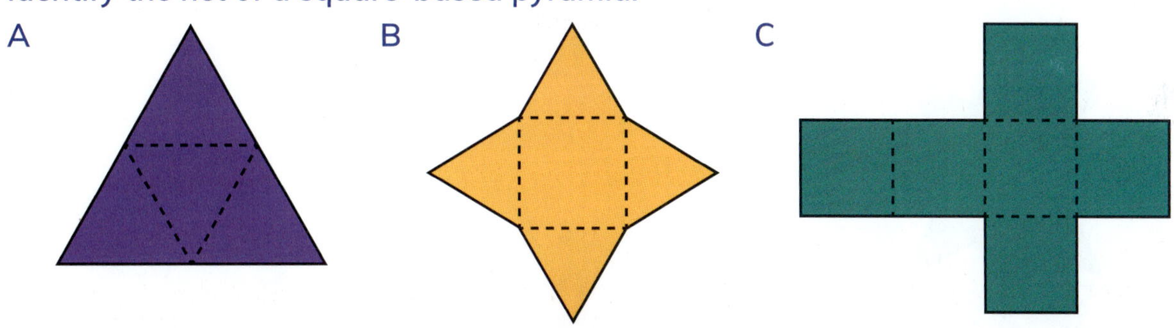

• A square-based pyramid has 5 faces.	Record the number of faces and the shape of the faces.
• It has 1 square face and 4 triangular faces.	Look for a net that has 1 square face and 4 triangular faces.

Answer: B is the net of a square-based pyramid.

3 Marcus has an octagon-based pyramid.

Tip

If more than one of the nets matches the correct number and shape of faces, try to visualise the faces folding up into the shape. The net should leave no gaps, and no faces should overlap when it is folded.

Which of these is a net of Marcus's shape?

A

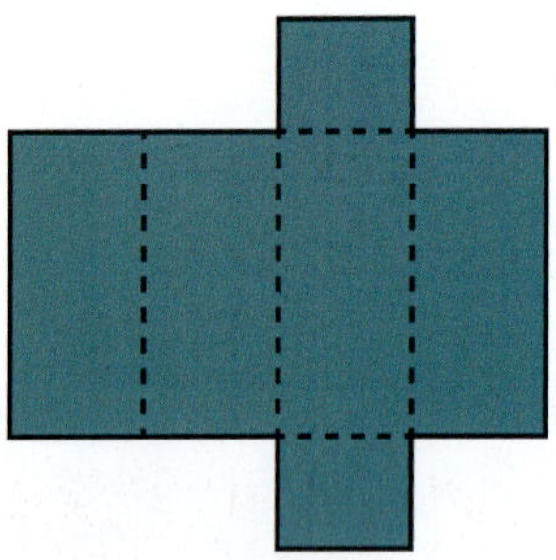

B

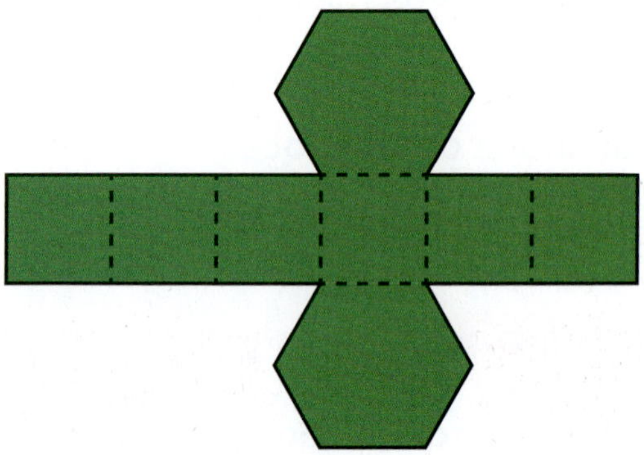

C

4 Identify the net of a pentagonal prism.

A

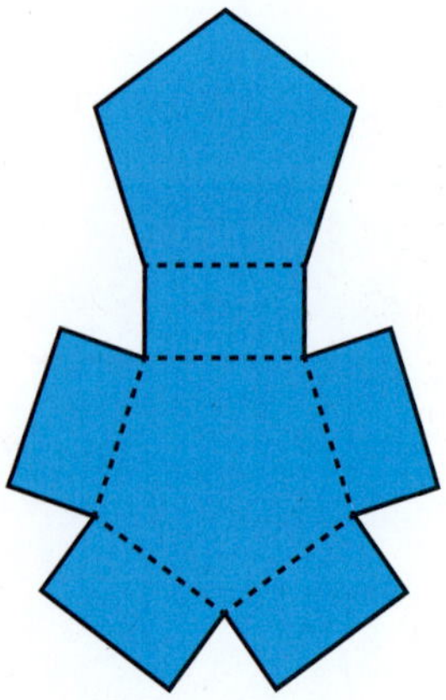

B

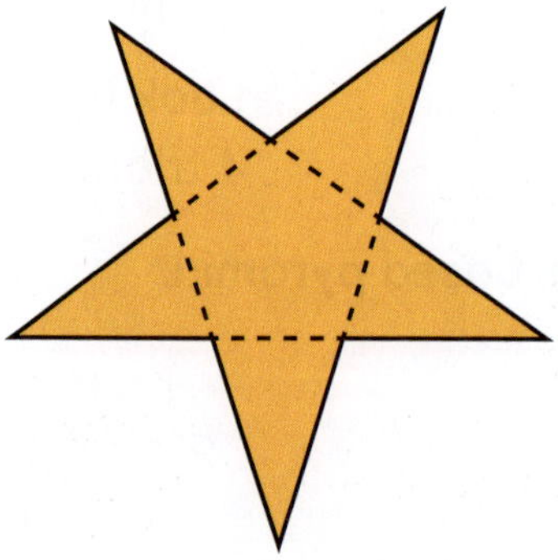

C

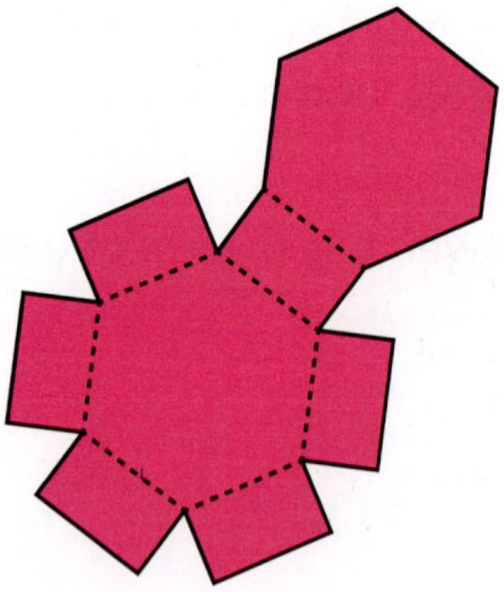

5 Name the 3D shapes made with these nets.

a

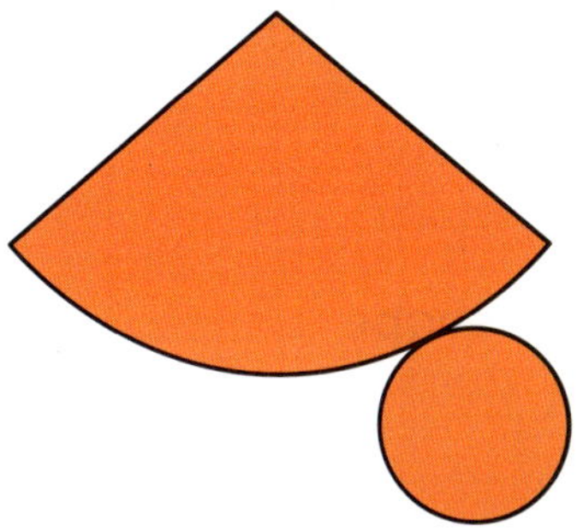

Cone

b

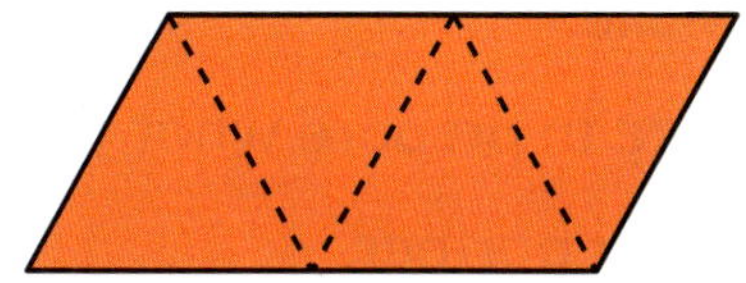

Tetrahedron

c

Cylinder

d

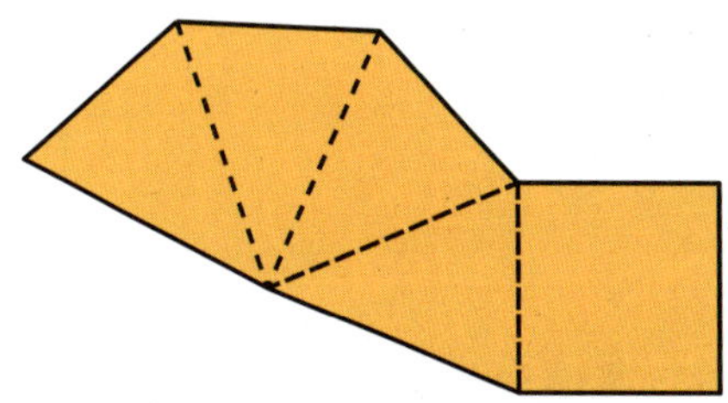

Square-based pyramid

Think like a mathematician

A triangle-based pyramid (tetrahedron) has 4 faces.

A square-based pyramid has 5 faces.

A pentagon-based pyramid has 6 faces.

a Continue the list to categorise the shapes:

A hexagon-based pyramid has _____ faces.

A heptagon-based pyramid has _____ _____ .

An _____-based pyramid has _____ _____ .

b Describe the link between the base shape of the pyramid and the number of faces.

Check this is true for a nonagon-based pyramid and a decagon-based pyramid.

c Investigate the number of faces of prisms in the same way.

d Generalise and describe the link between the base shape and the number of faces.

6 You will be explaining to your partner how to work out what 3D shape a net will make.

Take 1 minute to prepare what you will say.

Explain to your partner.

Ask your partner to explain how they work out what 3D shape a net will make.

Assess your own and your partner's explanations.

Did you include looking at:

- the number of faces
- the shape of the faces
- how to tell if a net will make a prism or a pyramid.

Write down what you did well and if there is anything you need to improve.

Look what I can do!

- [ ] I can match nets to the 3D shapes they make.

Check your progress

1 How many faces does a hexagonal prism have?

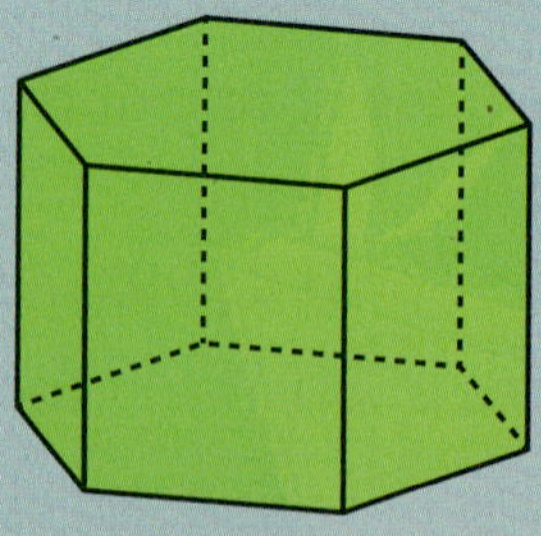

2 What are the shapes of the faces of a pentagon-based pyramid?

3 Describe a tetrahedron using the words 'edges', 'vertices' and 'faces'.

Continued

4 Which of these nets makes a pentagon-based pyramid?

A

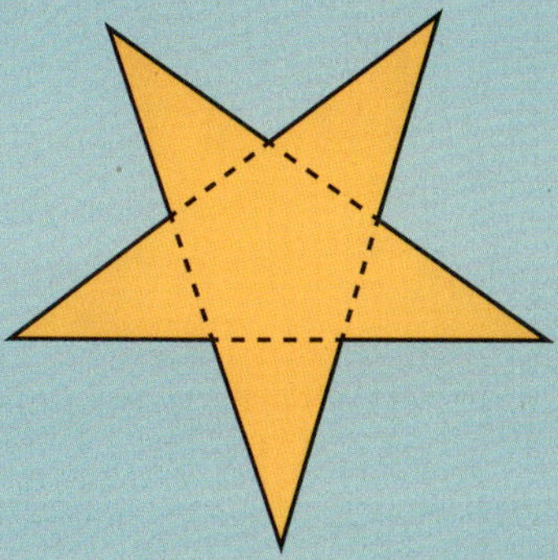

B

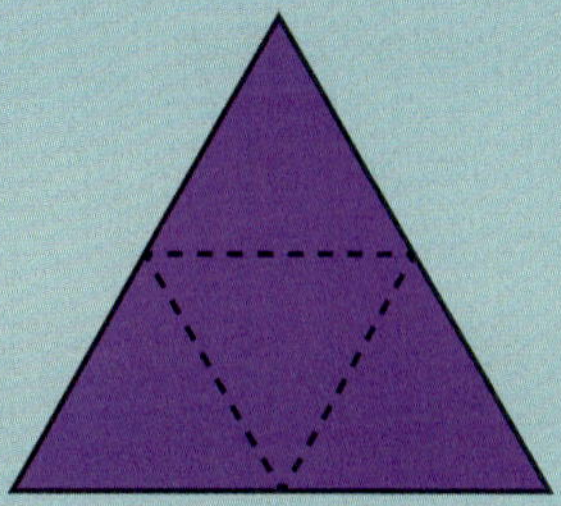

C

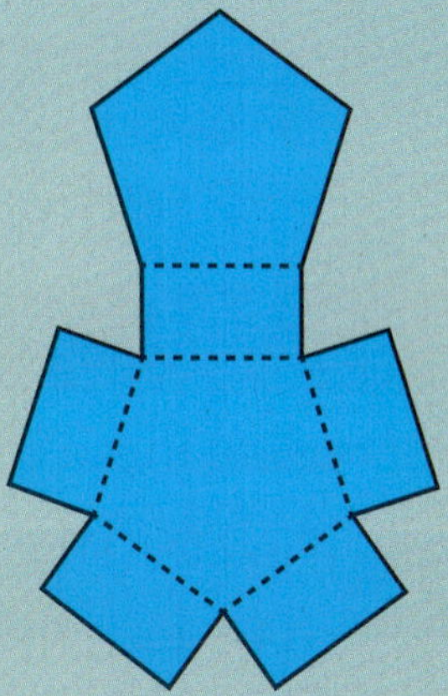

5 Name the shape that is made by this net.

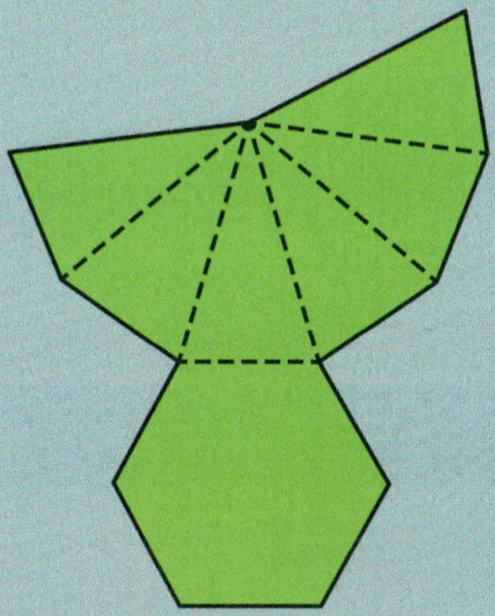

6 This is the net of a 3D shape, but one face is missing.

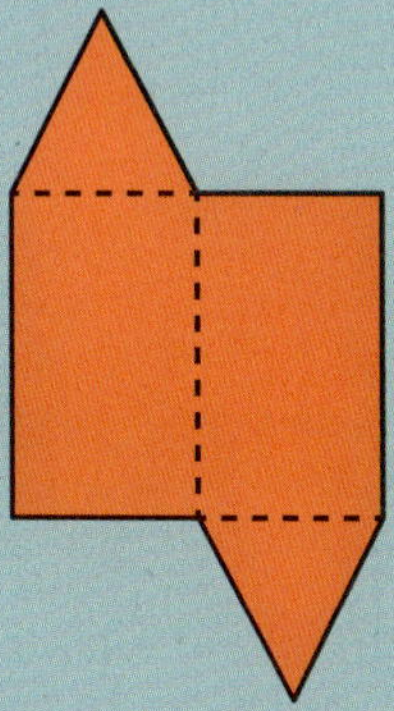

a What 3D shape should it make?

b What is the shape of the face that is missing?

13 Addition and subtraction

Getting started

1 Complete these calculations using an efficient method.

  a Find the sum of 318 and 425.

  b Find the difference between 425 and 318.

2 a A builder has 485 bricks.

  He uses 278 bricks.

  How many bricks does he have left?

  b There are 138 adults and 85 children at a concert.

  How many people are at the concert?

3 Find the missing numbers.

  a $\square + 605 = 1000$ b $1000 - \square = 316$

4 Complete these calculations.

  a $\frac{2}{5} + \frac{1}{5}$ b $\frac{5}{8} - \frac{3}{8}$

5 Find the missing numbers.

  a $\square + \frac{1}{5} = 1$ b $1 - \square = \frac{3}{8}$

We often do mathematical calculations at home, in the community, at school or at work.

Look at the picture. Which activities involve addition and subtraction? Discuss your ideas with your partner.

13.1 Adding and subtracting efficiently

We are going to . . .

- use a column method of calculation to add or subtract whole numbers.

In this unit, you will add and subtract whole numbers. You will revise methods you used earlier this year and extend them to include using a column method.

Being able to add and subtract quickly is a useful skill for everyday life. You might use addition to work out how much it costs to buy lunch in a café.

carry efficient

Worked example 1

Work out 367 – 185.

Method 1

	100s	10s	1s	
				Decompose the numbers.
367	300 +	60 +	7	
−185 =	− 100 +	80 +	5	
367	200 +	160 +	7	You need to regroup to subtract the tens.
−185 =	− 100 +	80 +	5	
367				Subtract and then compose the parts.
−185 =	100 +	80 +	2	
=	182			

Method 2

100s	10s	1s
3	6	7
−1	8	5
		2

Write the numbers in columns.

Subtract the ones:
7 ones – 5 ones = 2 ones

100s	10s	1s
[2]~~3~~	[1]6	7
−1	8	5
1	8	2

Regroup to subtract the tens:
3 hundreds and 6 tens is the same as 2 hundreds and 16 tens

Subtract the tens:
16 tens – 8 tens = 8 tens

Subtract the hundreds:
2 hundreds – 1 hundred = 1 hundred

Answer: 182

Exercise 13.1

For each of these questions, estimate the size of the answer then complete the calculation.

1 a Find the sum of 456 and 789.

b What is the total of 763 and 869?

c What is 678 more than 456?

2 a Subtract 456 from 789.

b Find the difference between 678 and 923.

c 906 minus 858.

A number of different words can be used instead of 'add' and 'subtract'. Some of these words have been used in questions 1 and 2. Can you think of other ways to write these calculations?

3 What is the difference between 1000 and the smallest 3-digit number that does not use the digit 0?

4 Write the missing number. You can use any method.

457 + ☐ = 713

5 Spot the mistakes and then do the calculations correctly.

a

	100s	10s	1s
	8	8	2
−	4	3	5
	4	5	3

b

	100s	10s	1s
	5	3	1
+	2	7	8
	7	0	9
	1		

6 Naomi has six digit cards.

1	2	3	4	5	6

She makes two 3-digit numbers and adds them together.

a What is the largest total Naomi can make?

b What is the smallest total she can make?

Discuss your answer with a partner.

Think like a mathematician

The numbers 1 to 9 are arranged as they are on a calculator.

- Choose a line of three numbers, for example 753.
- Reverse the numbers: 357.
- Add the numbers and record the result.
- Repeat the instructions with other lines of three numbers.

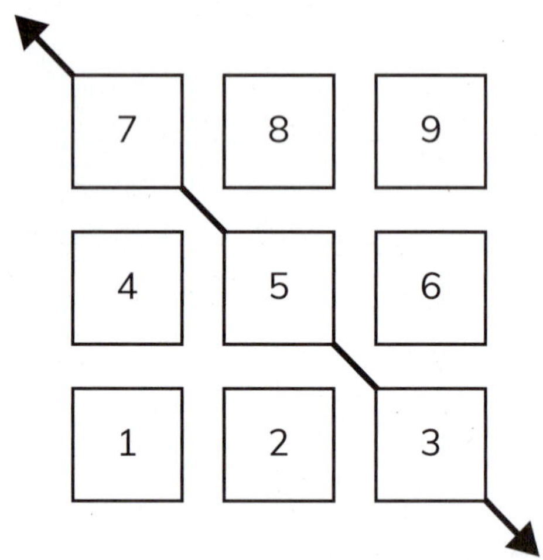

What do you notice about the results?

- You will show you are **specialising** when you find solutions to the problem.
- You will show you are **generalising** when you recognise patterns in your results.
- If you explain your results, you will show you are **convincing**.

Look what I can do!

- [ ] I can estimate the size of an answer before I do the calculation.
- [ ] I can add numbers using an efficient method.
- [ ] I can subtract numbers using an efficient method.

13.2 Adding and subtracting fractions with the same denominator

We are going to . . .

- add and subtract fractions with the same denominator including where the total is greater than 1.

improper fraction
proper fraction

A cake is divided into five equal pieces. Two people each have a piece and you want to know what fraction of the cake is left. You will need to use fractions to work this out.

$1 - \frac{2}{5} = \frac{3}{5}$

What other questions could you ask about this cake?

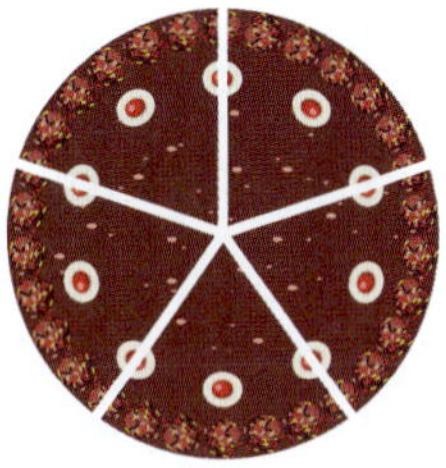

In Stage 3, you worked with fractions within a whole. In this unit you will add and subtract fractions where the total is greater than one.

Worked example 2

Here are four proper fractions. Circle two fractions that add up to 1.

$\frac{7}{10}$ $\frac{1}{10}$ $\frac{3}{10}$ $\frac{5}{10}$

Check to see that the denominators are all the same.

$\frac{10}{10} = 1$, so look for two numerators that sum to 10.

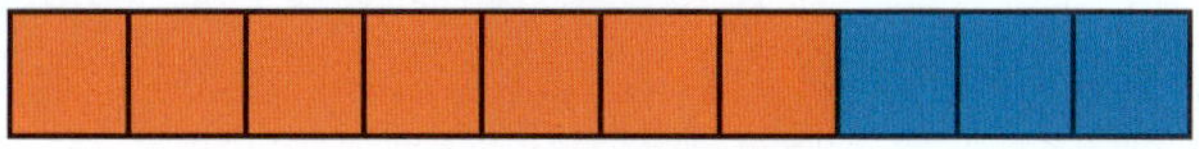

$$\frac{7}{10} + \frac{3}{10} = \frac{10}{10}$$

Answer:

$\frac{7}{10}$ (circled) $\frac{1}{10}$ $\frac{3}{10}$ (circled) $\frac{5}{10}$

Exercise 13.2

1 The chef serves $\frac{1}{6}$ of an apple pie.

What fraction of the apple pie is left?

2 Copy and complete these calculations.

a $\frac{3}{4} + \square = 1$ **b** $1 - \square = \frac{1}{8}$

3 For each grid write down the pairs of fractions that add up to 1.

For each pair of fractions, write two subtraction sentences.

For example:

$\frac{4}{5} + \frac{1}{5} = 1$ $1 - \frac{4}{5} = \frac{1}{5}$ $1 - \frac{1}{5} = \frac{4}{5}$

a

$\frac{1}{2}$	$\frac{1}{2}$	$\frac{5}{9}$	$\frac{4}{5}$
$\frac{2}{3}$	$\frac{1}{4}$	$\frac{1}{5}$	$\frac{6}{8}$
$\frac{5}{7}$	$\frac{3}{6}$	$\frac{3}{4}$	$\frac{2}{7}$
$\frac{2}{8}$	$\frac{4}{9}$	$\frac{3}{6}$	$\frac{1}{3}$

b

$\frac{1}{4}$	$\frac{2}{6}$	$\frac{1}{2}$	$\frac{4}{6}$
$\frac{1}{2}$	$\frac{2}{7}$	$\frac{1}{8}$	$\frac{6}{9}$
$\frac{2}{3}$	$\frac{7}{8}$	$\frac{3}{5}$	$\frac{2}{5}$
$\frac{3}{9}$	$\frac{5}{7}$	$\frac{1}{3}$	$\frac{3}{4}$

Check your answers with your partner.

4 Work out these calculations.

a $\frac{5}{9} + \frac{5}{9}$ **b** $\frac{4}{5} - \frac{1}{5}$ **c** $\frac{6}{7} - \frac{3}{7}$ **d** $\frac{5}{12} - \frac{1}{12}$

Look at your answer to part (a). It is an **improper fraction**. Why is it improper?

5 In the diagram, the fraction in each box is the sum of the two fractions below it.

Copy the diagram and fill in the missing fractions.

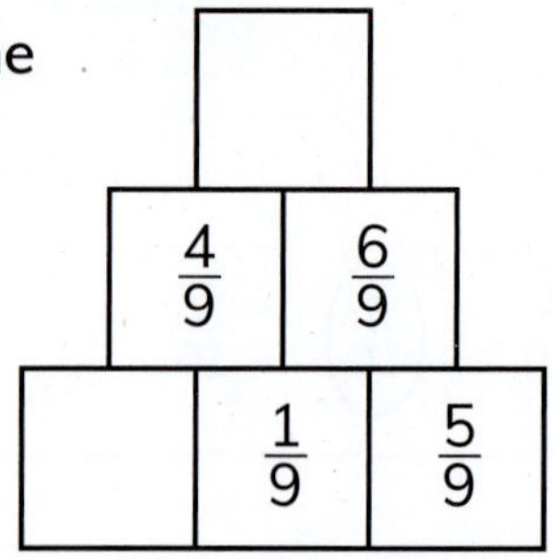

6 Yuri adds two fractions. This is his working.

$\frac{3}{9} + \frac{2}{9} = \frac{5}{18}$

Yuri is not correct. Explain what he has done wrong. What is the correct answer?

7 Fatima and Parveen work out the answer to $\frac{4}{5} + \frac{3}{5}$

Fatima says the answer is $\frac{7}{5}$

Parveen says the answer is $\frac{7}{10}$

Who do you agree with? Explain your answer.

Discuss your answer with a partner. Do you agree with their explanation? Can you draw a diagram to explain the correct answer?

Think like a mathematician

a Draw a square of edge 2 cm on square spotty paper.

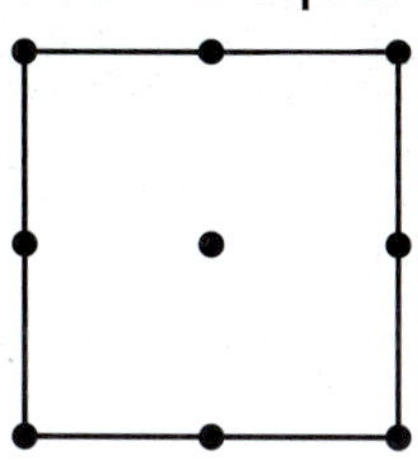

b Join any two dots on the perimeter (outside edge) with a straight line to split the square into two pieces.

What fraction of the whole have you split the square into?

c Record your results as a calculation, for example:

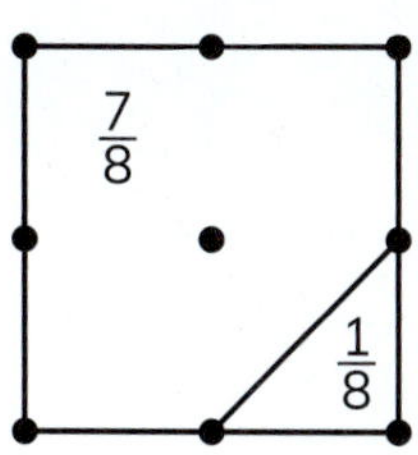

$\frac{7}{8} + \frac{1}{8} = 1$

d Find as many different ways as possible to split the square into two pieces.

Look what I can do!

- [ ] I can add and subtract fractions with the same denominator including where the total is greater than 1.

Check your progress

1 Subtract 255 from 600.

2 Maria baked 210 biscuits on Monday.

On Tuesday, Maria baked 35 more biscuits than she baked on Monday.

How many biscuits did Maria bake altogether on Monday and Tuesday?

3 Spot the mistake and then do the calculations correctly.

	100s	10s	1s
	7	1	2
−	4	8	6
	3	7	2

	100s	10s	1s
	4	5	6
+	3	5	2
	7	0	8
	1		

4 Leroy works out a calculation but he forgets to estimate his answer before he calculates it.

This is his working.

	100s	10s	1s
	5	0	6
+	7	8	9
1	2	9	5
		1	

Use rounding to show that Leroy's answer is reasonable.

5 Work out the missing fractions.

a $\frac{3}{8} + \square = \frac{15}{8}$

b $\frac{3}{8} - \square = \frac{1}{8}$

Continued

6 Which of these calculations are correct?

A $\frac{1}{5} + \frac{2}{5} = \frac{3}{5}$ B $\frac{1}{5} + \frac{2}{5} = \frac{3}{10}$ C $\frac{1}{5} + \frac{2}{5} = \frac{6}{10}$

Explain your answer.

7 Here are six fraction cards.

$\frac{2}{8}$ $\frac{3}{8}$ $\frac{4}{8}$ $\frac{5}{8}$ $\frac{6}{8}$ $\frac{7}{8}$

Use each card once to complete these number sentences.

$\square + \square = \frac{9}{8}$ $\square + \square = \frac{9}{8}$ $\square + \square = \frac{9}{8}$

14 Area and perimeter

Getting started

1 Calculate the perimeter of this rectangle, then copy and complete the sentence.

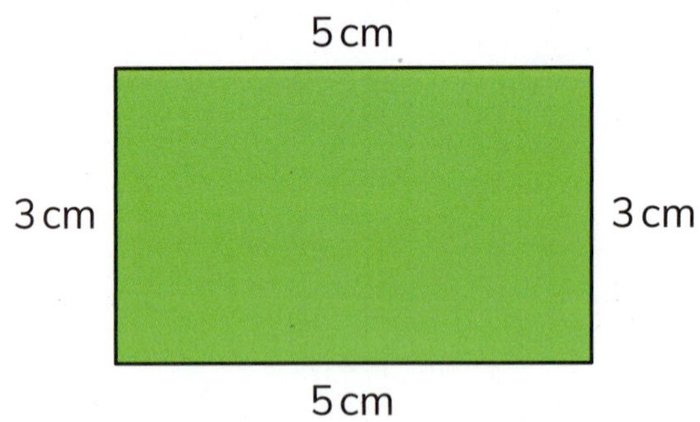

The perimeter is ______ ______.

2 Draw a rectangle with two sides that are 4 cm long and two sides that are 6 cm long.

3 Copy and complete the sentence.

The area of the blue shape is ______ square units.

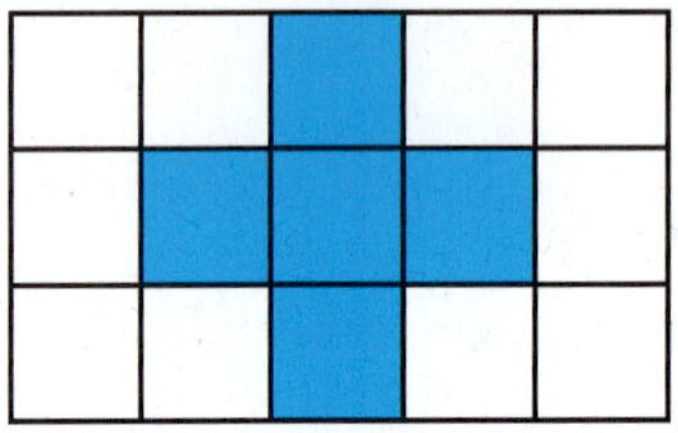

4 Copy and complete the sentence.

The area of the red shape is ______ square units.

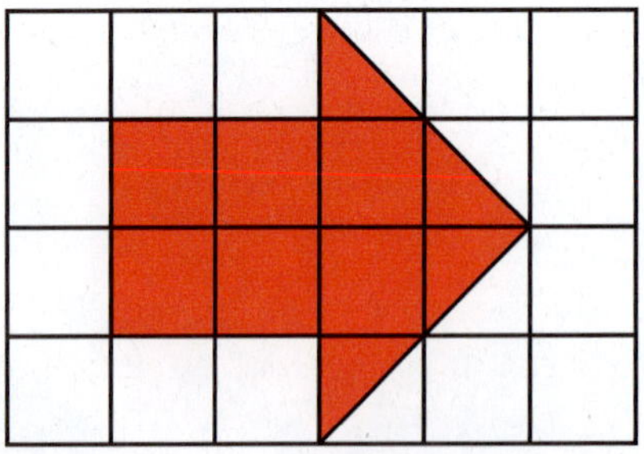

Understanding and using measurements of area and perimeter is useful in many everyday life situations.

How would you work out the number of fence panels you would need to go around this playground?

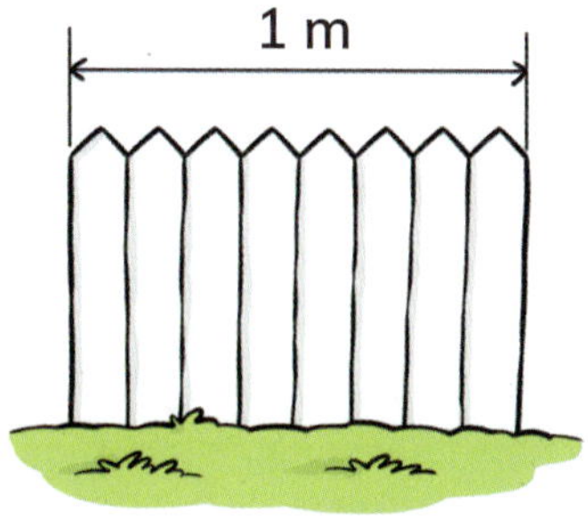

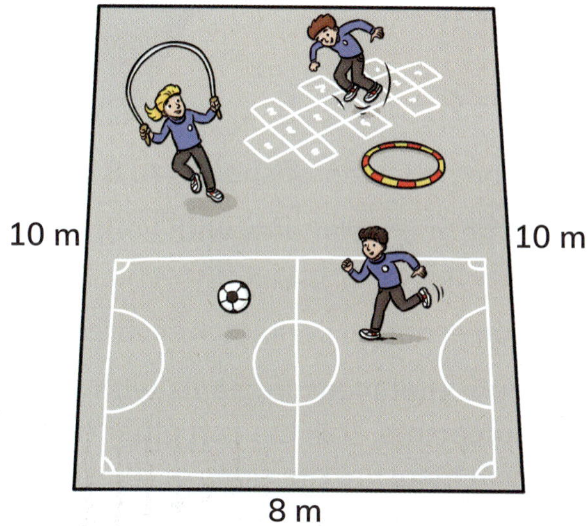

14.1 Estimating and measuring area and perimeter

We are going to . . .

- estimate and measure the perimeter of 2D shapes
- use mm, cm, m and km to record perimeter
- learn how to record area using mm^2, cm^2, m^2 and km^2
- estimate the area of shapes by counting part and whole squares
- add together the areas of different shapes to find the total area.

In this topic you will learn about the square units we use to record areas of different sizes. The units are important for describing the size of an area. Buying tiles to cover a wall that has an area of 8 square metres is very different to buying tiles to cover an area that is 8 square centimetres.

area
perimeter

Exercise 14.1

1 a Estimate the perimeter of these shapes in whole centimetres.

A

B
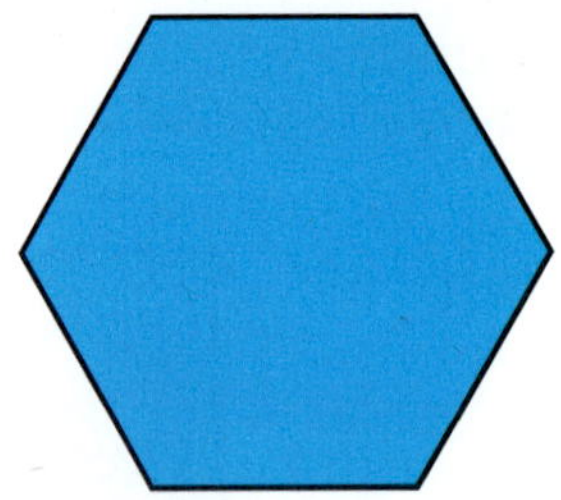
C
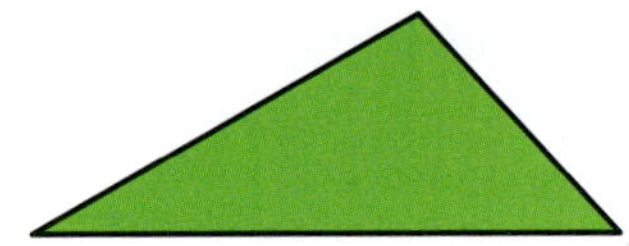

b Measure the perimeter of shapes A, B and C to the nearest whole centimetre.

- Compare your estimates with your partner's estimates.
  Talk to each other about how you estimate the perimeter of a shape.
- Can you estimate perimeter accurately?
- Compare your measurements with your partner's measurements. Talk to each other about how you measure the sides of the shapes.
- Can you measure perimeter accurately?

Tip

Remember:

1 cm = 10 mm

1 m = 100 cm

1 km = 1000 m

2 a The perimeter of a theme park is 5 km.
How long is the perimeter in metres?

b The perimeter of this stamp is 6 cm.
How long is the perimeter in millimetres?

c This is the floor plan of a room.
The length of each wall is given in metres.

i How long is the perimeter of the room in metres?

ii How long is the perimeter of the room in centimeters?

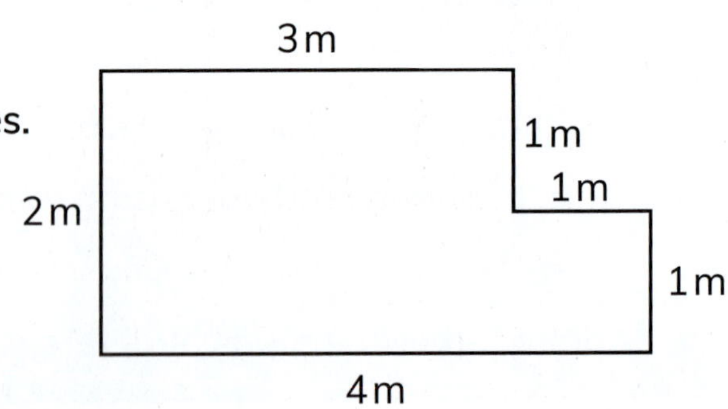

3 Which measurement should be used for the area of each of the following things: mm^2, cm^2, m^2 or km^2?

a A pond

b A puddle

c A sea

d A drop of water

Worked example 1

Count the squares to estimate the area of the juice spill on the tablecloth.

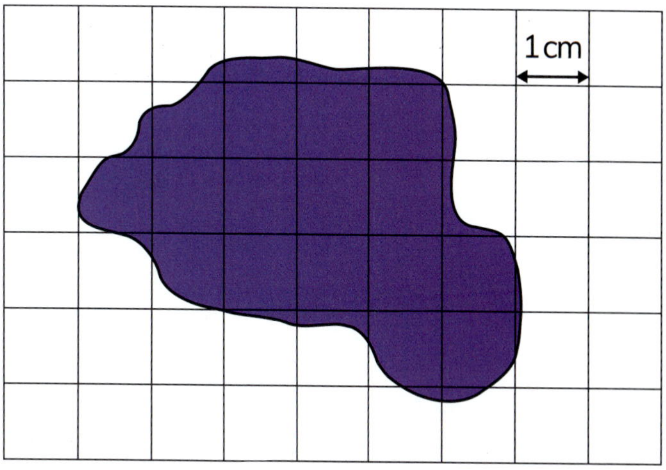

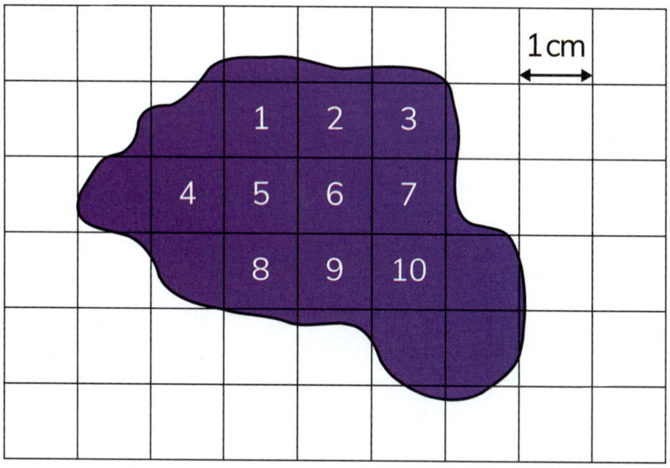

Count the number of whole squares covered by the spill.

There are 10 whole squares covered.

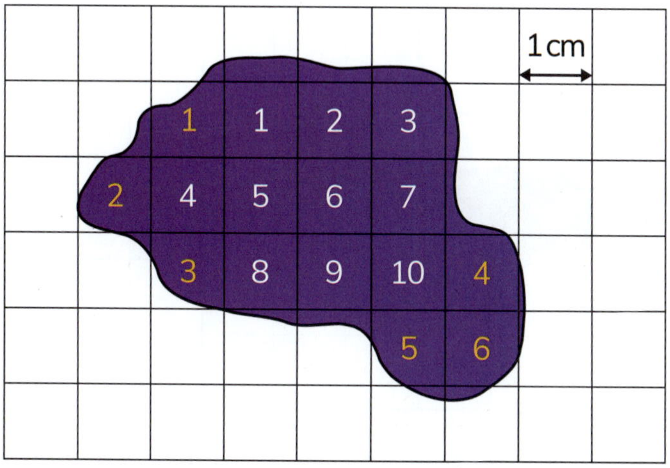

Count any squares that are more than half covered and add them to the whole squares.

There are 6 squares that are more than half covered. That is 16 squares altogether.

The squares are 1 cm wide. They are centimetre squares.

Check the units of area.

Answer: I estimate that 16 cm^2 is covered by spilt juice.

4 Count the squares to estimate the area of the island.

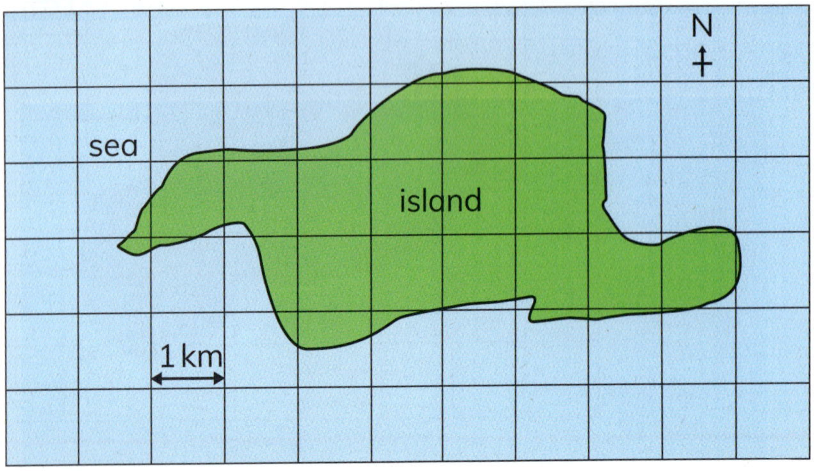

5 Count the squares to estimate the size of each stain on the baby's bib. Add together your estimates to find an estimate for the total area of the bib that is stained.

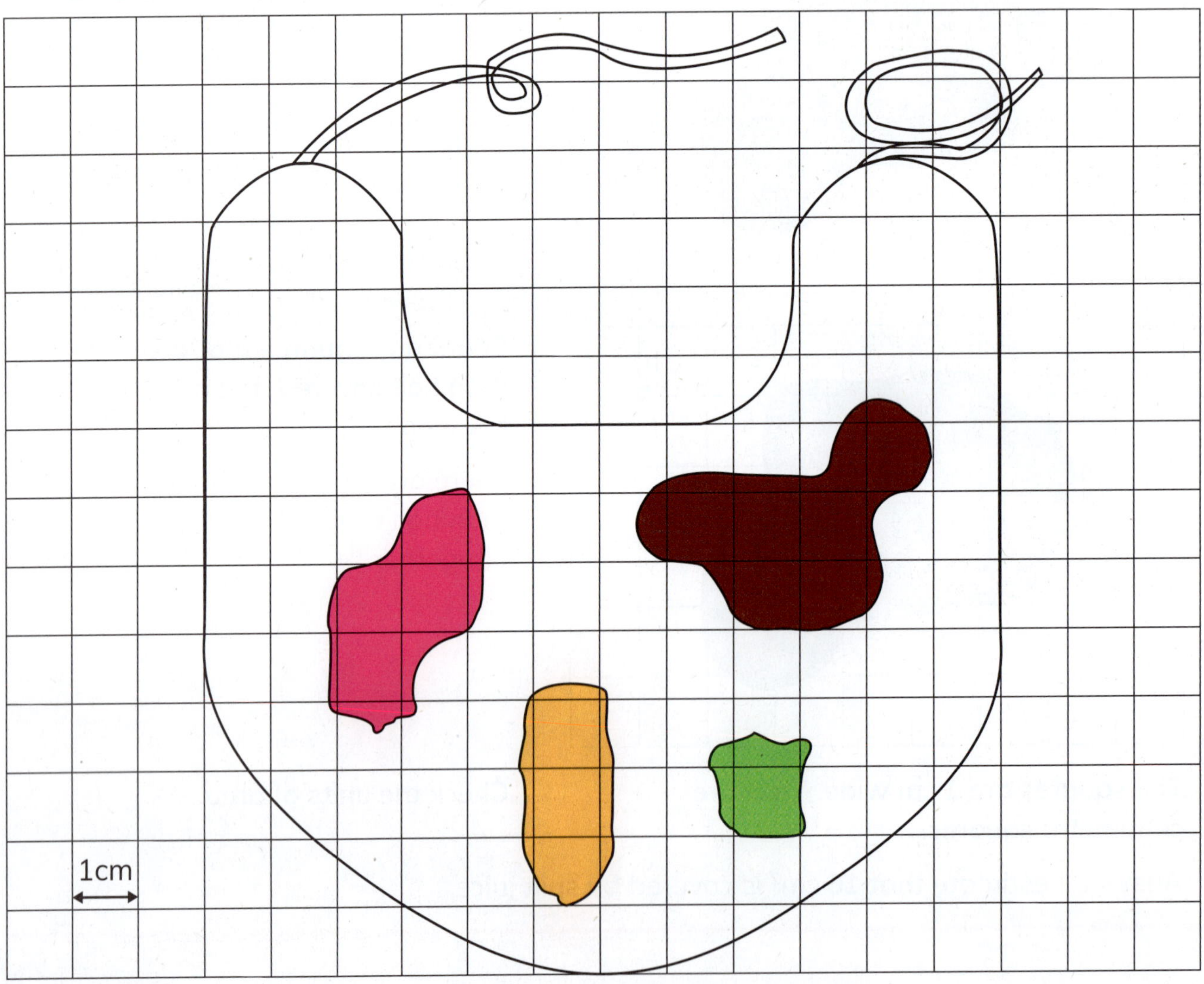

6 Lee says that to estimate an area you should only count whole squares.

Zaid says that to estimate an area you should count any square that is partly or wholly covered.

Jo says that to estimate an area you should only count the squares that are more than half covered.

Critique Lee, Zaid and Jo's ideas. Who will get the best estimate?

Explain why.

Reflect on how quickly and closely you are able to estimate an area to the nearest square unit. Think about:

- why it is important for an estimate to be made quickly
- why it is important for an estimate to be close to the actual measurement.

Look what I can do!

- [ ] I can estimate and measure the perimeter of 2D shapes.
- [ ] I can use mm, cm, m and km to record perimeter, and I can record area using cm^2, m^2 and km^2.
- [ ] I can estimate the area of shapes by counting part and whole squares and add together the areas of different shapes to find the total area.

14.2 Area and perimeter of rectangles

We are going to . . .

- draw rectangles and find their area and perimeter
- investigate ways to calculate the area of rectangles
- add together the areas of rectangles to find the total area.

Calculating the area of rectangles is useful in everyday life. The floors of rooms are usually rectangles, and floor coverings are bought in square units. Sometimes floor areas are shapes made up of two or more rectangles that are put together, so the areas need to be added together.

Worked example 2

Draw a rectangle with sides measuring 3 cm, 4 cm, 3 cm and 4 cm.
Work out the perimeter and area of the rectangle.

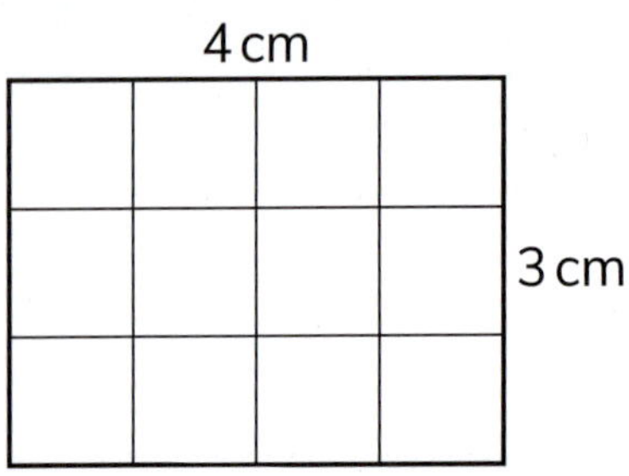

Draw the rectangle on squared paper using a pencil and ruler.

$3 + 4 + 3 + 4 = 14$

Add up the length of each side to find the total perimeter.

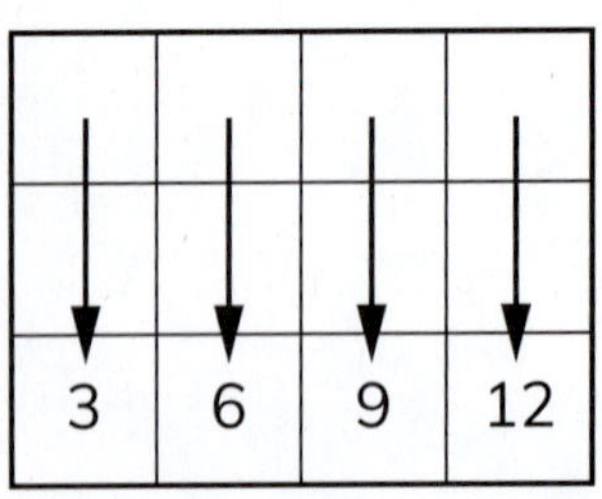

Count the squares to find the area. This rectangle has 3 squares in each column so you can count the squares in 3s.

Answer: The perimeter is 14 cm. The area is 12 cm^2.

Exercise 14.2

1 a Draw a rectangle with sides 2 cm, 5 cm, 2 cm and 5 cm on squared paper.

b What is the perimeter of the rectangle?

c What is the area of the rectangle?

2 a On squared paper draw a rectangle that is 6 cm long and 3 cm wide.

b What is the perimeter of the rectangle?

c What is the area of the rectangle?

3 a This rectangle has 5 squares in each row. Count in 5s to find out the area of the rectangle.

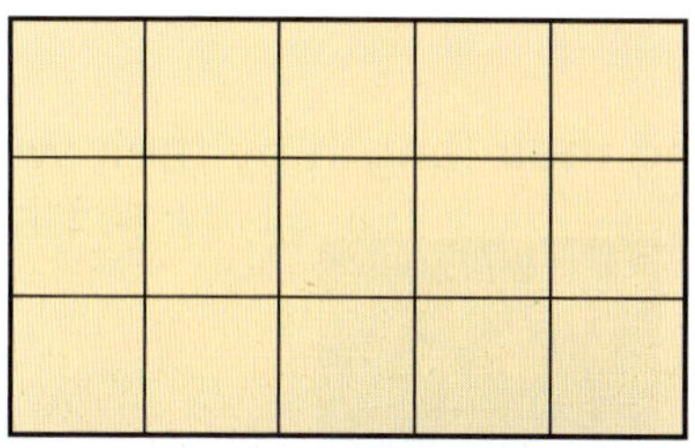

Key:  1 cm

b This rectangle has 4 squares in each column.
Count the squares in 4s to find out the area of the rectangle.

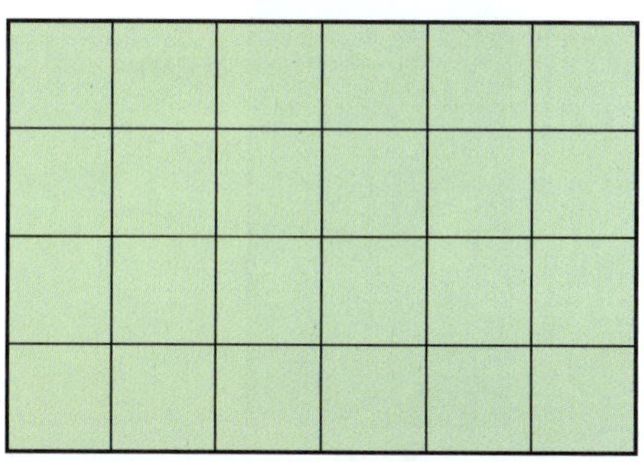

4 Count the squares in either rows or columns.
Calculate the area of the rectangles.

a

b

5 **a** Copy and complete this table for the rectangles in questions 3 and 4.

	Length	Width	Area
3a	5 cm	3 cm	cm^2
b		4 cm	cm^2
4a			cm^2
b			cm^2

b Talk to your partner about the connection between the length and width of the rectangle and the area. Copy and complete this generalisation about what you found out.

We have found out that ____ .

6 Calculate the area of these rectangles by multiplying their length by their width.

a

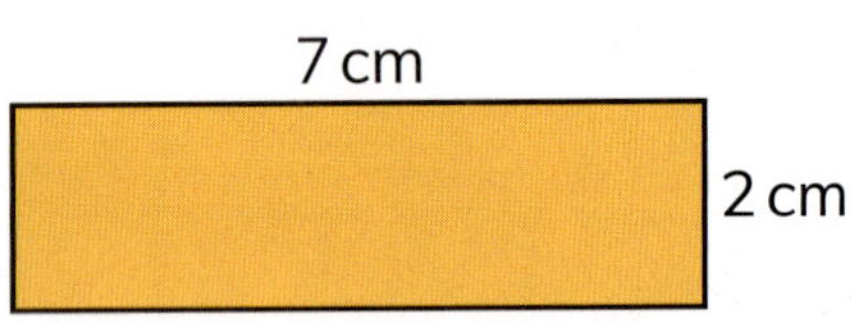

b

c

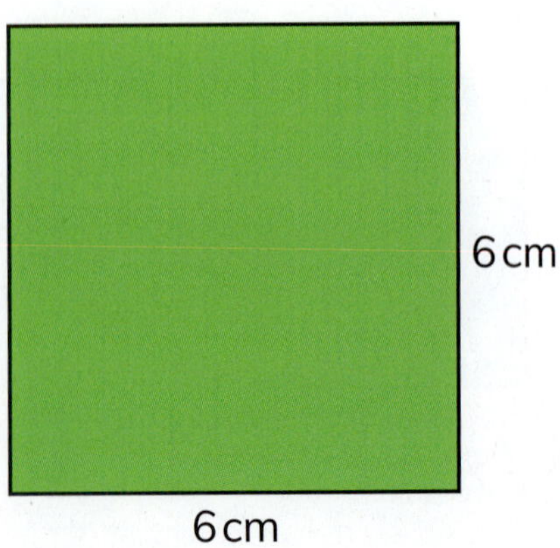

d

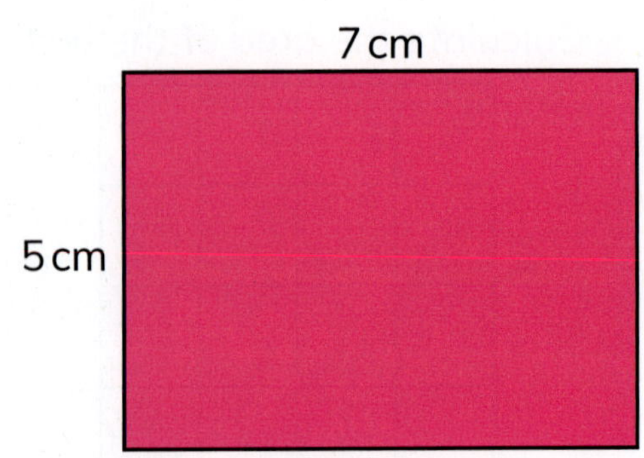

7 This rectangle has 3 rows of 8 squares.

$3 \times 8 = 24$. It has an area of $24\,cm^2$.

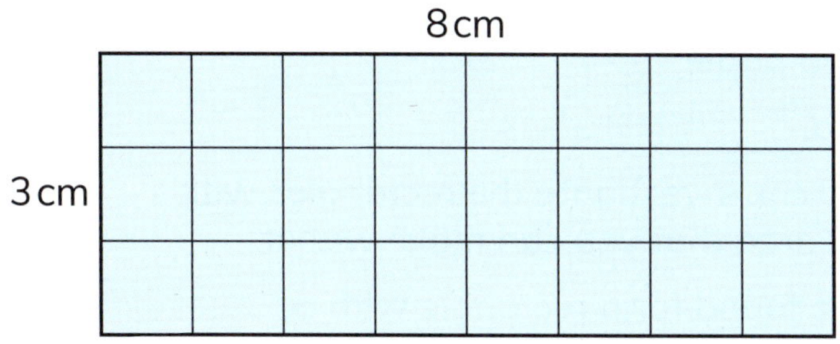

How many other rectangles can you draw with an area of $24\,cm^2$?

8 Lila says that she can work out the perimeter of a rectangle by measuring two of its sides and multiplying by 2.

Do you think that she is correct?

Check Lila's method by measuring the perimeters of these rectangles and by multiplying two of the sides by 2.

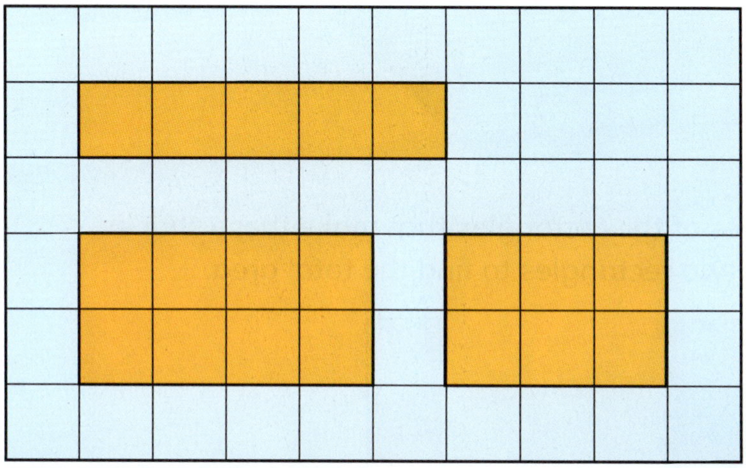

What did you find out?

Which of these things are you good at?
Which do you need to improve?

- Drawing rectangles.
- Calculating the area of rectangles.
- Finding the perimeter of rectangles.

When you have completed the Think like a mathematician questions, ask your partner how you can improve one of these skills.

Think like a mathematician

a Specialise by finding out what different rectangles with a perimeter of 16 cm you can draw on squared paper.

Label each rectangle with its area.

b A rectangle has a perimeter of 20 cm. Investigate the rectangles with the largest area and the smallest area that you can make with it.

What is the largest area you have found for a rectangle with a perimeter of 20 cm? How do you know it is the largest area?

What is the smallest area you have found for a rectangle with a perimeter of 20 cm? How do you know it is the smallest area?

Think about the skill you needed to improve.

Have you improved the skill?

How did you improve the skill?

What do you still need to improve?

9 Use a ruler to measure the sides of the rectangles that make these shapes. Add together the areas of the two rectangles to find the total area.

a

b

c

Look what I can do!

- [ ] I can draw rectangles and find their area and perimeter.
- [ ] I can calculate the area of rectangles.
- [ ] I can add together the areas of rectangles to find the total area.

Check your progress

1 Work out the perimeter of this garden.

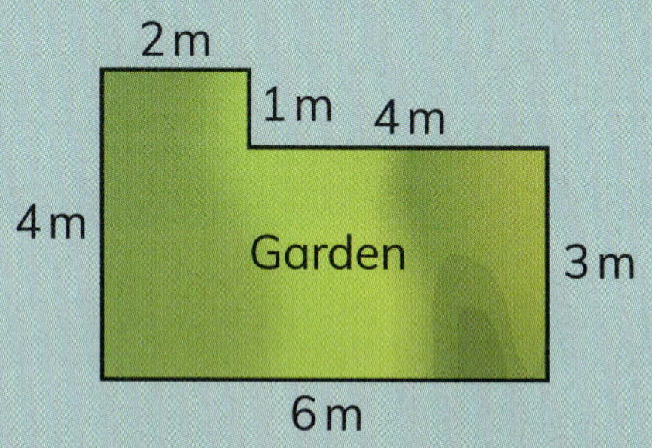

2 Measure the perimeter of this triangle in millimetres.

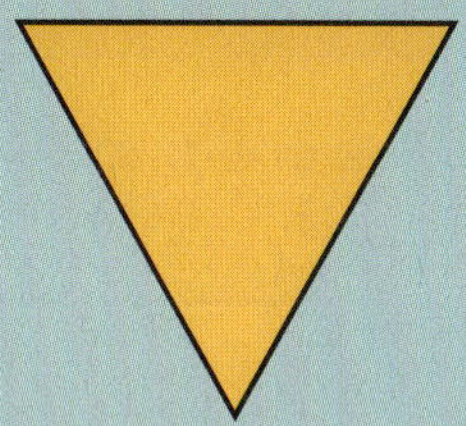

3 Estimate the area of this lake.

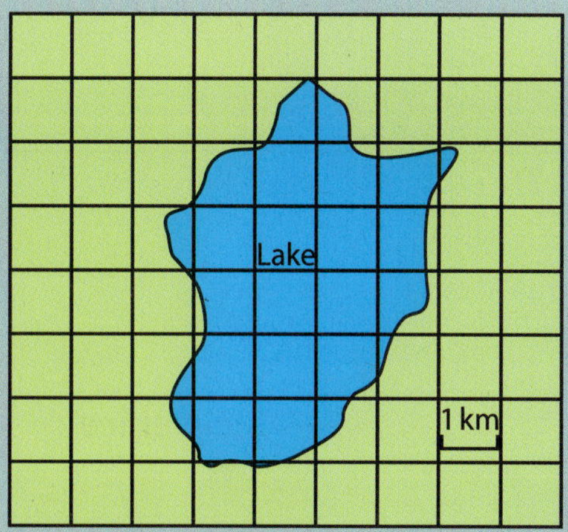

4 Draw a rectangle that has an area of $10\ cm^2$.

What is the perimeter of your rectangle?

Continued

5 Calculate the area of these rectangles.

a

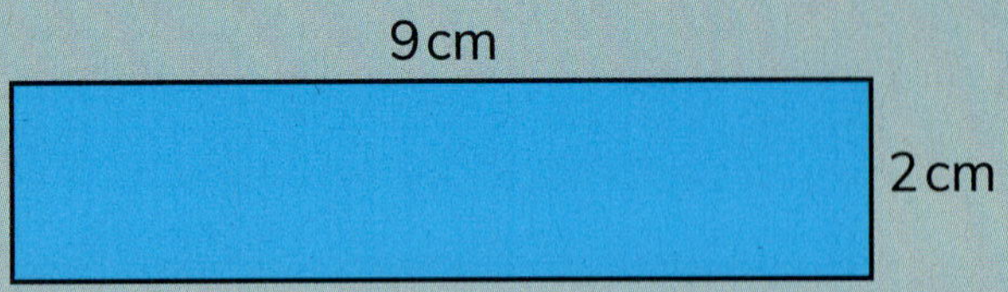

b

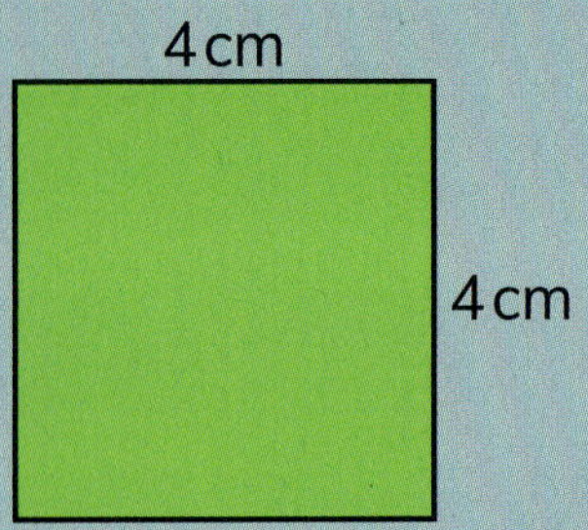

c

6 What is the total floor area of this building?

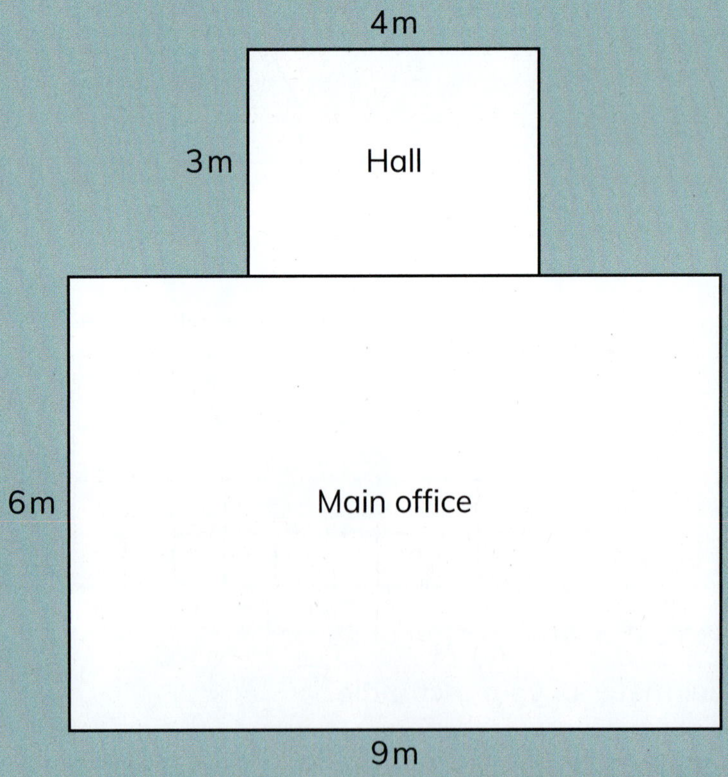

15 Special numbers

Getting started

1 Write each number that has both 2 and 3 as factors.

2 3 6 9 12

2 Write the missing number.

1, 4, 9, ☐, 25

3 Which of these numbers are multiples of 6?

2 3 4 6 12 18 24

4 a Write the following temperatures in order starting with the coldest.

−5 °C −2 °C 0 °C −1 °C 3 °C 1 °C

b Water changes to ice at 0 °C and below.
Write the temperatures from the list that would make ice.

5 What number goes in the box?

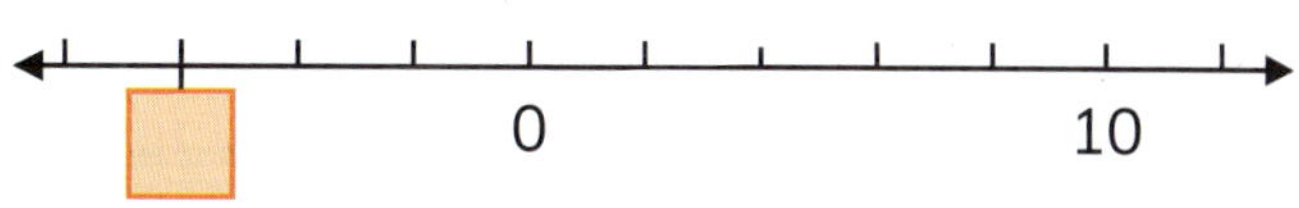

6 Write the letters of the statements that are true.

A 5 is a factor of 125

B $-5 > -3$

C 9998 is an even number

D 32 is a multiple of 4 and 8

E $0 < -1$

F 4 is a factor of 74

This unit is all about special numbers:

negative numbers

odd and even numbers

factors and multiples

square numbers

You have seen all of these special numbers before, but in this unit you will learn more about them.

Have you ever counted the petals on a flower?
Many flowers have 3 or 5 petals.

3 and 5 are both **odd** numbers.

Have you ever used a thermometer to measure the temperature in a freezer?
If you have, you probably used **negative** numbers.

You will learn the divisibility rules for 2, 5, 10, 25, 50 and 100. These rules allow you to test if one number is divisible by another without having to do much calculation.

15.1 Ordering and comparing numbers

We are going to . . .

- compare positive and negative numbers using the symbols <, > or =
- order positive and negative numbers.

This picture shows the height above sea level and the depth below sea level of an iceberg.

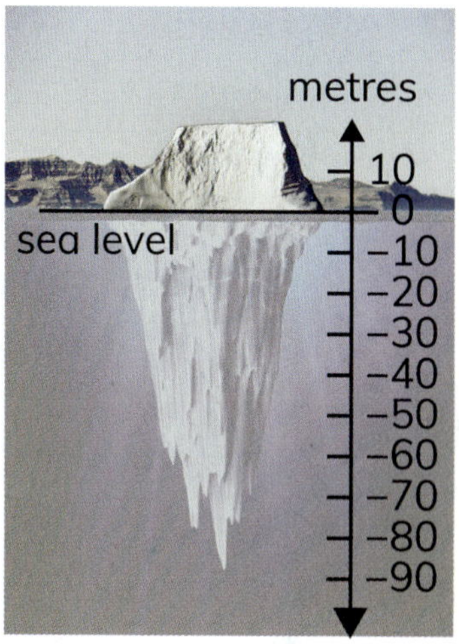

You can order numbers starting with the smallest or the largest. These numbers are in order according to their size:

–90, –80, –70, –60 ... (starting with the smallest)

10, 0, –10, –20 ... (starting with the largest)

You can compare two numbers using the symbols < and >.

For example:

$-30 < 0$ and $-50 > -60$

negative number
order

Worked example 1

Which is larger –5 or –3?
Write your answer using one of the symbols < or >

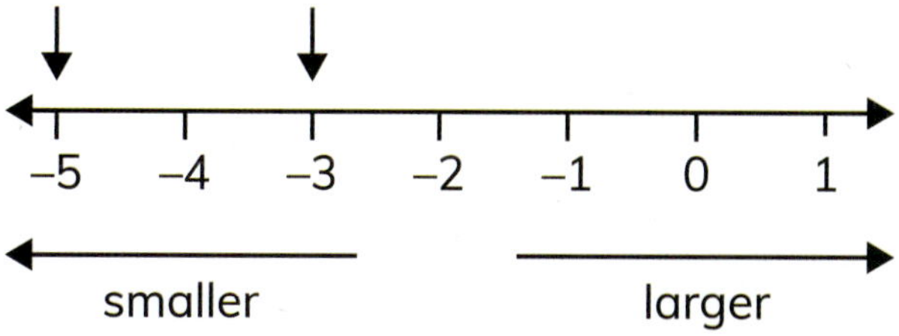

Mark the numbers on a number line.

The number on the right is greater.

Answer: –3 is greater than –5

$-3 > -5$

Exercise 15.1

1 Put these numbers in order starting with the smallest.

−1   −7   −2   −6   −5

2 The table shows the minimum temperature on four days.

Day	Temperature °C
Monday	−2
Tuesday	−1
Wednesday	3
Thursday	−4

a Which temperature is colder than −2 °C?

b Write the temperatures in order, starting with the coldest temperature.

3 a Put this set of numbers in order starting with the smallest.

−6   6   12   −12   0   −18

b Describe the number pattern.

c The pattern continues in the same way.
Will 121 be in the pattern? How do you know?

4 Write each pair of numbers using the symbol > or <.

a −3 ☐ 9   b 10 ☐ −1

c −15 ☐ 7   d −6 ☐ −9

Check your answers with your partner.
Make sure you are using the correct symbol.

5 If −5 < ☐ < −2 what whole number could ☐ be?

6 Here are six number cards. Three cards are blank.

−12		−4		−1	

Write a whole number on each blank card so that the six numbers are in order.

Can you find more than one answer to question 6?
*If you were asked to find **all** the possible answers what would you do?*
Could you ever find all the answers? Why not?

7 Here are four temperatures.

−4 °C	0 °C	5 °C	−2 °C

Use each temperature once to make this statement correct.

☐ < ☐ < ☐ < ☐

Think like a mathematician

Five negative whole numbers can be arranged to form a number pattern.
The numbers obey these rules:

- one number is between −4 and −6
- one number is between zero and −3 but is closer to zero than to −3
- one number is next to −8 and also next to −10
- one number is halfway between −5 and −9
- one number is halfway between 0 and −6

Arrange the numbers in order. Describe the pattern you have made.

Look what I can do!

- ☐ I can put positive and negative numbers in order.
- ☐ I can compare positive and negative numbers using the symbols < and >.

15.2 Working with special numbers

We are going to . . .

- use odd numbers and even numbers, factors and multiples, and square numbers.

In this section, we will work with these special numbers.

Even numbers
0, 2, 4, 6, 8, 10, . . .

Odd numbers
1, 3, 5, 7, 9, 11, . . .

Factors
The factors of 12 are 1, 2, 3, 4, 6 and 12

Square numbers

Multiples
The multiples of 5 are: 5, 10, 15, 20, 25, . . .

even
factor
multiple
odd
square number

Worked example 2

Write these numbers in the correct place on the Venn diagram.

5, 6, 7, 8, 10, 15, 20

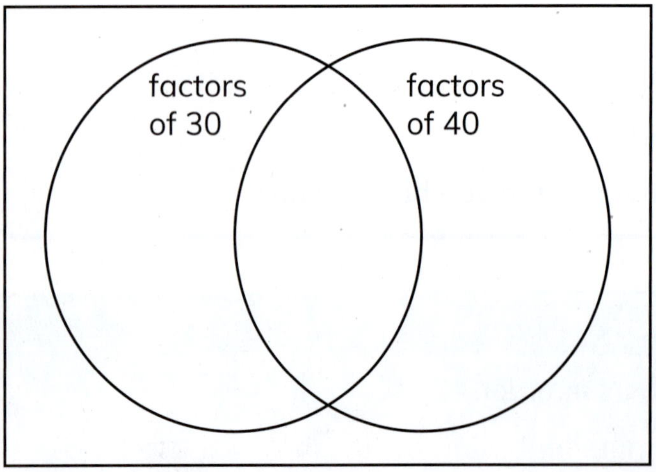

Continued

Find the factors of 30 and the factors of 40.
You can use a factor bug.

6 and 15 are factors of 30.

8 and 20 are factors of 40.

5 and 10 are factors of 30 and 40.

If a number is a factor of both 30 and 40 write it where the circles overlap.

7 is not a factor of 30 or 40.

If a number is not a factor of 30 or 40, write it outside the circles but inside the rectangle.

Answer:

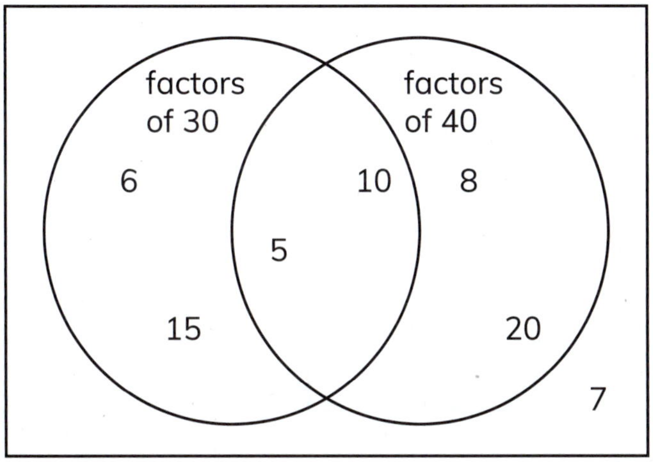

Exercise 15.2

1 Mia makes a number using the digits 4, 5 and 6.

- The number is even.
- The hundreds digit is greater than 4.
- The tens digit is greater than the hundreds digit.

What is Mia's number? Copy the boxes and write Mia's number in them.

2 Here is a Venn diagram for sorting numbers.

Copy and complete the diagram. Write each of these numbers in the correct place.

10 11 12 13 14 15 16

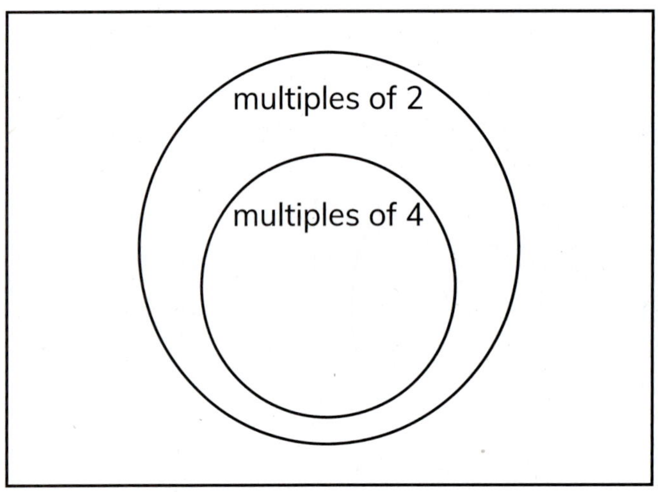

Compare your answer with your partner's answer.

Look at the diagrams for question 2 and for Worked example 2. What is the same and what is different?

One diagram is about factors and the other is about **multiples**, but they are also different in another way. Why are the diagrams different?

3 Here are four number cards.

30	32	33	35

Use each number once to make these statements correct.

a ☐ is a multiple of 3.

b ☐ is a multiple of 4.

c ☐ is a multiple of 5.

d ☐ is a multiple of 6.

4 Find two square numbers that have a sum of 100.

☐ + ☐ = 100

5 Copy and complete this sentence.

Every number with a factor of 6 must also have factors of ____, ____ and ____ .

6 Pablo writes a 3-digit number.

- All of the digits are odd.
- The sum of the digits is 7.

What is the smallest number Pablo can write?
Copy the boxes and write the number in them.

☐☐☐

7 Ingrid says, 'All numbers that end in a 4 are multiples of 4.'
Is Ingrid correct?
Explain how you know.

Think like a mathematician

Multiples

You will need these cards.

0	1	2	3	4	5	6	7	8	9

Choose a set of multiples, for example multiples of 4.

Now make as many different multiples of 4 as you can.

You can use each card only once.

You may not be able to use all the cards.

Example:

multiples of 4				unused numbers		
12	40	36	8	5	7	9

Choose other multiples to investigate.

You will show you are **specialising** when you find solutions to the problem.

Look what I can do!

- [ ] I can recognise and use odd and even numbers, factors and multiples, negative numbers and square numbers.

15.3 Tests of divisibility

We are going to . . .

- find numbers that are divisible by 2, 5, 10, 25, 50 and 100.

Knowing rules of divisibility can help you when you are calculating. They can also be used to check whether a product code is valid.

- Add the digits in even number positions:
  $7 + 9 + 0 + 5 + 4 + 9 = 34$
- Add the digits in odd number positions and multiply the result by 3:
  Sum $= 0 + 6 + 5 + 4 + 0 + 7 = 22$ and
  $22 \times 3 = 66$
- Add the two results: $34 + 66 = 100$
- Find the remainder when divided by 10: $100 \div 10 = 10$ remainder 0

0 76950 45047 9

If the remainder is zero, the code is valid.

divisibility rule   divisible

Worked example 3

Here are four digit cards.

2   3   4   5

Use the cards to make a total that is divisible by 5.

[ ][ ] + [ ][ ]

You can only use each card once.

A number is divisible by 5 if it has either 5 or 0 in the ones place.
This is a divisibility rule.

For these cards, the ones digits must add to 5.

Answer:

42 + 53 or 43 + 52

Exercise 15.3

1 Look at this set of numbers.
Write down:

a the numbers that are divisible by 100

b the numbers that are divisible by 10

c the numbers that are divisible by 5.

Discuss your answers with your partner.

5 100 25 700 40 650 530 10 300

2 Write down the numbers from this list that are divisible by 2.

13 42 163 21 48 284 6

How do you know they are divisible by 2?

3 Anton thinks that only numbers ending in 5 are divisible by 5.
Is he correct? How do you know?

4 a Sara counts in multiples of 50.

Which numbers does she say?

520 1250 255 1050 6700

b Vanda counts in multiples of 25.
Which numbers does she say?

525 1250 255 1050 6775

5 a Write down a number that is divisible by 5 and 10.

b Write down a number that is divisible by 2 and 5.

c Write down a number that is divisible by 2, 5, 10 and 100.

Think about how you answered part (c). If a number is divisible by 100, it is also divisible by all the factors of 100. 2, 5 and 10 are all factors of 100.

Copy and complete these sentences:

- If a number is divisible by 50 it is also divisible by ____.
- If a number is divisible by 25 it is also divisible by ____.

6 Use all the digits 0, 1, 5 and 6 in each part of this question.

   a Find the largest odd number divisible by 5.

   b Find the smallest number that is greater than 1000 and divisible by 5.

7 Pair these numbers so the difference between each pair is divisible by 5.

   74 48 89 66 23 39 64 91

   The first one is done for you:

   74 – 39 = 35 and 35 is divisible by 5.

Think like a mathematician

Hexagon maze

You need to go from the centre to one of the outside hexagons in two steps:

- Start in the centre.
- Move to a multiple of 2.
- Then move to a multiple of 5.

What are the possible paths you could take?

If you have worked on this maze before go to the next maze straight away.

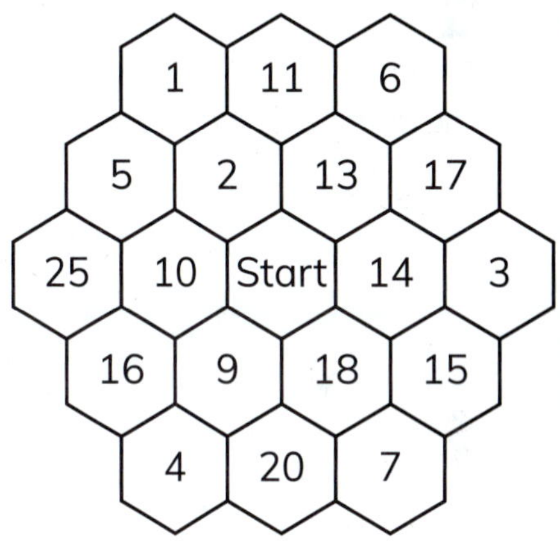

Now try using this maze.

Find your way through the maze.

- Start in the centre.
- Move to a multiple of 2.
- Then move to a multiple of 5.
- Finally, move to a multiple of 10.

You will need to be systematic to find all the solutions.

You will show you are **specialising** when you find solutions to the problem.

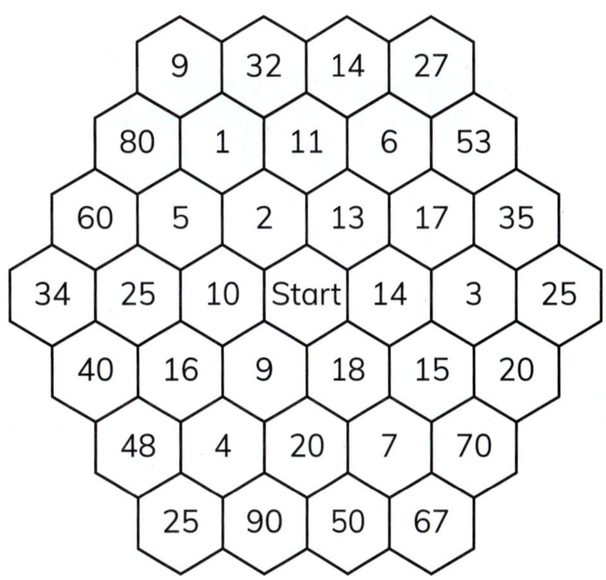

Look what I can do!

- [ ] I can find numbers that are divisible by 2, 5, 10, 25, 50 and 100.

Check your progress

1 Look at this set of numbers.

Write down:

a the numbers that are divisible by 100

b the numbers that are divisible by 50

c the numbers that are divisible by 10

d the numbers that are divisible by 5.

700 125 530 5 10 60 100 305 350

2 What is the largest even number you can make using the digits 5, 7, 6 and 3?

3 Which whole numbers can □ represent in the following number statement?

$-7 > \square > -10$

4 Here are four numbers.

24 25 26 27

Copy and complete these statements.
Use each number once.

a □ is a multiple of 2

b □ is a multiple of 3

c □ is a multiple of 4

d □ is a multiple of 5

5 Heidi says, 'Factors come in pairs, so all numbers have an even number of factors.'

Is she correct?

Explain your answer.

Continued

6 Copy the Venn diagram and write each number in the correct place.

6 8 12 24 36 40

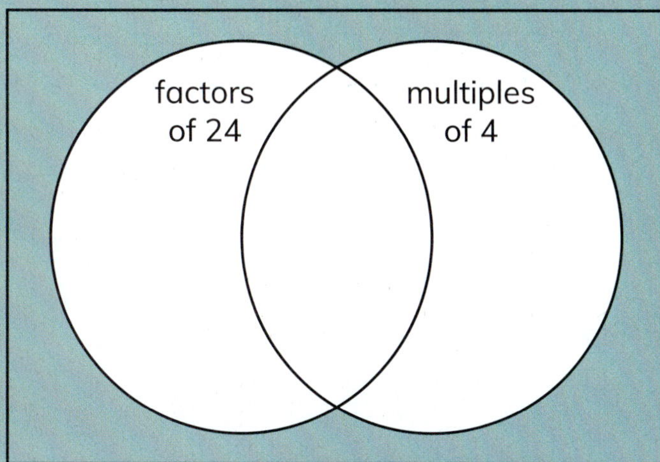

Project 6

Special numbers

Here we have three squares made of purple and yellow tiles:

Tell your partner about the squares.

- How many tiles are there in each of the three squares? How did you work it out?
- How many tiles would be added to the smallest square to make the middle square?
- How many tiles would be added to the middle square to make the biggest square?
- What do you notice?
- How many tiles would you have to add to make the next square? How do you know?
- Five can be added to which square number to make the next square number?
- Nineteen can be added to which square number to make the next square number?
- What can you find out by continuing the pattern of squares?
- Can you explain what you have noticed?

16 Data display and interpretation

Getting started

1 Copy the Carroll diagram.

Draw and colour two shapes in each section to match the headings.

	Red	Not red
Triangle	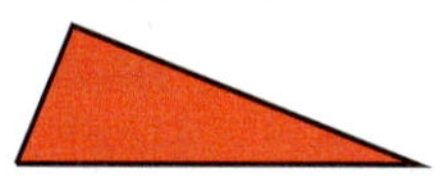	
Not triangle		

2 This is a Venn diagram.

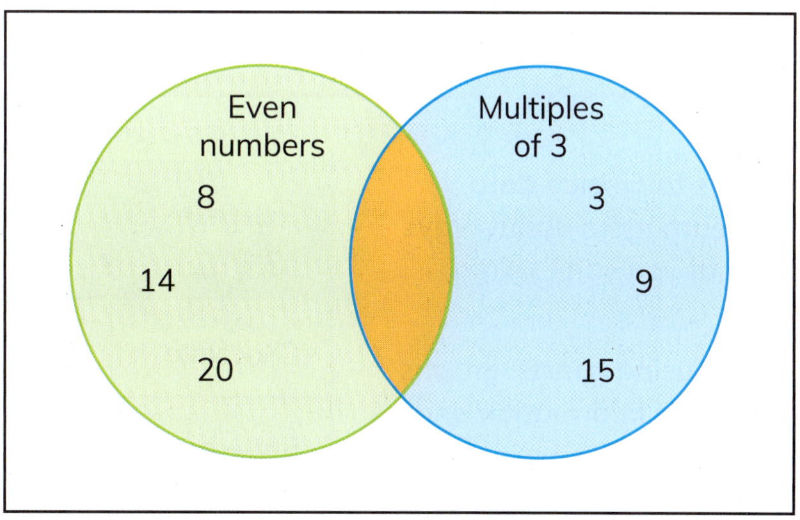

a Write three numbers that could be in the yellow section of the diagram.

b Write three numbers that could be written outside the circles.

Continued

3 Class 4 counted the number of different creatures they found on a patch of grass.

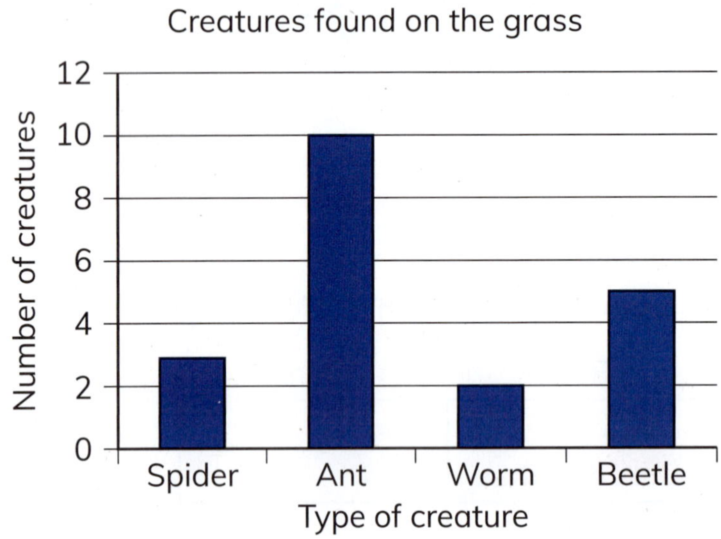

a How many spiders did they find?

b Which type of creature did they find twice?

c Which creatures did they find more than three times?

d How many more ants than beetles did they find?

There are lots of ways to display data. In this unit you will learn more about ways to display data so that you can explain information clearly.

When you show data using charts, graphs or diagrams it makes the information and patterns easier to see.

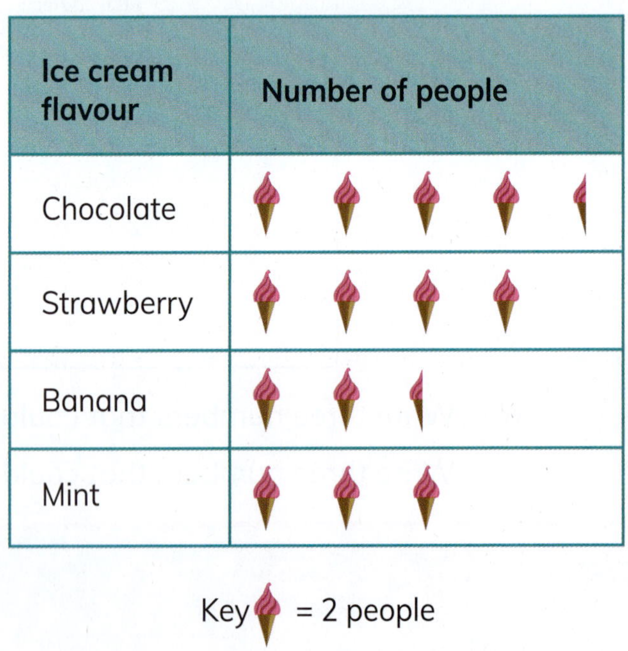

The data here is shown in a pictogram.

What information can you work out from the pictogram?

How many other ways can you think of to display data?

16.1 Displaying and interpreting data

We are going to . . .

- record, organise and represent data in diagrams and charts
- interpret and compare data to answer statistical questions.

In this unit you will explore and use a variety of ways to display data so that you can understand and interpret it more easily. You will use Carroll diagrams and Venn diagrams for sorting data. You will use bar charts and pictograms to help you compare different sets of data.

bar chart
Carroll diagram
pictogram
Venn diagram

Worked example 1

Put these shapes into the Venn diagram.

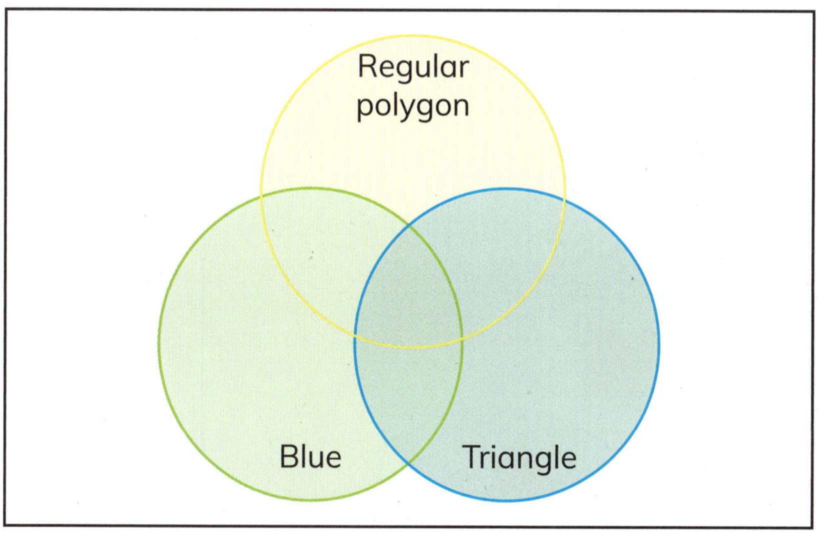

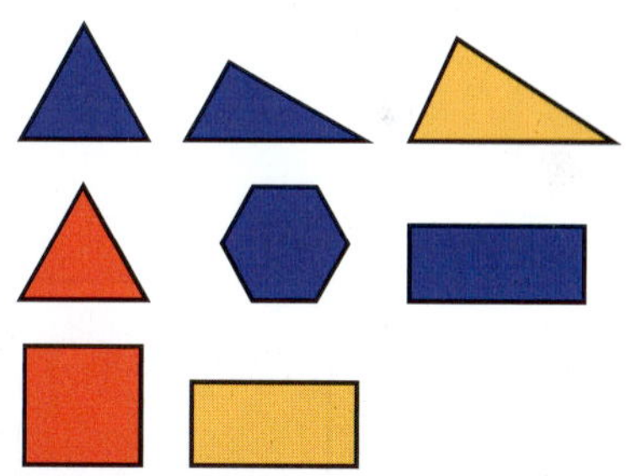

Continued

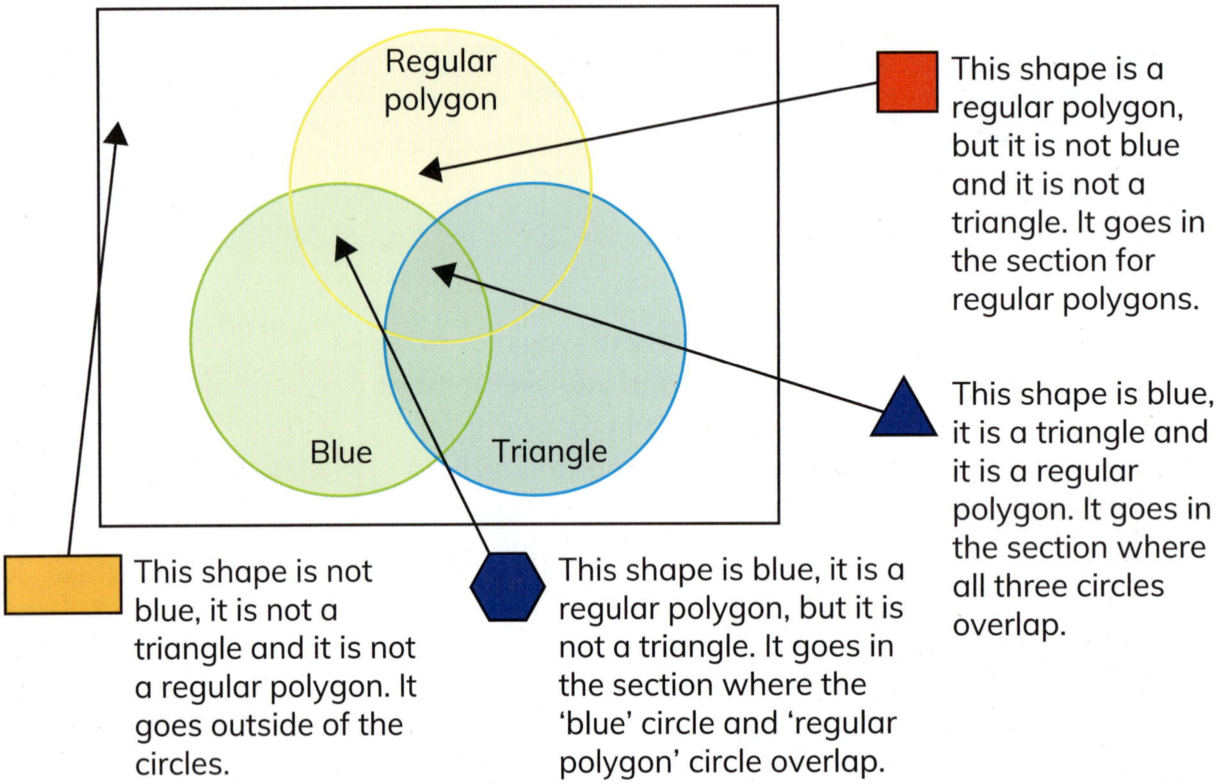

Answer:

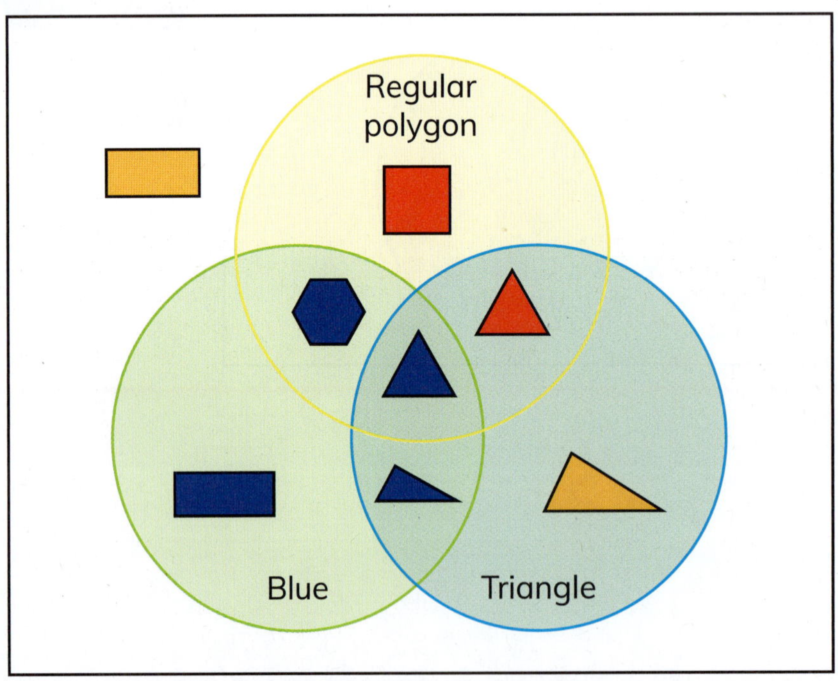

Exercise 16.1

1 Look at the children.

Copy the Venn diagram and sort each child into the correct section.

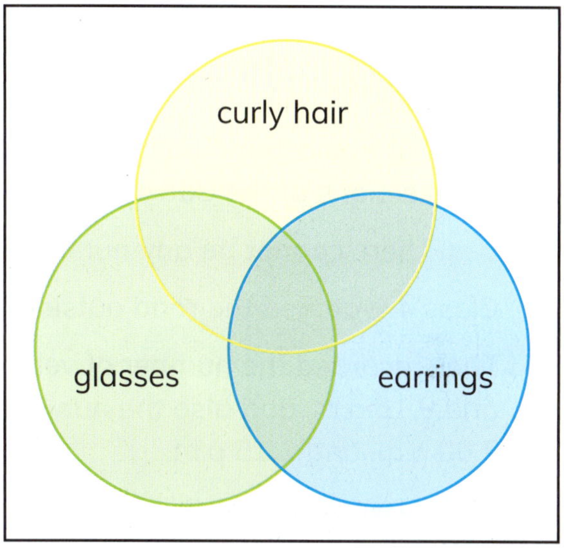

2 Copy the Venn diagram and fill in the numbers 1 to 30.

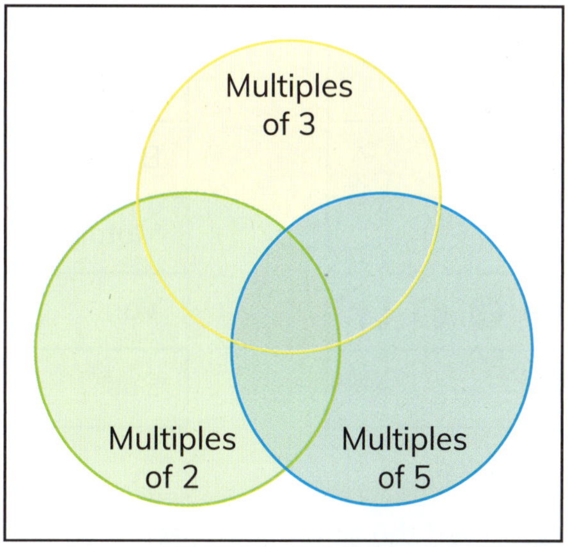

3 a Copy and complete the Carroll diagram.
Put the numbers 1 to 20 into the Carroll diagram.

	even	not even
multiple of 10		
not a multiple of 10		

b Copy and complete this sentence to explain why one of the sections of the Carroll diagram does not contain any numbers.

There cannot be any number in the section ____ because ____.

4 Class 4 watched the road outside their window.

They recorded the number of vehicles that passed between 9.00 a.m. and 9.15 a.m. and also the number of vehicles that passed between 2.00 p.m. and 2.15 p.m.

These two pictograms show the results.

Number of vehicles passing between 9.00 a.m. and 9.15 a.m.

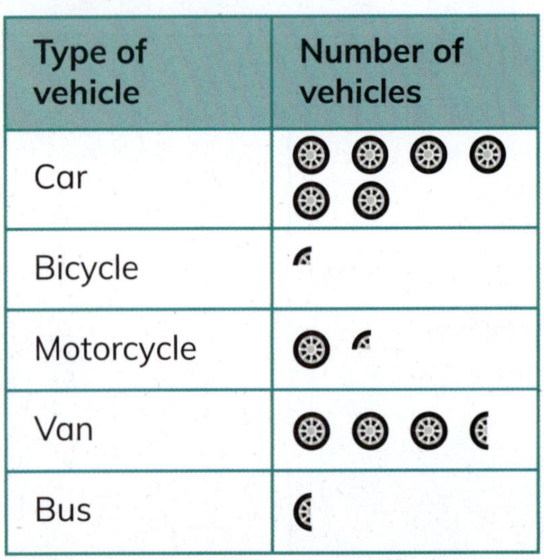

Key: ⊛ = 4 vehicles

Number of vehicles passing between 2.00 p.m. and 2.15 p.m.

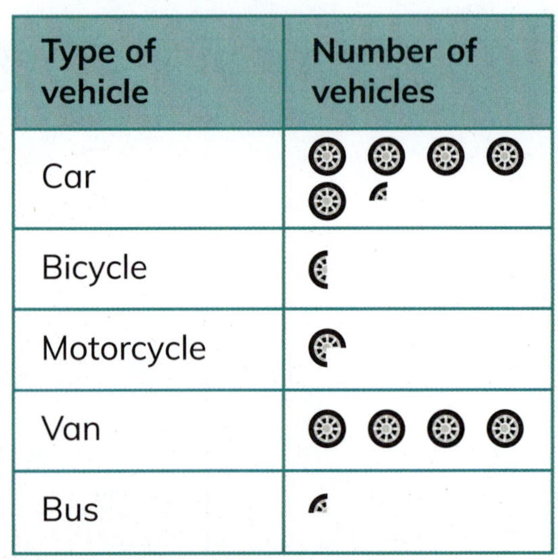

Key: ⊛ = 4 vehicles

a How many cars passed the school between 9.00 a.m. and 9.15 a.m.?

b How many buses passed the school between 2.00 p.m. and 2.15 p.m.?

c During which time did most vans pass the school?

d How many more motorcycles passed the school between 9.00 a.m. and 9.15 a.m. than between 2.00 p.m. and 2.15 p.m.?

e How many vehicles passed the school in total between 9.00 a.m. and 9.15 a.m.?

f During which time was the road outside the school busiest? Explain how you know.

5 Thirty children voted for their favourite singer.

Thirty adults also voted for their favourite singer.

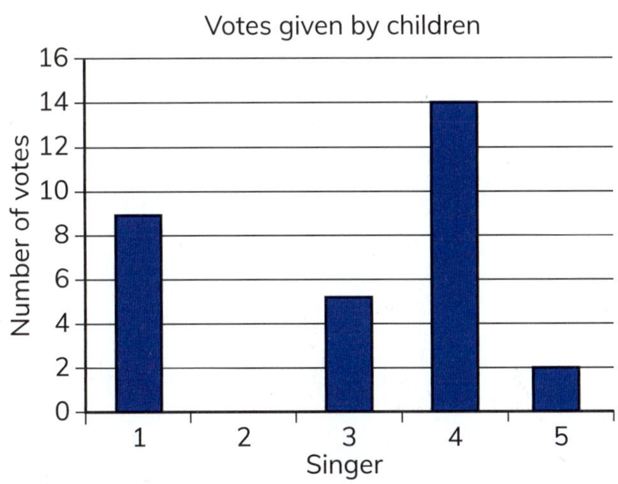

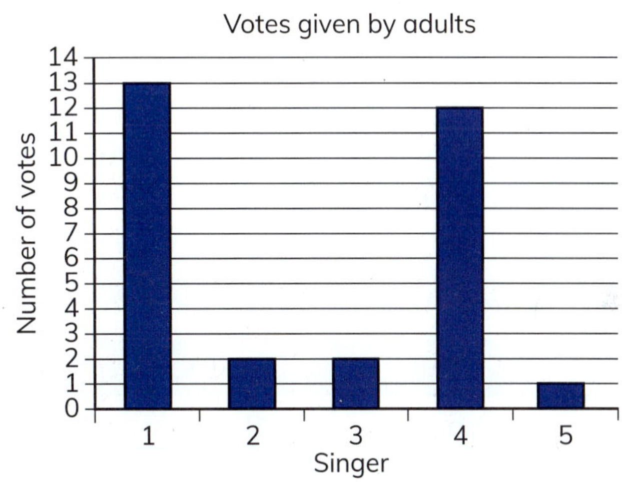

a Which singer received 13 votes from the adults?

b How many children voted for singer 2?

c How many more children than adults voted for singer 3?

d How many people in total voted for singer 4?

e Copy the sentence and complete it by writing something that is similar about the data in the two graphs.

Both the adults and children _____.

f Conjecture about the differences in the data between the two graphs. Copy and complete the sentence by writing what is different about the data in the two graphs.

The children _____, but the adults _____.

g Copy and complete the sentence to give a possible reason why the data in the graphs is different.

I think that the data for the children's vote and the data for the adults' vote is different because _____.

6 Ahmed used a tally chart to collect data about the number of people in households.

Number of people living in a household	Tally	Frequency
1 to 3	卌	5
4 to 6	卌 卌 卌 II	17
7 to 9	卌 III	8

a How many households had between 7 to 9 people?

b Ahmed says that his data shows that 17 households had 4 people in them. Is he correct? Explain your answer.

Draw a tally chart and collect data from people in your classroom about the number of people in their households.

Write two sentences describing what is different and what is similar between the data in your table and the data in the table above.

7 Three students used a table to record the scores in a test.

Learner	Score
Moira	138
Olivia	121
Parveen	154

The three graphs show this information.

Which one shows the results best?

Explain your answer.

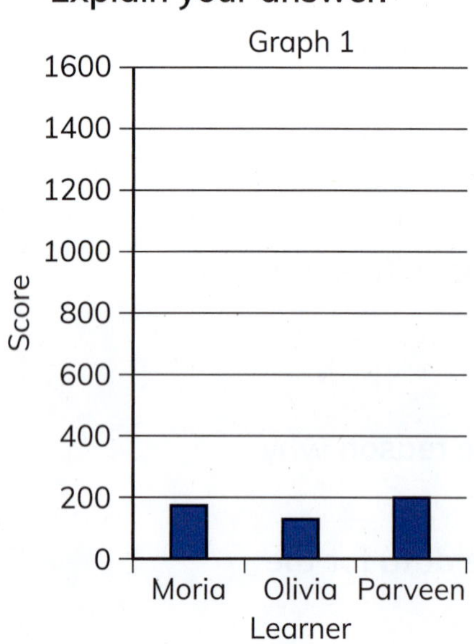

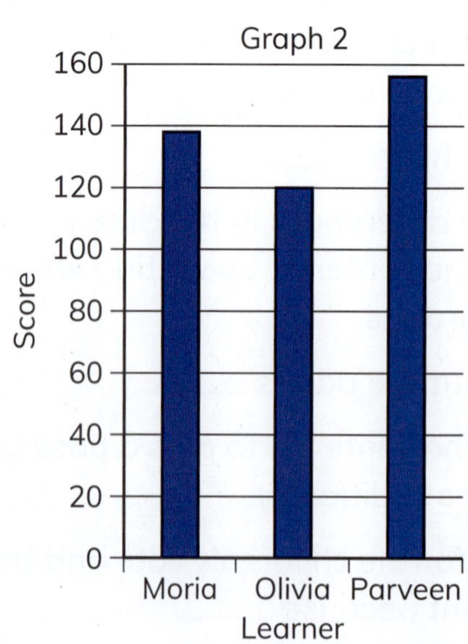

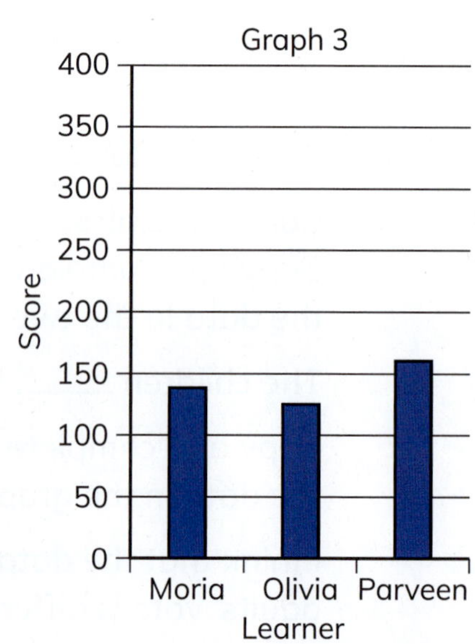

8 Class 1 and Class 2 took a Maths test. These frequency tables show how many children got each score on the test.

Class 1

Score	Number of children
0	2
1	3
2	2
3	4
4	11
5	8

Class 2

Score	Number of children
0	0
1	2
2	2
3	6
4	9
5	11

a Would a Carroll diagram or a pictogram be better for displaying this data?

b A bar chart would also be a good way to represent the data.
Draw two bar charts to display the data.

You will need to:

- choose a scale
- add a title
- label the horizontal axis and the vertical axis.

c Describe one way that the data in the graphs is similar.

d Describe one way that the data in the graphs is different.

e Why do you think that more children in Class 2 had higher scores?

Look at the bar charts you have made. Use this checklist to assess how well you have displayed the data.

- Have you used a ruler to make the chart neat and clear?
- Have you added a title to your chart?
- Have you labelled the horizontal axis and the vertical axis?
- Does the scale you have chosen make it easy to see the height of each bar and compare them?

Copy and complete this sentence.

I can improve how I draw bar charts by ____.

Think like a mathematician

Work with a partner, or in a small group.

Create a poster showing the different ways of displaying data and when they can be used. Show the different characteristics of each and critique their advantages and disadvantages. Include:

- Venn diagram
- Carroll diagram
- tally chart
- frequency table
- dot plot
- pictogram
- bar chart.

Look what I can do!

- [ ] I can sort and compare items in Carroll diagrams and Venn diagrams.
- [ ] I can record, organise and represent data in a bar chart.
- [ ] I can interpret and compare data to answer questions using graphs and charts.

Check your progress

1 Copy and complete the Carroll diagram below.
Put the numbers 1 to 30 into the Carroll diagram.

	odd	not odd
multiple of 7		
not a multiple of 7		

2 a Copy and complete the sentences to describe what you know about these shapes from the Venn diagram.

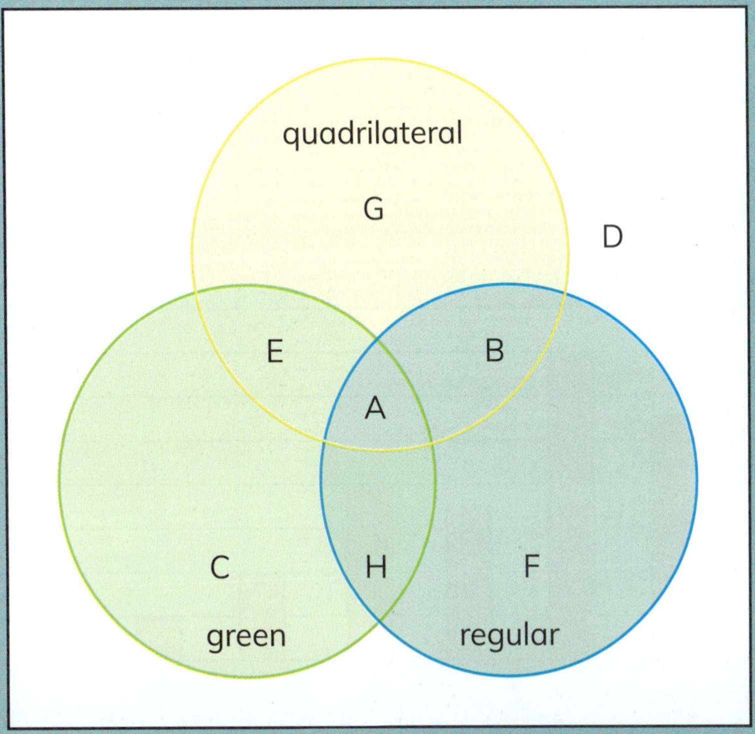

Shape A is ____.

Shape B is ____.

Shape C is ____.

Shape D is ____.

b Which shape is a regular green polygon, but not a quadrilateral?

Continued

3 Look at these two bar charts.

A graph showing the number of letters in the words of one page of Book 1

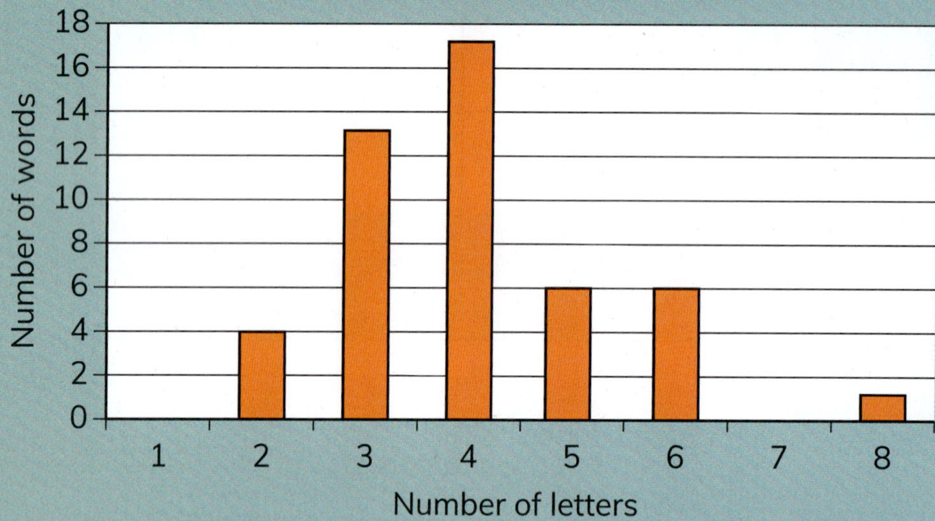

A graph showing the number of letters in the words of one page of Book 2

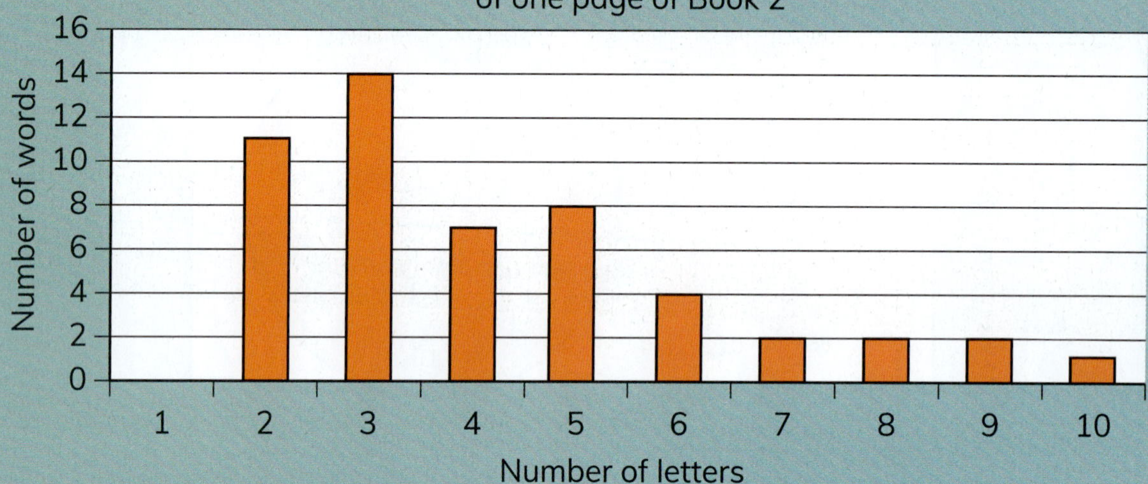

a How many words on the page in Book 1 had four letters?

b How many words on the page in Book 2 had ten letters?

c How many words were there in total on the page in Book 1?

d How many words were there in total on the page in Book 2?

Continued

e Write one thing that is similar between the number of letters in words in Book 1 and those in Book 2.

f Write one thing that is different between the number of letters in words in Book 1 and those in Book 2.

g There are more words on the page in Book 2 than on the page in Book 1.

There are more words that are longer than 6 letters on the page in Book 2 than on the page in Book 1.

Write about why there might be those differences between the books.

4 This frequency table shows the number of badges collected by five children.

Child	Number of badges
Kevin	12
Todd	21
Tia	18
Raquel	16
Amanda	27

Display the information in a pictogram.

Use this key:

 = 4 badges

17 Multiplication and division

Getting started

Use an efficient method to answer these questions.

1 Calculate the product of 76 and 5.

2 486 × 6

3 76 ÷ 4

4 87 ÷ 7

5 Paper plates are sold in packs of 8.

Ahmed needs 27 plates.

How many packs must he buy?

6 Anna has some hexagons and triangles.

She uses 7 hexagons and 8 triangles to make a flower.
Anna makes some more flowers.
She uses 128 triangles altogether.
How many flowers does she make?
How many hexagons does she use?

You can use multiplication and division in lots of everyday situations.

Here are four number stories A, B, C and D.

A Krysta has some red tulips.
She places 8 tulips in each vase.
She has 4 vases of tulips.

How many tulips does she have altogether?

B There are 32 learners in the class.
At the end of term, they divide into teams of 4 to enter a competition.
All of the learners enter the competition.

How many teams of 4 are there?

C

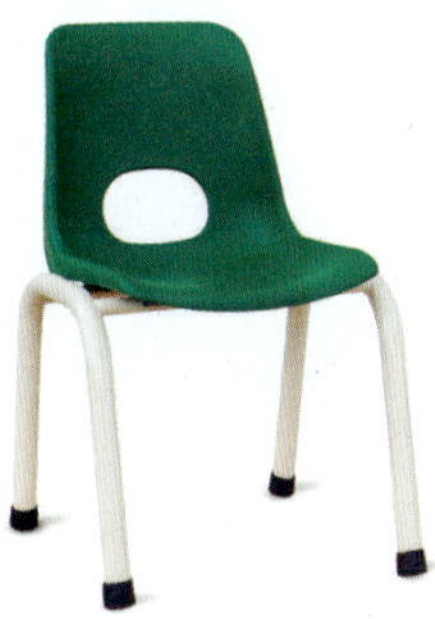

Hassan and Khalid set out chairs in the hall.
They put out 32 chairs.
They arrange the chairs in 4 rows with the same number of chairs in each row.

How many chairs do they put in each row?

D Ollie enjoys drawing pictures using coloured pens.
He has 8 packets of pens.
Each packet holds 4 pens.

How many pens has Ollie got altogether?

Match one number sentence connecting 4, 8 and 32 to each number story.

$32 \div 4 = \square$	$8 \times 4 = \square$	$32 \div 4 = \square$	$4 \times 8 = \square$
Sharing 32 between 4	4 lots of 8	**Grouping** 32 into 4s	8 lots of 4

Think of some number stories to match multiplication and division number sentences.

17.1 Using an efficient column method for multiplication

We are going to . . .

- estimate the answer to multiplying a whole number up to 1000 by a 1-digit number
- multiply a whole number by a 1-digit number.

We all learn how to multiply numbers in school and many people use multiplication in their jobs.

Imagine you are in charge of putting fuel in a plane.

To work out how much fuel is needed you need to multiply the amount of fuel burned every hour by the journey time.

If you get the calculation wrong the plane will not be able to reach its destination.

estimate product

Worked example 1

Calculate 346 × 9.

Estimate: 350 × 10 = 3500

Make an estimate.

Step 1:

Work from right to left.

$$\begin{array}{r} 3\ \ 4\ \ 6 \\ \times\qquad 9 \\ \hline 4 \\ \hline {}_{5}\quad \end{array}$$

6 × 9 = 54 (put 4 on the answer and carry 5 tens).

Continued

Step 2:

	3	4	6
	×		9
		1	4
	4	5	

40 × 9 = 360. Add 50 to give 410 (put 1 in the tens column and carry 4 hundreds).

Step 3:

	3	4	6
	×		9
3	1	1	4
	4	5	

300 × 9 = 2700. Add 400 to give 3100 (put 1 in the hundreds column and 3 in the thousands column).

Check your answer is close to your estimate.

Answer: 345 × 9 = 3114

Exercise 17.1

Remember to make estimates before you calculate.

1 There are 12 months in a year. How many months are there in 8 years?

2 Write the answers that are odd numbers.

A 27 × 5 B 13 × 8 C 58 × 4 D 33 × 9

3 One screw has a mass of 6 grams. What is the total mass of 408 screws?

4 Multiply 288 by 8.

5 Find the product of 428 and 9.

6 Here is a number machine.

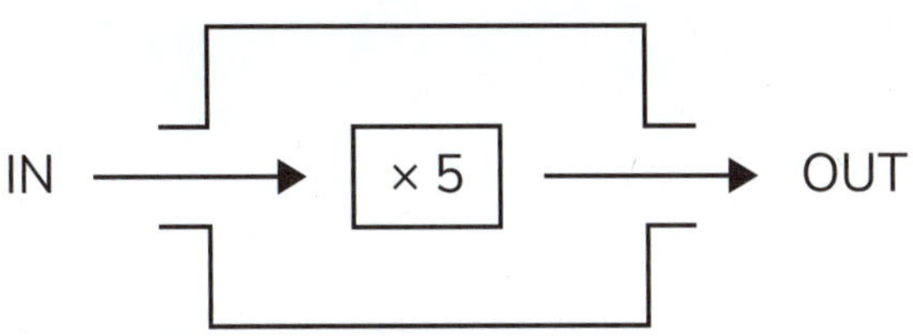

Copy and complete the table.

IN	123	345	567
OUT			

7 Copy the following and write the **same** digit in each box to make the calculation correct.

	3	□	6
	×		□
1	3	8	4

How did you work out your answer?
What facts did you use to help you?

8 A 6-day ski lift pass for an adult costs \$209.

There are 8 adults in the ski group.
What is the total cost of the ski lift passes?

9 Tara says, 'A 3-digit number multiplied by a 1-digit number will always give a 4-digit number'.

Is she correct?

Explain your answer.

What approximations did you make before calculating the answers in this exercise?

Explain to your partner how you estimated and worked out your answers.

Think like a mathematician

Use the first triangle to find the rule, then use the rule to complete the other two triangles.

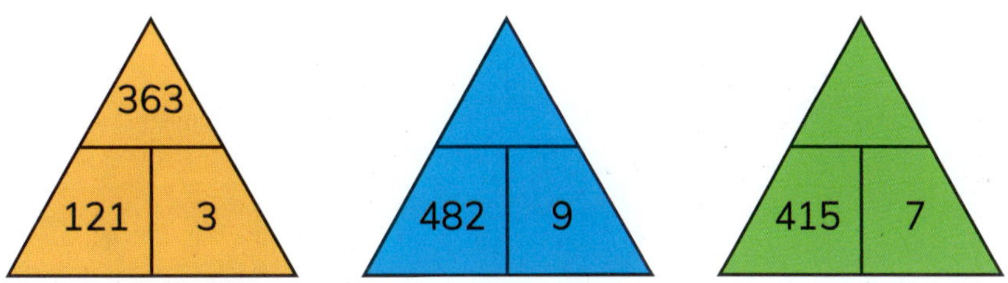

You will show you are **generalising** when you find the rule.

Look what I can do!

- [ ] I can estimate the answer to multiplying a whole number up to 1000 by a 1-digit number.
- [ ] I can multiply a whole number by a 1-digit number.

› 17.2 Using an efficient method for division

We are going to . . .

- estimate the answer to a division of a 2-digit number by a 1-digit number
- divide a number up to 100 by a 1-digit number
- decide whether to round up or down after division to give an answer to a problem.

You can use division to solve problems.

There are 224 players entered into a 7-a-side football competition. Dividing 224 by 7 tells you how many teams entered the competition.

dividend **divisor** **quotient** **remainder**

Worked example 2

Calculate 75 ÷ 4.

Estimate: 40 ÷ 4 = 10 and 80 ÷ 4 = 20 so the answer is between 10 and 20 and closer to 20.

	10	+8 r3	
4	40	+35	

Answer: 18 r3

Split 75 into 40 + 35

There are ten fours in forty and eight fours in thirty-five with a remainder of 3.

	1	8	r3
4	7	$^{3}5$	

Answer: 18 r3

Using the estimate, write 1 to show ten fours, and write 3 next to the 5 to show that you carry 30 over.

There are eight fours in thirty five with a remainder of 3.

Answer: 18 r3

Exercise 17.2

1 Parveen needs 28 balloons.
A shop sells balloons in packs of 5.

How many packs does Parveen need to buy?

2 56 children arrange themselves in teams of 4.
How many teams do they make?

3 A carton of orange juice fills 6 cups.
Erik wants to fill 50 cups with orange juice.
How many cartons does Erik need?

4 A group of friends earn $96 by washing cars.
They share the money equally.
They get $8 each.
How many friends are in the group?

5 Correct the errors in these calculations.

$$3\overline{)86}\quad \text{answer } 22 \qquad\qquad 3\overline{)57}\quad \text{answer } 52$$

Discuss with your partner how the errors may have happened.

6 Copy this calculation and find the missing digit.

$$\begin{array}{r} 2\;6 \\ 3\;\overline{)\;\square\;8} \end{array}$$

How did you work out your answer? Can you think of different ways? You could use trial and improvement or you could use multiplication. Show how you could use multiplication.

7 a What is the highest remainder possible when you divide by 3?

b What is the highest remainder possible when you divide by 4?

c Make a general statement comparing the divisor (the number you are dividing by) and the remainder.

8 Petra has two strips of card. Each strip is 24 centimetres long.
One strip is divided into 3 equal parts.
The other strip is divided into 4 equal parts.

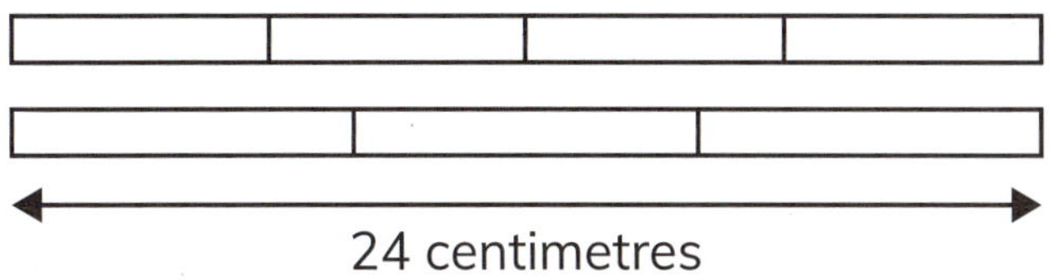

Petra uses the two strips to make this shape.

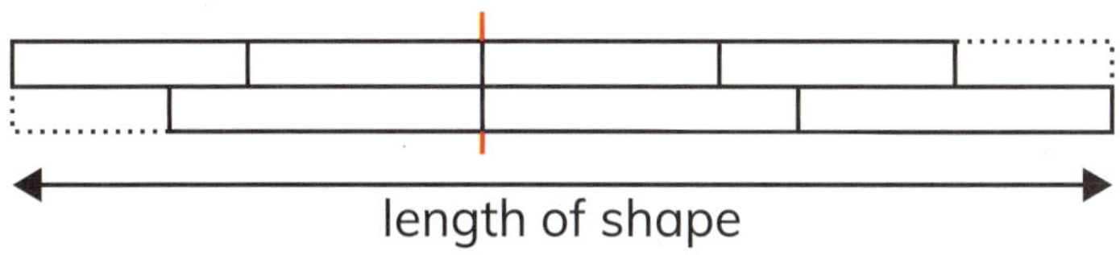

What is the total length of Petra's shape?
Check your method and your answer with that of your partner.

Think like a mathematician

Imagine you have a set of number cards from 0 to 9.

Use 4 different cards to make division sentences like this.

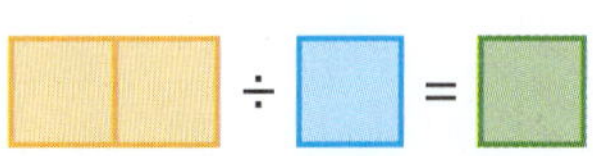

Find all the possible solutions.

Look what I can do!

- ☐ I can estimate the answer to a division of a 2-digit number by a 1-digit number.
- ☐ I can divide a number up to 100 by a 1-digit number.
- ☐ I can decide whether to round up or down after division to give the answer to a problem.

Check your progress

1 Peng estimates the answer to 399 × 6 to be 2400.
Is this a good estimate? Explain your answer.

2 Plants are sold in trays.
Each tray holds 15 plants.
Orla buys 7 trays of plants.
How many plants does she buy?

3 a Divide 93 by 6.

b Find the product of 93 and 6.

4 Amul uses a number machine. Every number he puts in is multiplied by the same number.

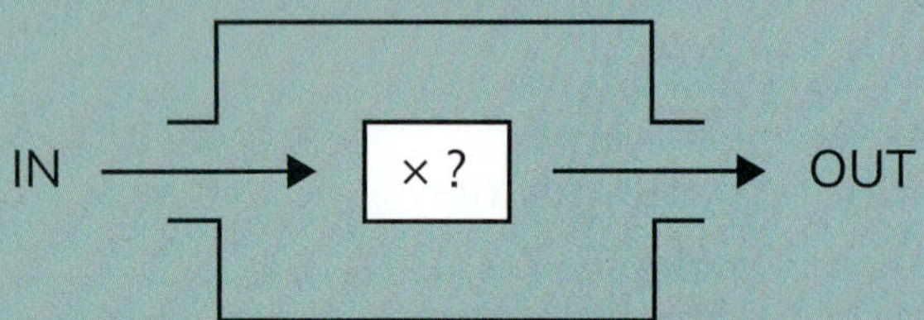

Amul puts four numbers in to the machine. The numbers 21, 49, 70 and 84 come out. What could the machine be multiplying by?

5 Copy and complete these calculations.

	4	1	5
	×		7

8	9	7	

6 Pierre has some number cards.

a He holds up a card and says, 'If I multiply the number on the card by 5, the answer is 45.'
What number is on the card?

b Pierre holds up a different card and says, 'If I divide the number on this card by 3, the answer is 5.'
What number is on the card?

Continued

7 Lan has 74 apples. She makes bags of 6 apples.

How many full bags can Lan make?

8 Here is a number machine.

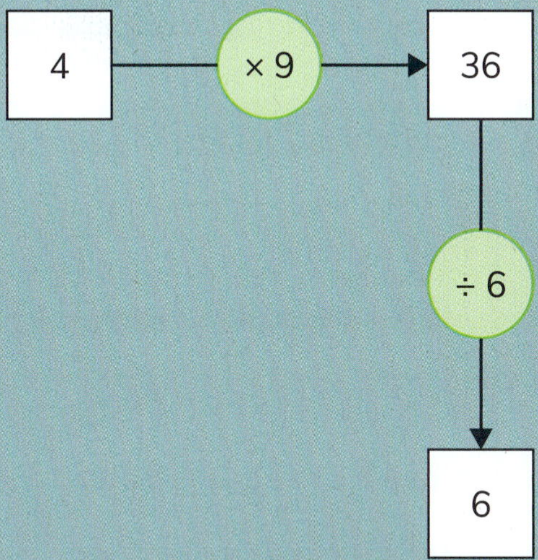

Copy and complete this number machine.

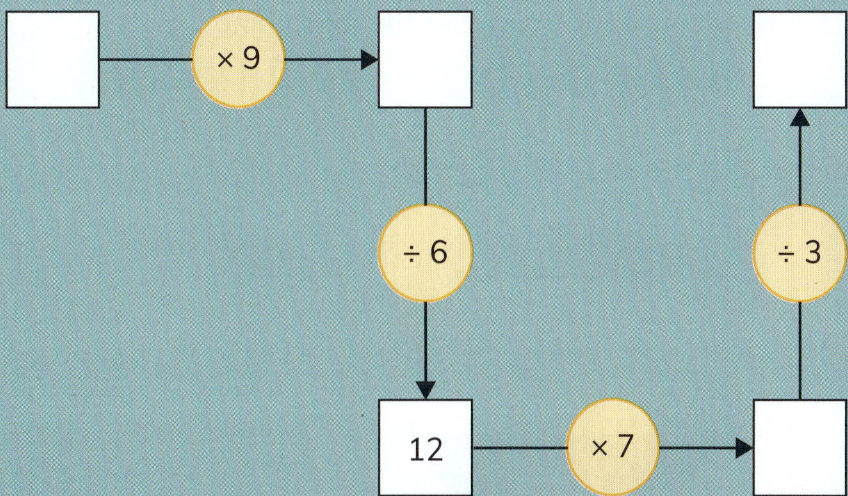

18 Position, direction and movement

Getting started

1 Copy the compass. North is labelled. Label the other arrows: 'South', 'East' and 'West'.

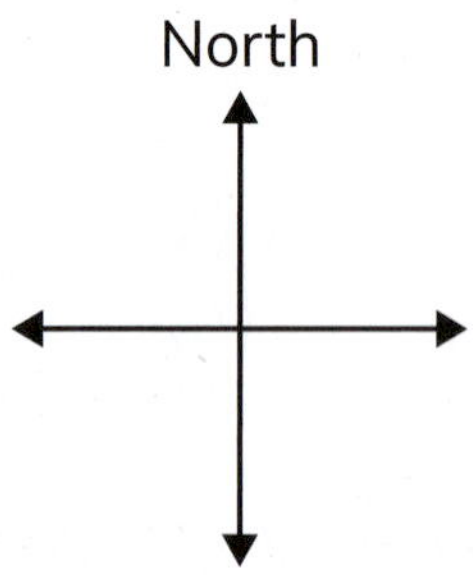

2 Put your finger on the X. Follow the instructions.

What letter is your finger on at the end?

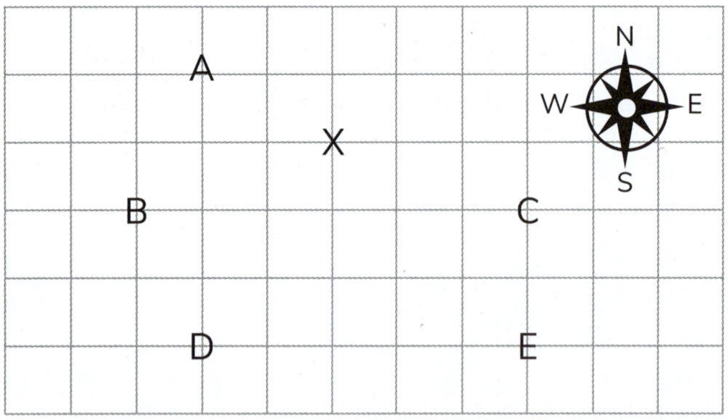

Instructions

Move one square North.

Move five squares West.

Move four squares South.

Move three squares East.

3 Which triangle has been reflected correctly over the mirror line?

Mirror line

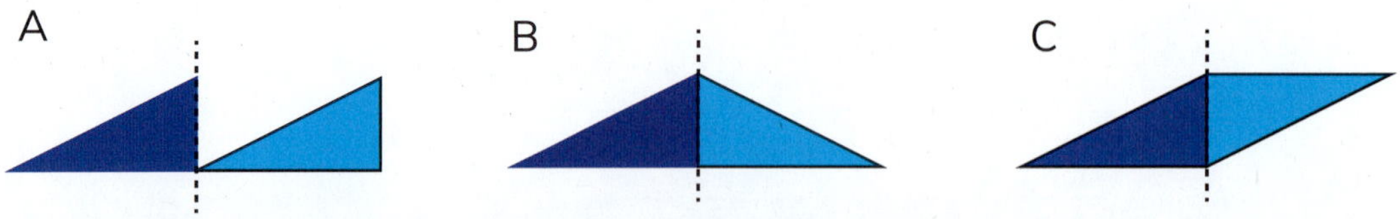

4 Use a ruler and pencil to copy this shape and the mirror line.

Reflect the shape over the mirror line.

In this unit you will learn about clear and useful ways to record position. You will explore movement in different directions and learn more about how to reflect shapes.

These ideas are useful for designing patterns for displays and fabrics.

These ideas will also help you to read maps and plan how to get to places.

This is a map of the area around Cambridge in England. Choose two places on the map. Plan a route to get from one place to another along the roads.

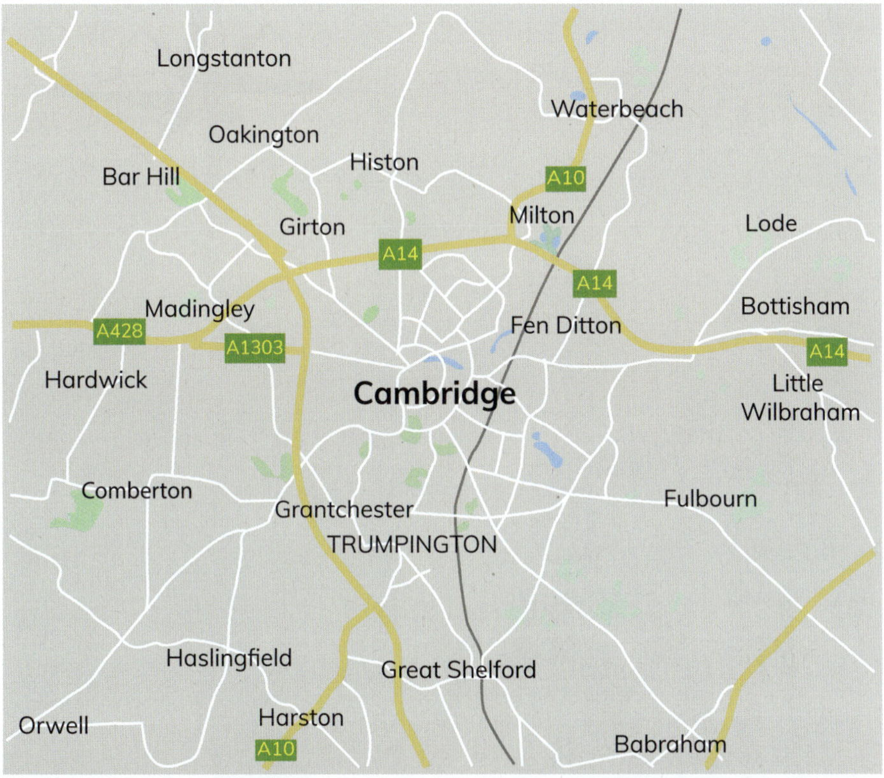

Imagery ©2020 CNES / Airbus, Getmapping plc, Infoterra Ltd & Bluesky, Landsat / Copernicus, Maxar Technologies, The GeoInformation Group, Map data ©2020

18.1 Position and movement

We are going to . . .

- use eight compass directions to describe direction
- use coordinates to describe position.

This section is about using coordinates to describe a position and using compass directions to describe movement.

A compass is useful for finding your way at sea or in unfamiliar places.

compass   coordinates   quadrant

Exercise 18.1

1 What do the letters NE stand for on a compass?

2 What compass direction is missing from this compass?

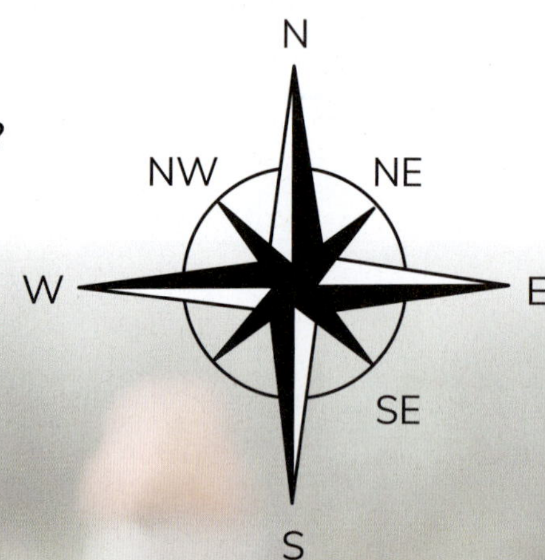

3 **a** Use the map to see where Arnold is standing.
If Arnold travels north-west, what town will he reach?

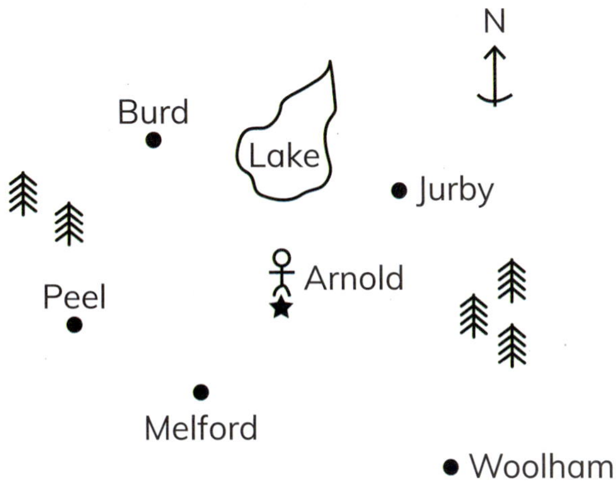

b What direction does Arnold walk to get to each of these places?

i Woolham **ii** Jurby **iii** Melford

4 This map shows the roads between Ibri and Sheki.
One way to get from Ibri to Sheki is to travel:
1 square north-west, 1 square north-east,
1 square north-west, 1 square north-east.
List all the different ways you can to describe travelling back from Sheki to Ibri using compass directions.

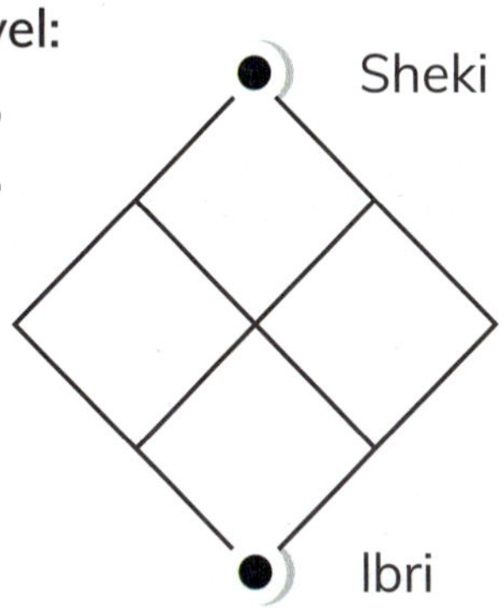

Swap your answer to question 4 with a partner.

- How many ways has your partner found to travel from Sheki to Ibri?
- Check that the routes are correct.
- Has your partner listed the routes systematically so that they know they have found every route?
- How is your partner's work different to your work?

Talk to your partner about your answers and agree what you can both do to improve.

Worked example 1

Mark the coordinates (3, 5) with an X.

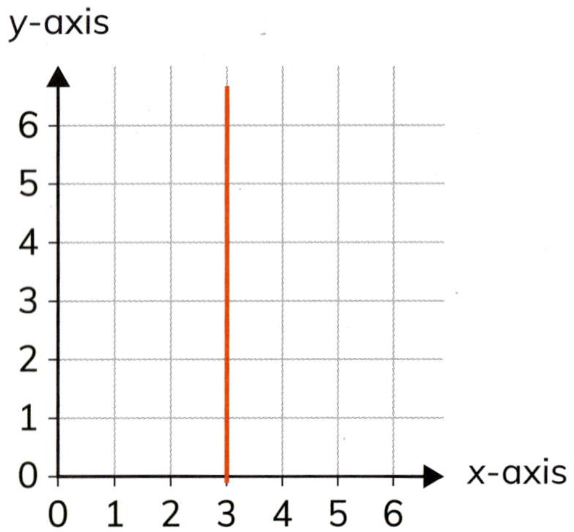

The first number of the coordinates is the distance horizontally. Find the line that goes through '3' on the horizontal (**x**) axis.

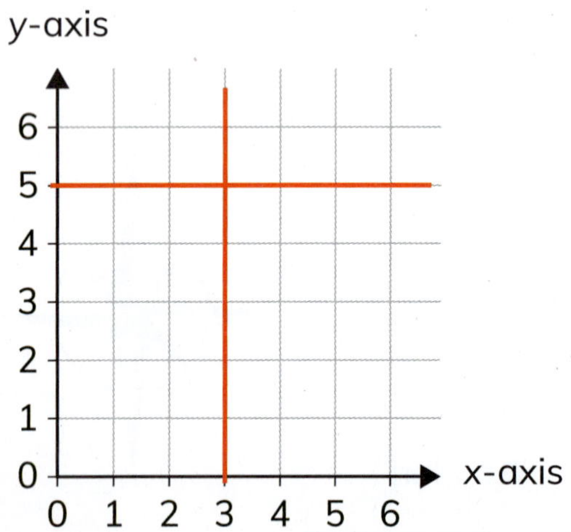

The second number of the coordinates is the distance vertically. Find the line that goes through '5' on the vertical (**y**) axis.

Where the lines cross is the point with the coordinates (3, 5).

Mark (3, 5) with a cross.

Answer:

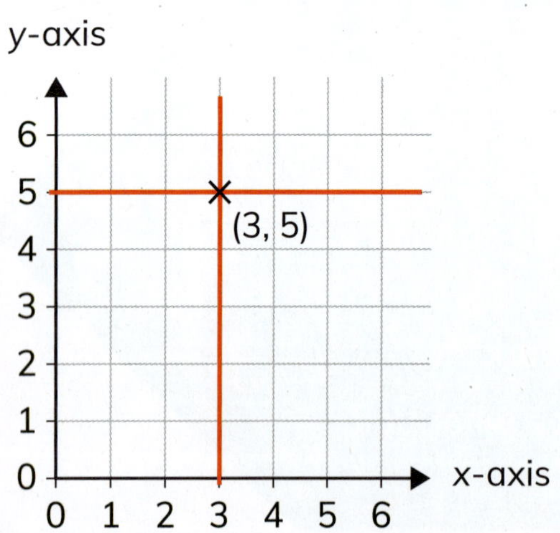

5 Write the coordinates of the four points that are marked on this grid.

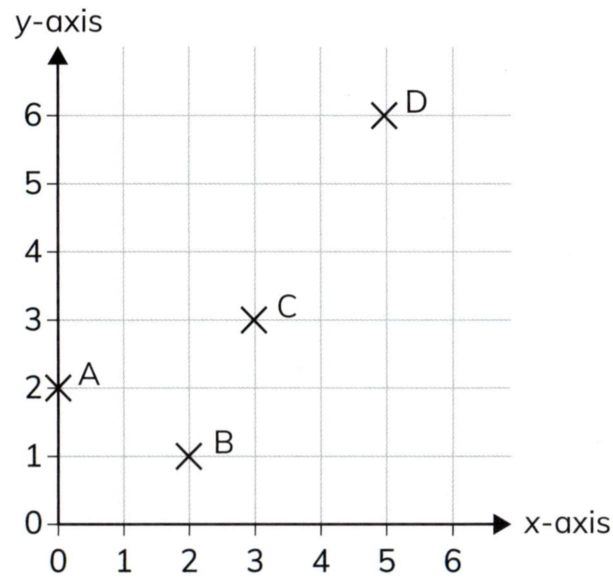

6 Safiya says that the point marked on this grid has coordinates (4, 1).
Explain why she is wrong.

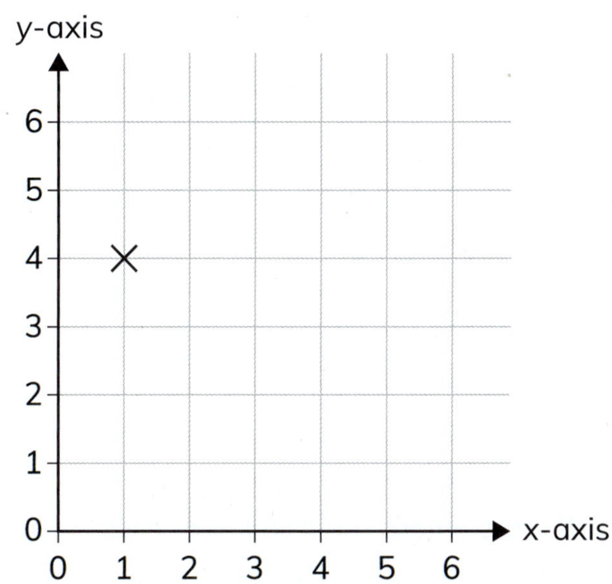

Safiya has made a common mistake with coordinates.

How will you make sure that you do not make the same mistake in the future?

Think of a way to remember that the first number of the coordinates is the horizontal distance and the second number of the coordinates is the vertical distance.

7 Copy this grid.

Mark these coordinates on your grid with a cross, X.

(5, 3) (1, 1) (4, 6) (3, 0)

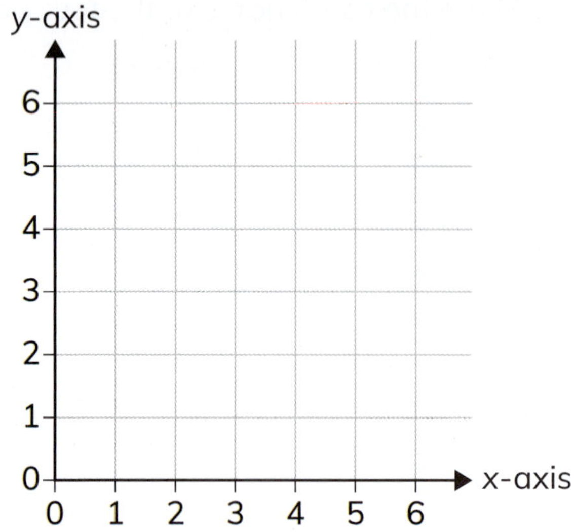

Think like a mathematician

1 With your partner, draw a coordinate grid from 0 to 6 on the horizontal (x) axis and from 0 to 6 on the vertical (*y*) axis.

2 Choose one of the numbers on the *y*-axis.
Draw a horizontal line through the number and the quadrant.

3 Work together to write down all the coordinates you can name on that line.

4 Discuss what is similar and different about the coordinates on that line.
Generalise about what they all have in common.

5 Choose one of the numbers on the x-axis.
Draw a vertical line through the number and the quadrant.

6 Work together to write down all the coordinates you can name on that line.

7 Discuss what is similar and different about the coordinates on that line.
Generalise about what they all have in common.

8 Write down the coordinates where the two lines cross.

9 Tell another pair of learners the coordinates where your two lines cross.
Can they work out the coordinates of the points that are on your two lines?

Look what I can do!

- [ ] I can use eight compass directions to describe direction.
- [ ] I can use coordinates to describe position.

18.2 Reflecting 2D shapes

We are going to . . .

- sketch the reflection of a 2D shape on a grid.

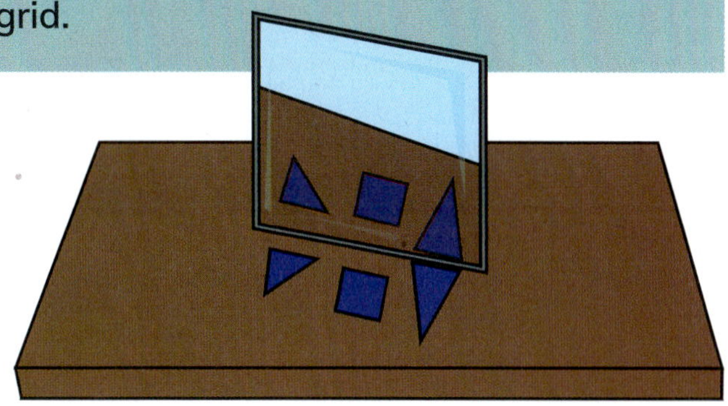

In this section you will improve the accuracy of how you reflect shapes over a mirror line by using a grid of squares.

When you know how to reflect a shape, you can create interesting patterns and designs.

Exercise 18.2

mirror line
reflection

1 Sketch this shape and the mirror line on plain paper. Draw the reflection of the shape over the mirror line.

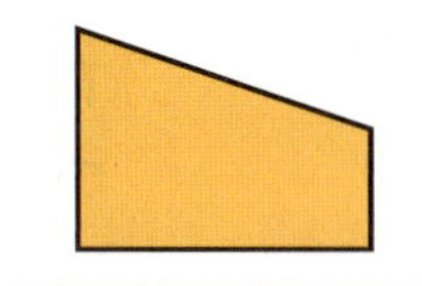

Place a mirror along the mirror line to check the reflection is accurate.

Worked example 2

Reflect this shape over the mirror line on the grid.

This is a vertical mirror line.

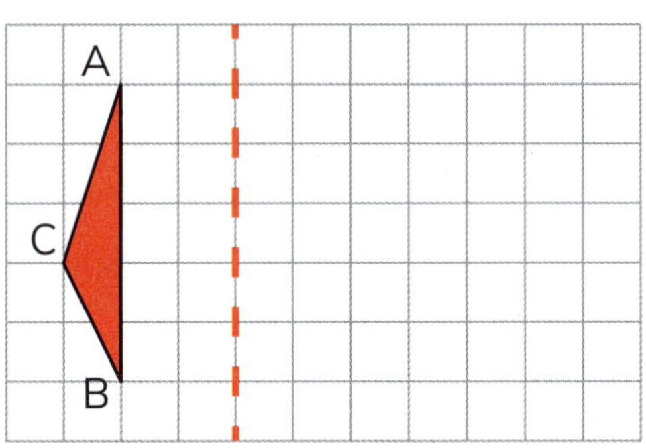

Continued

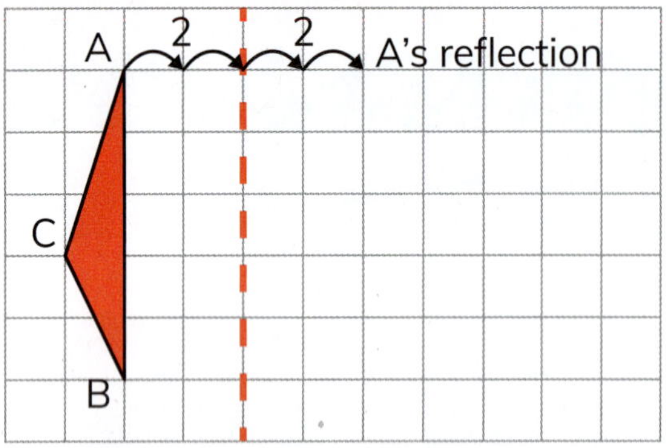

The vertex A is two squares from the mirror line. Its reflection will be two squares from the mirror line, on the other side of the mirror.

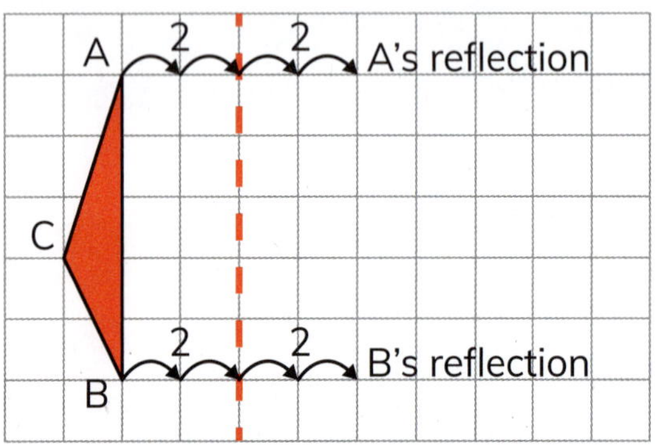

The vertex B is also two squares from the mirror line. Its reflection will be two squares from the mirror line, on the other side of the mirror.

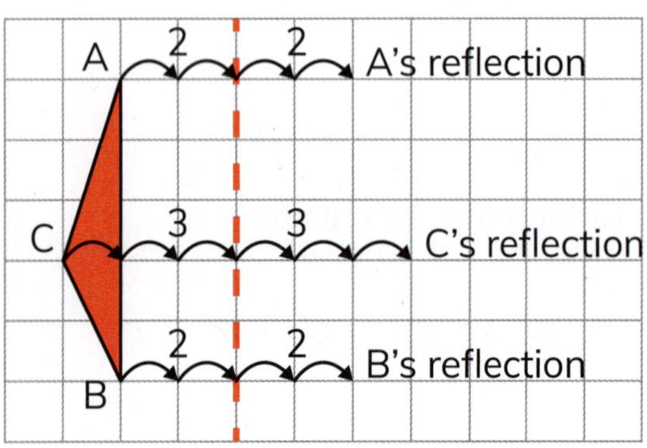

The vertex C is three squares from the mirror line. Its reflection will be three squares from the mirror line, on the other side of the mirror.

Join the vertices to make the reflection of the whole shape.

Answer:

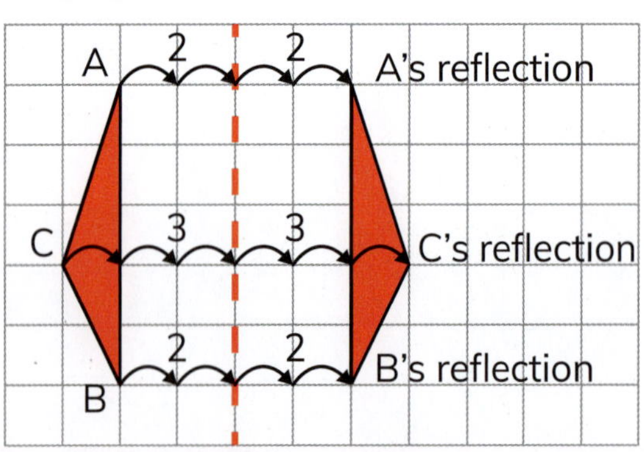

2 Draw each shape and mirror line on squared paper.

a

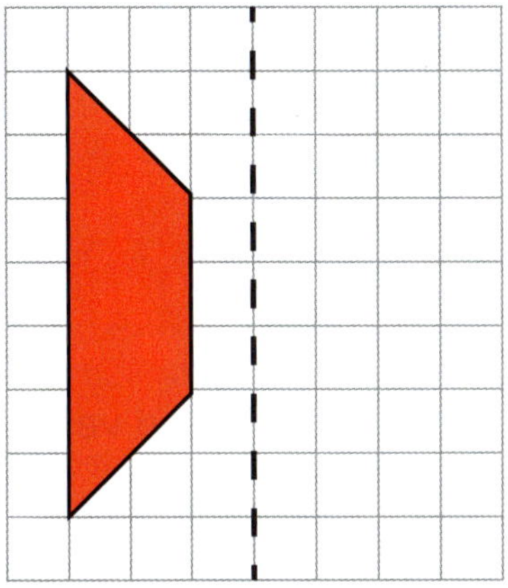

b

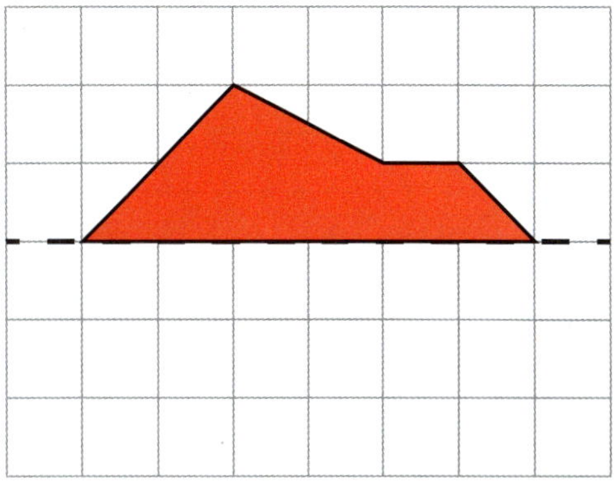

Reflect each shape by counting the squares between the vertices and the mirror line.

3 When a shape is reflected over a mirror line that is along one of its edges, the original shape and the reflected shape make a new shape together.

Example:

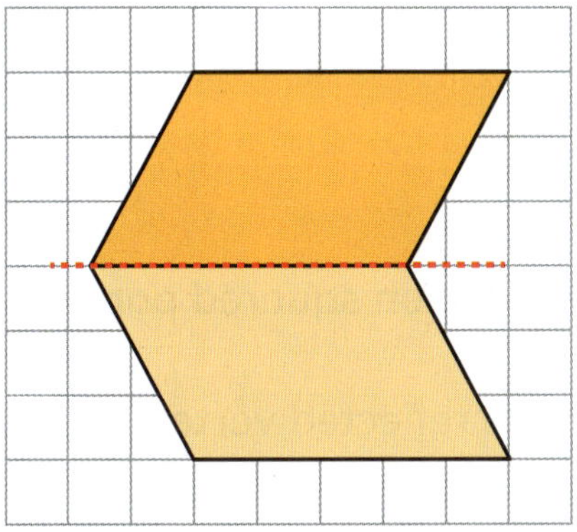

The parallelogram and the reflected parallelogram combined have made a hexagon.

a For each shape predict what the new combined shape will be after the reflection.

A

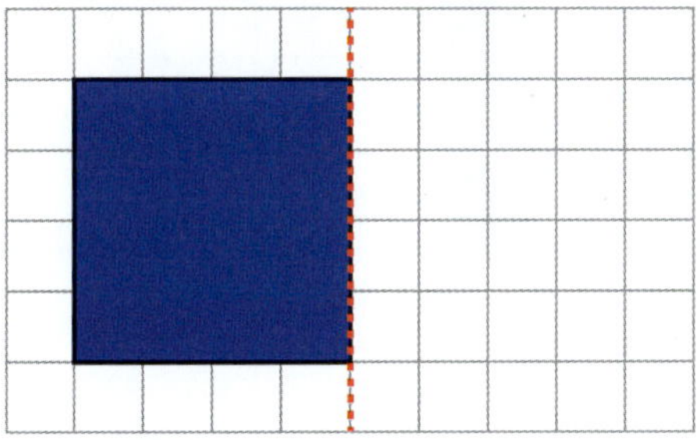

B

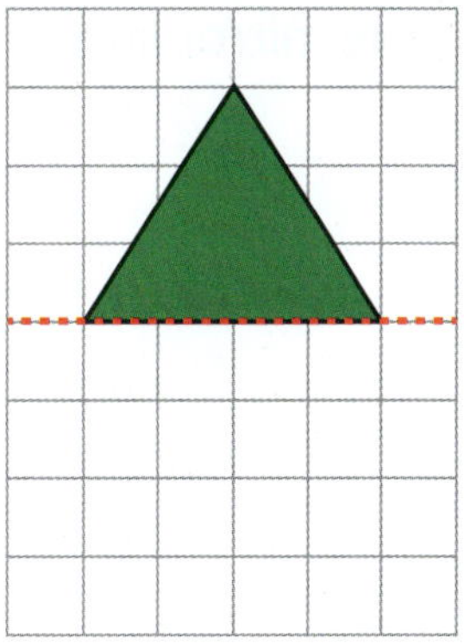

C

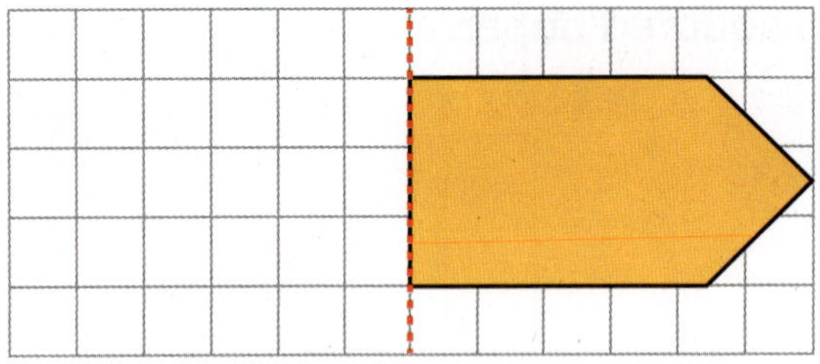

b Sketch and reflect the shapes to check your predictions.

4 Raj has reflected this pentagon over the vertical mirror line.
He has drawn red lines between each original vertex and its reflected vertex.

Describe the red lines.

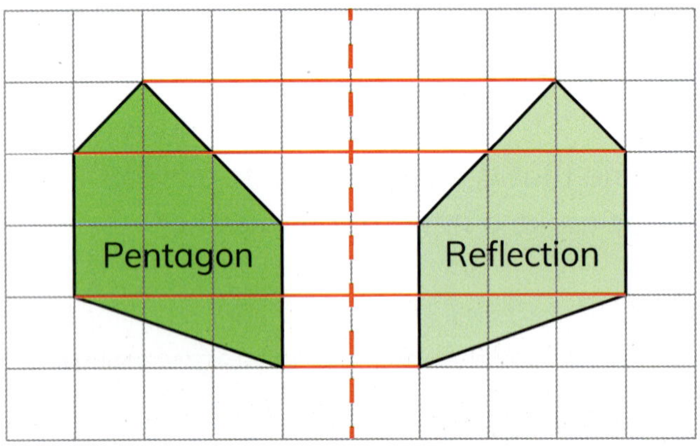

5 Draw your own shape and a horizontal mirror line on squared paper.
Reflect the shape over the mirror line.
Draw lines between each original vertex and its reflected vertex.
Describe the lines.

6 The vertices of this rectangle have coordinates (0, 2), (0, 5), (1, 2) and (1, 5).
Conjecture what will happen then investigate to find the coordinates of the vertices of the shape when it is reflected over the mirror line.

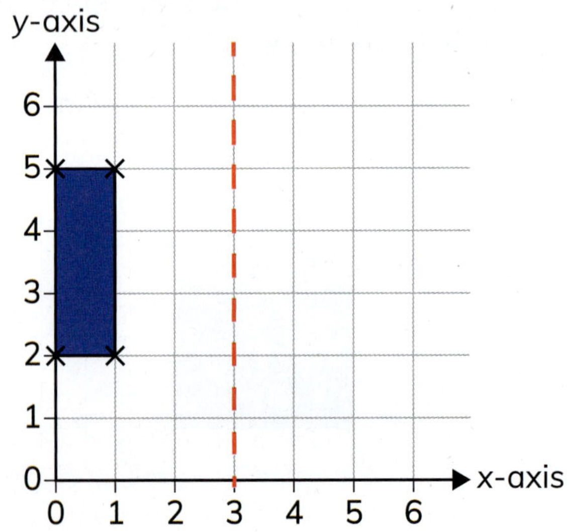

Think like a mathematician

a With your small group discuss the question:

> Does a reflected shape have a greater, smaller or the same area as the original shape?

b Investigate the question by reflecting rectangles.

c Make a poster showing your conclusions. Include a generalisation about what you have found out.

d Swap your poster with another group. Assess the understanding you can see in the poster.

- Has the group answered the question set in the investigation?
- Has the group used diagrams to illustrate or demonstrate their answer?
- Has the group written a convincing explanation?
- What advice can you give to help the group improve their poster?

Think about your poster and the poster you have assessed. How will you improve your poster?

Look what I can do!

☐ I can sketch the reflection of a 2D shape on a grid.

Check your progress

1 What compass directions should the boat follow to travel along the river to the sea?

2 Copy this grid.

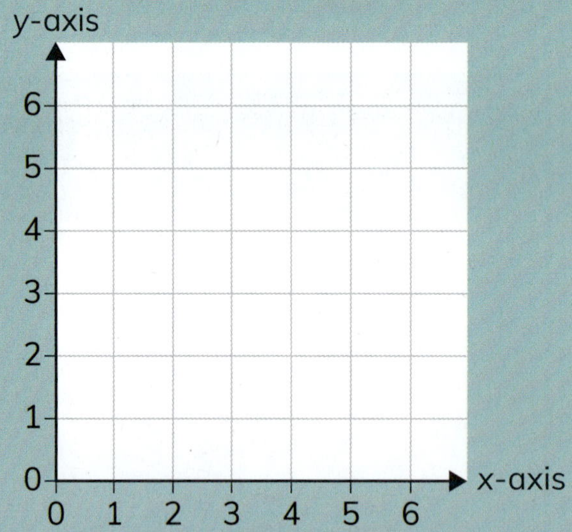

Mark these coordinates on your grid with a cross, X.

(3, 1) (0, 4) (2, 6) (5, 0) (2, 2)

Continued

3 This hexagon is reflected over the mirror line.

What new shape is made from the original hexagon and the reflected hexagon combined?

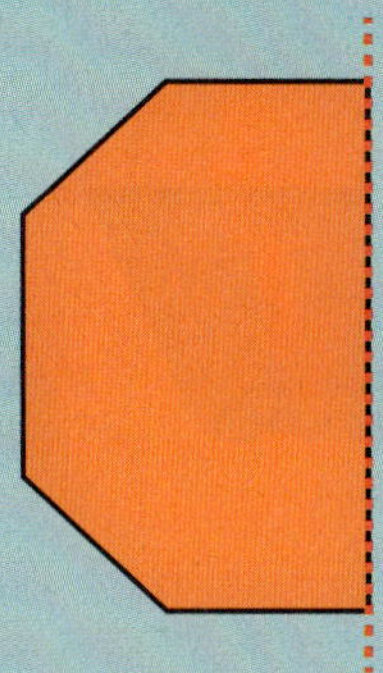

4 Copy the triangle and the mirror line.
Reflect the triangle over the mirror line.

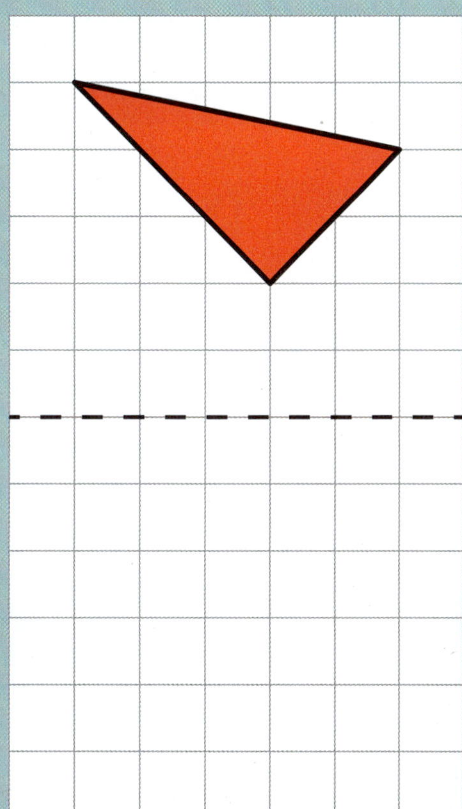

Continued

5 The parallelogram will be reflected over the mirror line.

What are the coordinates of the vertices of the reflected parallelogram?

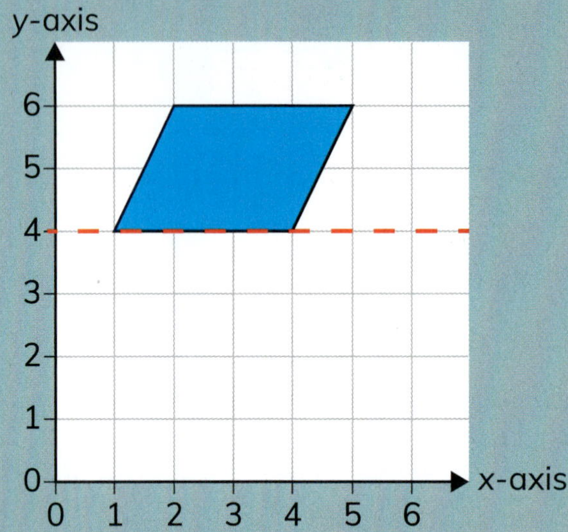

Glossary

2D shape a flat shape. It has two dimensions (2D) 76

a.m. a time in the morning between midnight and midday 29

acute angle an angle less than 90 degrees 104

analogue clock a clock with an 'hour hand' and a 'minute hand' 29

angle the size of turn from one line to the other line where two lines meet 100

area the space a surface covers. It is measured in square units, such as square metres or square centimetres. 167

array objects or numbers arranged in rows and columns 63

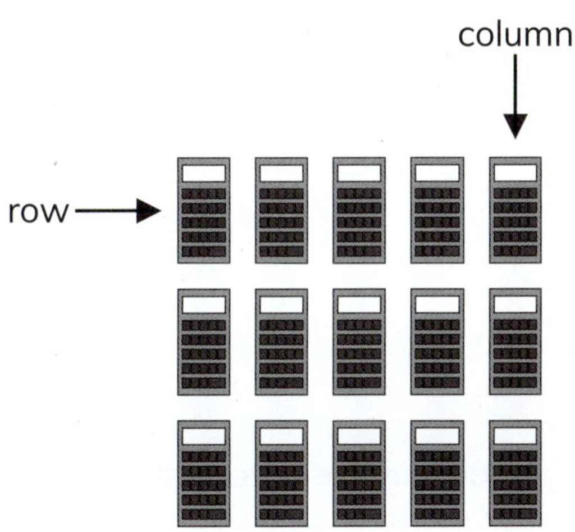

associative law when more than two numbers are added or multiplied you can do the calculations in any order. For example: 67

$8 + 3 + 4 = 8 + 3 + 4$ $\qquad$ $5 \times 2 \times 3 = 5 \times 2 \times 3$

$11 + 4 = 8 + 7$ $\qquad$ $10 \times 3 = 5 \times 6$

$15 = 15$ $\qquad$ $30 = 30$

bar chart — a graph that uses bars to show data — 197

calendar — a chart showing the days of the week and the months of the year — 33

Carroll diagram — a two-way table used for sorting items such as objects, shapes or numbers — 197

carry — lift a number and take it to another place. You carry numbers when you do column addition. For example: — 67

$$\begin{array}{r} 4\ 8 \\ +\ 4\ 7 \\ \hline 9\ 5 \\ \hline 1 \end{array}$$

7 add 8 is 15
Write the 5 in the 'ones' column
Carry 1 ten to the tens column

certain — an event will definitely happen — 56

compare — to say what is the same and what is different, or to say which is greater or smaller — 100

compass — an instrument that shows direction. For example, North, South, East, West. — 222

compose — put together, for example 600 + 30 + 2 = 632 — 21

cone — a 3D shape with a circular base and a curved surface that goes to a vertex — 145

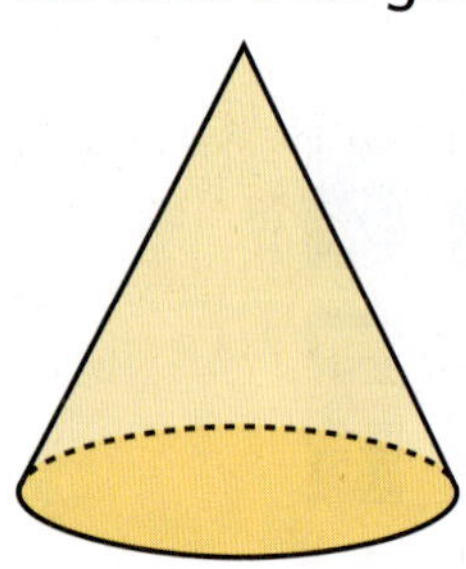

coordinates — a pair of numbers inside brackets, for example (2, 5). They are used to show a position on a grid. — 222

counter-example — an example that shows a general statement is wrong, for example: — 50

General statement: All multiples of 5 end in 5.
Counter-example: 10 is a multiple of 5 that does not end in 5.

data a collection of information 126

decompose break down a number into parts.
For example, 456 is 400 + 50 + 6 21

degrees a unit of measurement for angles 100

denominator the bottom number of a fraction. It tells you how many equal parts a shape has been divided into. For example, 89

$\frac{3}{5}$ 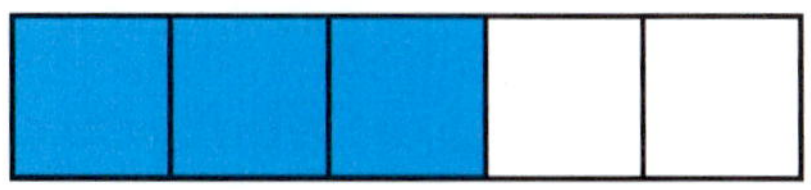

5 is the denominator.
The shape is divided into 5 equal parts.

difference to find the difference you subtract the smaller quantity from the larger quantity 45

digital clock a clock that uses numerals to tell the time 29

dividend the number being divided, for example: 214

31 ÷ 3 = 10 r1

↑

dividend

divisibility rule a rule for finding out whether one whole number is divisible by another. For example, a number can be divided by 2 if the last digit is divisible by 2, or by 5 if the last digit is 5 or 0, or by 10 if the last digit is 0. 189

divisible can be divided without a remainder.
For example, 14 is divisible by 2. 189

division sharing or grouping a number into equal parts 118

divisor a number that divides another number, for example: 214

31 ÷ 3 = 10 r1

↑

divisor

dot plot a way of representing data on a graph using dots 126

Term	Meaning	Page
edge / edges	a line on a 3D shape where 2 faces meet	145
efficient	work in an organised way	157
equivalent	equal in value	21
equivalent fraction	fractions that are equal in value. For example, $\frac{2}{4}$ and $\frac{1}{2}$ are equivalent fractions:	133

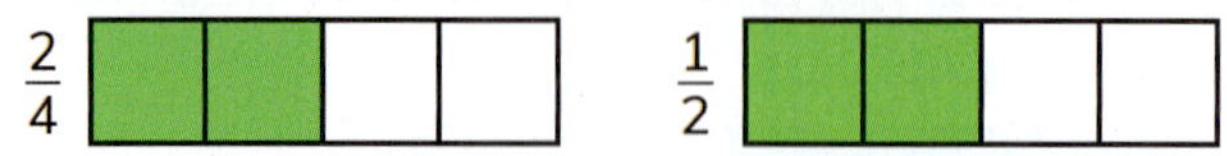

Term	Meaning	Page
estimate	a rough calculation based on what you already know and rounding	107
even	a multiple of 2. Even numbers end in 2, 4, 6, 8 or 0. For example 6, 22 or 108. An even number is divisible by 2 without a remainder.	50
even chance	it is equally likely and unlikely that an event will happen	56
face / faces	one flat surface of a 3D shape	145
factor	a whole number that divides exactly into another number. For example: $2 \times 3 = 6$, so 2 and 3 are factors of 6.	63
fraction	any part of a group, number or whole.	89

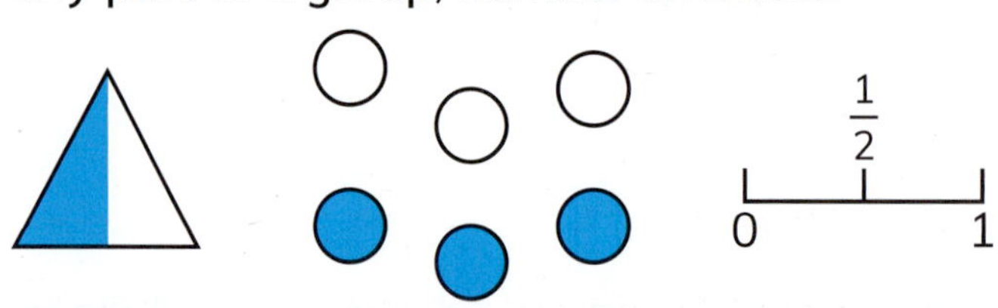

$\frac{1}{2}$ the triangle is shaded

$\frac{1}{2}$ the circles are shaded

$\frac{1}{2}$ is a position on the number line

Term	Meaning	Page
generalisation (general statement)	a statement that works for all examples. For example, 'two odd numbers added together give an even number'	50
good chance	it is likely that an event will happen	56
horizontal	a straight line parallel to the horizon	81
hour	a unit of time equal to 60 minutes. There are 24 hours in a day.	29

hundred thousand	a 6-digit number that is 10 times larger than ten thousand	21

100 000s	10 000s	1000s	100s	10s	1s
1	0	0	0	0	0

x 10

improper fraction	a fraction where the numerator is greater than or equal to the denominator. For example, $\frac{5}{3}$ (five thirds) and $\frac{3}{3}$ (three thirds).	161
inverse operations	operations that are the opposite of each other. For example: the inverse of add 2 is subtract 2. The inverse of multiply by 5 is divide by 5.	63

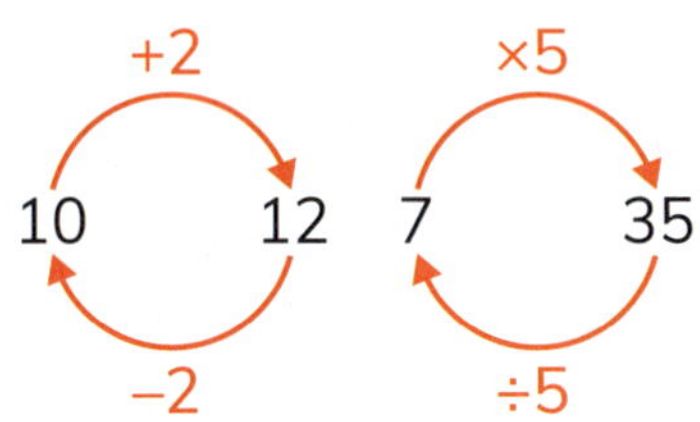

likelihood	how likely something is to happen	56
likely	something that will probably happen or is expected	56
leap year	a normal year has 365 days but a leap year has 366 days (one extra day in February). A leap year occurs every four years.	33
line of symmetry	the imaginary line where you could fold the shape or pattern so that both halves match exactly	81
linear sequence	a number pattern which increases (or decreases) by the same amount each time. For example, the pattern 2, 6, 10, 14, ... follows the rule 'add 4 to the previous term'.	12
maybe	something is possible or might be true	56
million	a 7-digit number that is 10 times larger than a hundred thousand	21

minute a unit of time equal to 60 seconds. There are 60 minutes in an hour. 29

mirror line a line midway between an image and its reflection 227

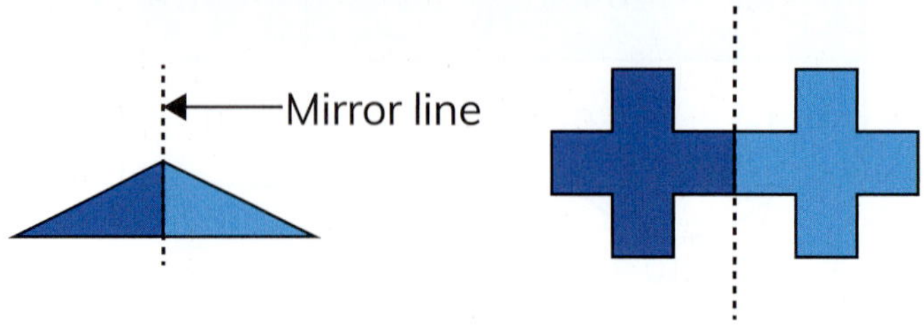

multiple the result of multiplying a number by a whole number. The first few multiples of 3 are: 3, 6, 9, 12, 15, 18, 21, 24, 27, 30, 33, 36 . . . 3 will divide exactly into any of these multiples. 63

negative number a number less than zero. You use a negative sign (–) to show a negative number: 12

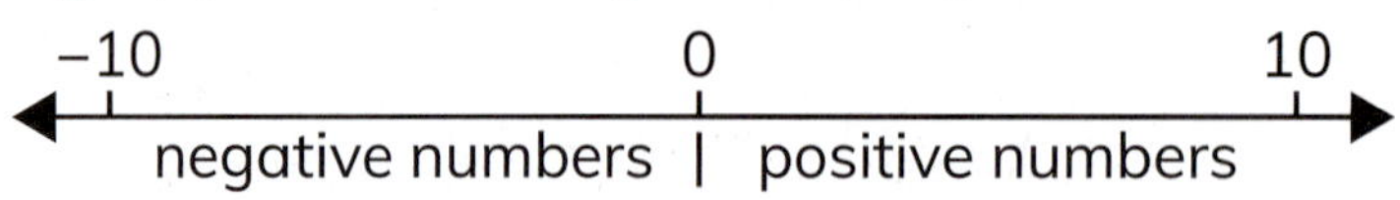

net a 2D flat shape that can be folded up into a 3D solid shape 150

no chance an event is impossible 56

non-linear sequence a number pattern where the numbers do not increase or decrease by the same amount each time. 12

For example, in this sequence the numbers double each time: 2, 4, 8, 16, ...

numerator the numerator is the number above the line of a fraction. It shows you how many parts we have. 89

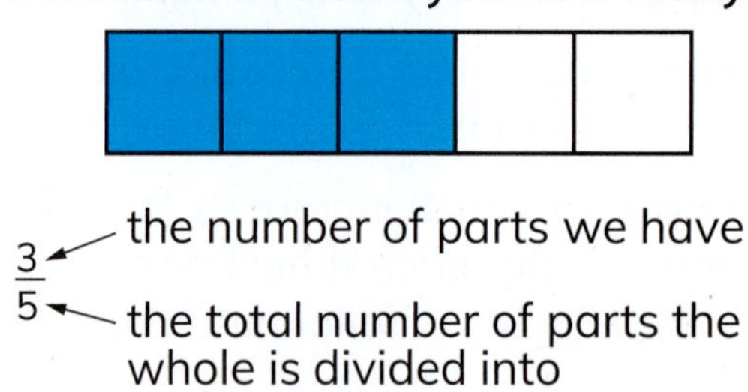

obtuse angle an angle greater than 90 degrees and less than 180 degrees 104

odd odd numbers end in 1, 3, 5, 7 or 9. For example 5, 103 or 7689. Odd numbers are not divisible by 2. 50

operator to find the fraction of an amount, you use the fraction as an operator on the amount. The fraction acts like division, for example $\frac{1}{4}$ of a pizza means a whole pizza divided by 4. 94

order arrange according to size, amount or value. For example, 1, 2, 3, 4 or: 114

outcome the result of an event in a probability experiment 56

p.m. a time in the afternoon or evening between midday and midnight 29

parallel lines that are the same distance apart all the way along their length 76

percent the number of parts in a hundred. The word 'percent' or the symbol % is used with a number, for example 3 percent can be written as 3%. 137

percentage the number of parts out of a hundred. For example, this diagram shows 25% which is equivalent to $\frac{25}{100}$. 137

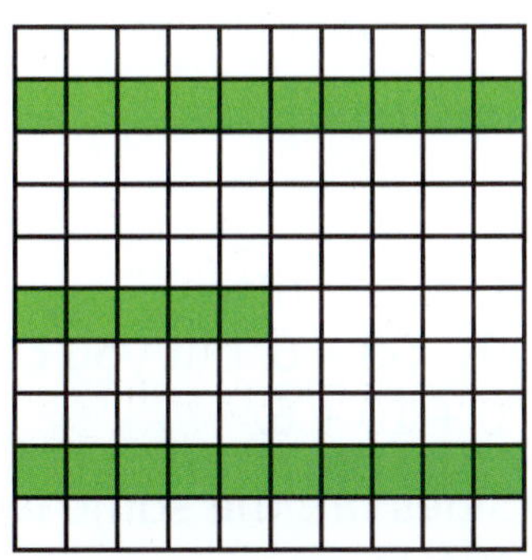

perimeter the distance around the outside of a shape. It is measured in units of length, such as metres or centimetres. 167

pictogram a graph that uses pictures to represent quantities 197

place holder use of zero to hold other digits in the correct position. For example, in the number 804 the '0' acts as a place holder for the tens. 21

polygon — a flat shape with 3 or more straight sides and no curved sides — 76

poor chance — it is unlikely that an event will happen — 56

prism — a 3D shape with two identical faces at opposite ends of the shape. All of the other faces are rectangles. — 145

probability — a number indicating how likely an event is — 54

product — the answer when two or more numbers are multiplied together. For example: the product of 3 and 5 is 15 because $3 \times 5 = 15$. — 63

proper fraction — a fraction smaller than a whole. The numerator is smaller than the denominator. For example, $\frac{1}{5}$. — 133

pyramid — a 3D shape with any 2D shape as a base.
All of the other faces are triangles.
The triangular faces all meet at a vertex. — 145

quadrant — an area on a grid between the two axes — 222

quotient — the result of a division — 214

$31 \div 3 = 10$ r1

↑ (pointing to 10)

quotient

reflection — a mirror image — 227

regroup — change the way a number is written.
For example, $456 = 400 + 50 + 6$, but you can change this to $400 + 40 + 10 + 6$. — 45

regular — a shape where all the sides are the same length and all the angles are the same — 76

remainder — the amount left over after dividing a number, for example: — 118

$31 \div 3 = 10$ r1 ⟵ remainder

right angle — an angle of 90 degrees — 104

round — change a number to a simpler value when an accurate answer is not needed — 114

round to the nearest — you can round a number to the nearest 10, 100, 1000 and so on. For example: 658 rounded to the nearest 10 is 660: 114

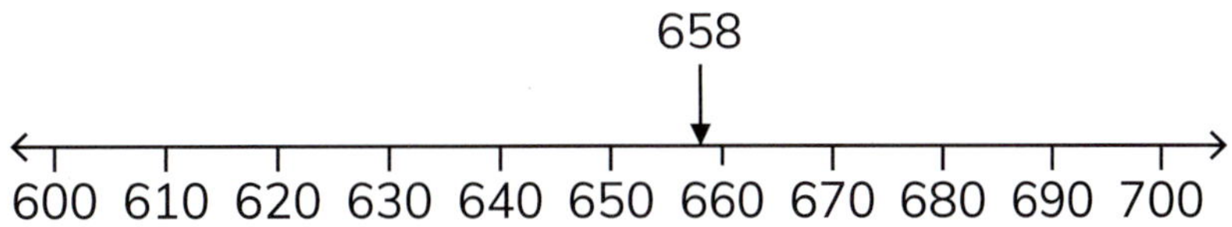

round up / round down — when the answer to a division has a remainder, you can round up to the next whole number or round down by removing the remainder: 118

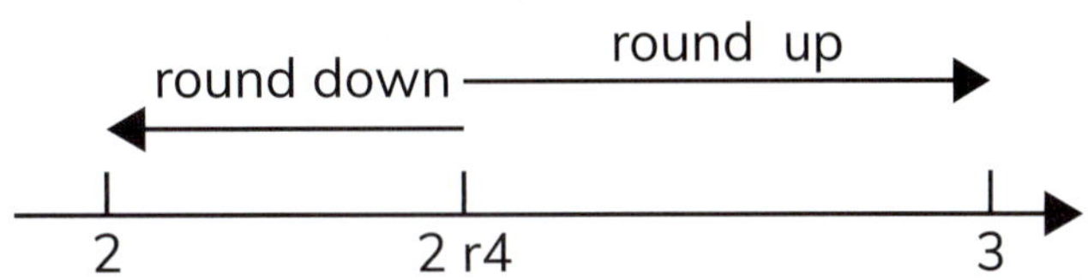

Example: Tina has 20 cakes and boxes that hold 8 cakes.

20 + 8 = 2 r4

How many boxes can Tina fill? Answer: 2 boxes (round down)

Tina puts all the cakes into boxes. How many boxes does she need? Answer: 3 boxes (round up)

rule — a pattern or relationship between numbers 12

second — a unit of time. There are 60 seconds in 1 minute. 29

sequence — numbers in a particular order 12

spatial pattern — a pattern that includes drawings. For example, these patterns show square numbers: 12

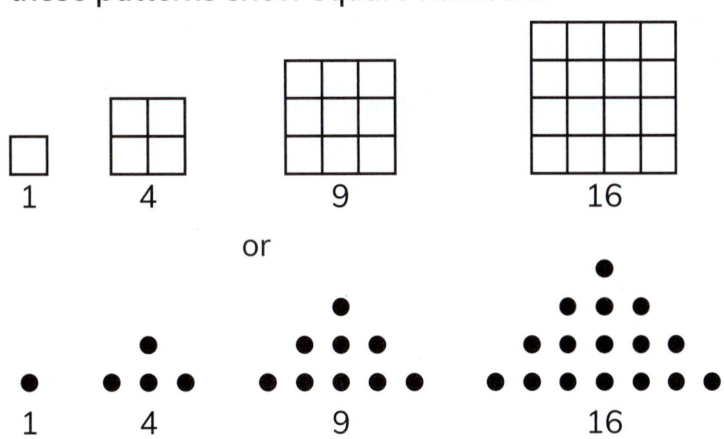

square number the number you get when you multiply a whole number by itself. For example, $4 \times 4 = 16$. 16 is a square number. 12

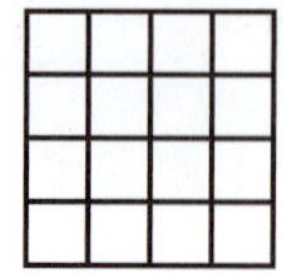

statistical question a question that can have different answers, so you need to collect data in order to answer it 126

symbol a thing that represents something else. For example, □, ○ and △ are symbols that could represent a missing number or operation. 41

symmetry one half of a shape is a mirror image of the other half 81

temperature how hot or cold something is. You can use a thermometer to measure temperature in degrees Celsius. 17

ten thousand a 5-digit number that is 10 times larger than a thousand 21

10 000s	1000s	100s	10s	1s
1	0	0	0	0

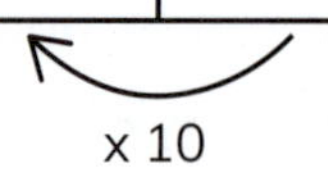

term part of a sequence separated by commas. For example, in the sequence 1, 2, 3, 4, . . . the first term is 1 and the third term is 3 and the tenth term would be 10. 12

term-to-term rule a rule you can use to find out how to get from one term to the next. For example, in the sequence 7, 10, 13, . . . the term-to-term rule is 'add 3 to the previous term'. 12

tessellation a pattern of shapes fitting together without any spaces between them 76

tetrahedron a special pyramid that has a base that is a triangle, just like its other faces 150

thousand	a 4-digit number that is 10 times larger than a hundred	21

1000s	100s	10s	1s
0	0	0	0

x 10

time interval	the length of time between two given times	33
timetable	a table of information showing when things will happen	33
unit fraction	a fraction with a numerator of 1. For example, $\frac{1}{2}$ or $\frac{1}{5}$.	94
Venn diagram	a diagram using curved shapes to sort items such as objects, shapes and numbers	197
vertex / vertices	the point where two or more edges meet	145
vertical	a straight line at a right angle to the horizon	81
zero	another name for nothing or nought. On a number line it is the point where numbers change from positive to negative:	17

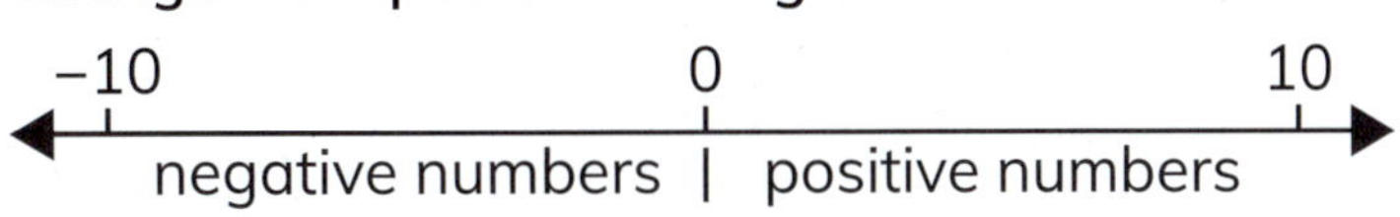

Acknowledgements

It takes a number of people to put together a new series of resources and their comments, support and encouragement have been really important to us.

From Mary Wood: With thanks to Katherine Bird, my editor, for her wise words, to my son, David for his willingness to talk mathematics and respond to my IT needs and to my husband, Norman, for being there when it was tough going.

From Emma Low: With thanks to Katherine and Caroline for their indispensable ideas and feedback, and also to Andy and our daughters Natasha, Jessica and Phoebe for their love and support and occasional very helpful puzzle and problem testing.

From Cambridge University Press:

We would like to thank the following people: Katherine Bird and Suzanne Thurston for their support for the authors; Lynne McClure for her feedback and comments on early sections of the manuscript; Thomas Carter, Caroline Walton, Laura Collins, Charlotte Griggs, Gabby Martin, Elizabeth Scurfield, Berenice Howard-Smith, Zohir Naciri, Emma McCrea and Eddie Rippeth as part of the team at Cambridge preparing the resources. We would also like to particularly thank all of the anonymous reviewers for their time and comments on the manuscript and as part of the endorsement process.

The authors and publishers acknowledge the following sources of copyright material and are grateful for the permissions granted. While every effort has been made, it has not always been possible to identify the sources of all the material used, or to trace all copyright holders. If any omissions are brought to our notice, we will be happy to include the appropriate acknowledgements on reprinting.

Thanks to the following for permission to reproduce images:

Cover illustration: Omar Aranda (Beehive Illustration);

Grant Faint/Getty Images; Richard McManus/Getty Images; the-lightwriter/Getty Images; Lastovetskiy/Getty Images; MirageC/Getty Images; discan/Getty Images; Prykhodov/Getty Images; Peter Dazeley/Getty Images; FotoSpeedy/Getty Images; Loren Zemlicka/Getty Images; Gary Conner/Getty Images; rubberball/Getty Images; Nirian/Getty Images; Simon McGill/Getty Images;Wataru Yanagida/Getty Images; Grant Faint/Getty Images; BSIP/Getty Images; KempMartin/Getty Images; jyu-akc/Getty Images; David Malan/Getty Images; xavierarnau/Getty Images; ullstein bild /Getty Images; Bildagentur-online/Getty Images; Jacky Parker Photography; Xinzheng/ Getty Images; nonnie192/Getty Images; the_burtons/Getty Images; mipan/Getty Images; Jed Share/Getty Images; Izzet Keribar/Getty Images; Jeff Foott/Getty Images; Roger T. Schmidt/Getty Images; DNY59/Getty Images; Richard Drury/Getty Images; yuanyuan yan/Getty Images; Antonio Lopez Martinez / EyeEm; DEA / G. NIMATALLAH/Getty Images; Kwanchai Lerttanapunyaporn / EyeEm/Getty Images; Westend61/Getty Images; Boris SV/Getty Images; Simon McGill/Getty Images; Peter Cade/Getty Images; Afriandi/Getty Images; /Getty Images; FBF_BsAs/Getty Images; Ralf Hiemisch/Getty Images; elzauer/Getty Images; MirageC/Getty Images; Ellen van Bodegom Getty Images; Tritooth//Getty Images; Photodisc/Getty Images;akinbostanci/Getty Images; pepifoto/Getty Images; Snap Decision/Getty Images; AlinaMD/Getty Images; DNY59/Getty Images; artvea/Getty Images; the_burtons/Getty Images; JAG IMAGES/Getty Images; njekaterina/Getty Images; PhoTon/Getty Images; PhoTon/Getty Images; Helena Wahlman/Getty Images; Busà; hotography/Getty Images; Kenny Williamson/Getty Images; Jan Hakan Dahlstrom/Getty Images; Yih Chang Chew / EyeEm/Getty Images; Sasirin Pamai / EyeEmGetty Images; emptyclouds/Getty Images; njekaterina/Getty Images; Robert Kneschke/EyeEm/Getty Images; njekaterina/Getty Images; Kwanchai ; erttanapunyaporn / EyeEm/Getty Images; laf Simon / EyeEm/Getty Images; Ivan Spasic / EyeEm/Getty Images; Wolfgang Werner/Getty Images; Yobro10/Getty Images; dejan Jekic/Getty Images; Lawrence Manning/Getty Images; Ulrich Baumgarten /Getty Images; Maciej Gorzelinski / EyeEm/Getty Images; Monkey Business Images/Getty Images; Vasko/Getty Images; TravelCouples/Getty Images; oxygen/Getty Images; Boris SV/Getty Images; Peter Cade/Getty Images; © Philippe LEJEANVRE/Getty Images; CSA Images/Getty Images